I0889404

A Place for Humility

THE IOWA WHITMAN SERIES

Ed Folsom, series editor

A Place for Humility

Whitman, Dickinson, and the Natural World

by Christine Gerhardt

University of Iowa Press • Iowa City

University of Iowa Press, Iowa City 52242

www.uiowapress.org
Printed in the United States of America
Design by Omega Clay

Library of Congress Cataloging-in-Publication Data
Gerhardt, Christine.
A Place for Humility: Whitman, Dickinson, and the Natural World / Christine Gerhardt.
pages cm. — (Iowa Whitman Series)
Includes bibliographical references and index.
ISBN 978-1-60938-271-1 (pbk), 978-1-60938-291-9 (ebk)
1. Whitman, Walt, 1819–1892—Criticism and interpretation.
2. Dickinson, Emily, 1830–1886—Criticism and interpretation.
3. American poetry—19th century—History and criticism.
4. Nature in literature. 5. Environmentalism in literature.
6. Poetics. I. Title.
PS3242.N2G47 2014
811.009'36—dc23 2014006256

The University of Iowa Press is a member of Green Press Initiative and is committed to preserving natural resources.

Printed on acid-free paper
ISSN: 1556-5610

For Jeanne

Contents

Acknowledgments

Many colleagues, friends, and mentors have helped me in the process of writing this book, and it makes me happy to bring all of them together here and thank them. The beginnings of this project go back to an inspiring class on ecocriticism that Bob DeMott taught at Ohio University in 1996, and to discussions with the colleagues and friends I met during my year there, including Jim Thompson and Dean McWilliams, and of course, Mitch Boucher, Neil Browne, and Alice Rozic. At the University of Dortmund, it was my teacher, mentor, and friend Walter Grünzweig who suggested that an ecocritical study on Whitman and Dickinson was doable, and whose extremely valuable comments on this manuscript have helped me to see many unexpected connections between Whitman and Dickinson and between the nineteenth century and ours. To be able to grow up, academically, with someone who cherishes the unique possibilities of scholarly work and loves to bring like-minded people together from all over the word was a beautiful gift, and I thank him for his steady encouragement and generous support. Also at the University of Dortmund, the colleagues and friends who have joined our weekly *Oberseminare* over the years were often the first who read and commented on different parts of this book, and I am grateful for their ideas, camaraderie, and overall support; of this committed and fun group, special thanks go to Randi Gunzenhäuser, Sibylle Klemm, Ariane Köster, Uwe Küchler, and Miriam Strube.

During different research trips to the United States, several people have provided assistance and thoughtful advice. My warm thanks go to Jimmie Killingsworth for discussing a number of central aspects of ecocriticism and Whitman's ecological outlook with me in 2001 and 2002. His generosity and encouragement were invaluable in giving this project direction at its early stages. I was also extremely fortunate to have enjoyed many inspiring conversations with Ed Folsom, in Dortmund and especially during my stay in Iowa in 2006. I am very grateful for his carefully weighed thoughts on how to read Whitman and Dickinson together, for helping me to sound out the ambiguities of several key poems and for his enthusiasm and most kind generosity. Additionally, I would like to thank Don Les for showing me the herbaria at the University of Connecticut, and Julie Mulroy and Steve Hill for discussing herbaria and botany with me and for helping me find important publications in these and other fields.

Many thanks also go to the colleagues and friends I met at different ASLE and EASLCE conferences and related meetings and workshops. Apart from the lively conversations I enjoyed with them, I am grateful to Sylvia Mayer in particular for being interested in my ecocritical ideas from very early on and for so freely sharing her own research; to Jon and Gail Smith for their perceptive critique of two of my essays; and to Heinz Tschachler for co-organizing the first green workshop with me. And Hannes Bergthaller, Catrin Gersdorf, Wolfgang Hochbruck, Vera Norwood, Nirmal Selvamony, and the members of the research network "The Futures of (European) American Studies" have all shaped my thinking about literature and the environment in various ways.

In terms of financial and institutional support for this project, the eighteen-month Lise Meitner research grant generously provided by North-Rhine Westfalia's Ministry for Innovation, Science, and Research was most important, because it allowed me to focus on the manuscript at a crucial stage. I also wish to express my gratitude to the Houghton Library, especially for letting me see Dickinson's herbarium, and to the libraries of Emory University, Oglethorpe University, and the University of Iowa for allowing me to use their resources.

My thanks also go to my colleagues at the University of Freiburg for sharing their ideas and offering comments and advice, and to the Carl-Schurz-Haus / German-American Institute in Freiburg, for allowing me to organize lecture series and other events on American environmentalism that kept me involved with the latest developments in the field. In my new academic home, the University of Bamberg, my colleagues in the English Department and others have been so welcoming and supportive that it feels as if I had been here much longer than I have; I thank Nicole K. Konopka and Judith Rauscher for their fantastic work and good spirits, which were particularly crucial when I revised the final draft. I am also grateful to those who have, in Connecticut, Dortmund, and Bamberg, generously helped with proofreading the manuscript at different stages or provided other vital support: thanks to Selma Erdogdu, Judy Marco, Nina Schewe, Claire Scott, and Tom Whalen.

I have been more than fortunate to enjoy the warm friendship of Claudia Nichelmann, Daniela Strezinsky, Kathrin Pionschek, Petra Meurer, Bruno Wittke and Andreas Müller-Heydenreich, Suzanne Seger, Melanie Schäpers, Ruth Meierling, Thomas Rennebaum and Klaus Rohnke, Edith Lamersdorf, Iris Hermann, Lale Behzadi, and Sigrid Lohneis. All of them, and their often overlapping circles of friends, have sustained me much more than they perhaps realize. Finally, my love and gratitude go to my father, Heinz Gerhardt, for sharing his fascination with other languages and cultures with me as a child, and for having always continued our conversation; to my mother, Susanne Gerhardt, for showing me that I could do what I set my mind on, and for providing the most loving support and sustenance; and to Dietrich Otto, whose encouragement to take that first academic position when the option offered itself made such a difference. My deepest thanks go to Jeanne Cortiel, for her love and companionship during this wonderful journey together—for being part of this project from its beginning, for helping me come to my own, and for never ceasing to inspire me.

Abbreviations

Works by Emily Dickinson

Fr *The Poems of Emily Dickinson*. Ed. R. W. Franklin. 3 vols. Cambridge, MA: Harvard University Press, 1998. Citation by poem number.

L *The Letters of Emily Dickinson*. Eds. Thomas H. Johnson and Theodora Ward. Cambridge, MA: Harvard University Press, 1986 (1958). Citation by letter number.

Works by Walt Whitman

CPCP *Complete Poetry and Collected Prose*. Ed. Justin Kaplan. Washington, DC: Library of America, 1982.

LG "The Text of *Leaves of Grass*, 1891–92." *Leaves of Grass, and Other Writings*. Ed. Michael Moon. New York: Norton, 2002. 2–491.

LG 1855 "*Leaves of Grass* (1855 Text)." *Leaves of Grass, and Other Writings*. Ed. Michael Moon. New York: Norton, 2002. 662–751.

A Place for Humility

Introduction

Emily Dickinson and Walt Whitman are widely acknowledged as two of America's foremost nature poets. This recognition rests largely on their explorations of natural phenomena as suggestive symbols for cultural developments, for individual experiences, and for poetry itself. In Dickinson's lyric meditations, natural phenomena constitute key metaphors for life and death, for a new religion, and for the power of the creative imagination, while in Whitman's expansive vision, the grass, the sea, and a mockingbird's song resonate in terms of America's democratic inclusiveness, the presence of death, and the poet's evolving voice. Yet for all their metaphorical suggestiveness, Dickinson's and Whitman's poems about the natural world neither preclude nor erase nature's relevance as an actual living environment. To the contrary, many of Dickinson's poems are deeply invested in New England's landscapes, and for all her interest in transcending geographical parameters of perception, poems such as "Who robbed the Woods –" (Fr57) and "A – Field of Stubble, lying sere" (Fr1419) offer intriguing perspectives on natural phenomena and on the vagaries of human-nonhuman relationships. Similarly, key passages in Whitman's *Leaves of Grass* are informed by the speaker's attention to Long Island's topographies, and when he deals with the cutting of California's old-growth forests in "Song of the Redwood Tree," or envisions an interconnected globe in "Passage to India," he is as concerned with nature's symbolic power as with his culture's ways of interacting with the actual earth. In their respective poetic projects, the natural world matters both figuratively and as a living environment, as a realm of the imagination and as the physical ground of human existence profoundly affected by human action. This double perspective, and the ways in which it intersects with their formal innovations, points beyond their traditional status as curiously disparate icons of American nature poetry. That both of them not only approach nature as an important subject in its own right but also address human-nature relationships in ethical terms invests their work with important environmental overtones.

Dickinson and Whitman developed their environmentally suggestive poetics at roughly the same historical moment, a time when a major shift occurred in their culture's general view of the natural world. Precisely when they achieved poetic maturity, an existing countervoice to America's dominant attitude toward nature was gaining strength; as Max Oelschlaeger observed, "a shift transpired from viewing wild nature as merely a valuable resource [. . .] and obstacle [. . .] toward a conception of wilderness as an end in its own right and an endangered species in need of preservation" (4). This book examines Dickinson's and Whitman's poetry in conjunction with this important change in environmental perception, and explores the links between their poetic projects in the context of nineteenth-century environmental thought from the perspective of a modern ecological awareness that makes such a reading possible. It is my argument that both Dickinson's and Whitman's poetry participate in this shift in different but related ways, and that this interlocking involvement with their culture's growing environmental sensibilities constitutes an important connection between their disparate bodies of work. There may be few direct links between Dickinson's "letter to the World" (Fr519) and Whitman's "language experiment" (*American Primer* vii), but through a web of environmentally oriented discourses, their poetry engages in a cultural conversation about the natural world and the possibilities and limitations of writing about it—a conversation in which their thematic and formal choices meet on a number of levels.

One of the most resonant connections that emerges from such an approach is that Dickinson and Whitman share a platially oriented environmental poetics. Both poets imagine nature symbolically and as a complex physical presence, frequently addressing human-nature interactions in specific geographical contexts; indeed, it is their similar awareness of nature and human-nature relationships on different geographical scales that yields surprisingly specific lines of connection between their work and the time's intensifying environmental discussions. Moreover, Dickinson and Whitman not only try to grasp natural phenomena as interwoven, autonomous entities and to picture more egalitarian human-nonhuman relationships, but they do so by way of certain modes—from parallel gestures of noticing minute natural details to shared ways of envisioning the entire globe—that echo and revise the ways in which environmentally concerned scientists, essayists, and activists were approaching nature on different geographical scales. Finally, Dickinson and Whitman also speak back to their time's evolving green debates by unsettling the idea of human knowledge and control so prevalent even in proto-ecological discourses. Reading the two of them together in such a way suggests that both explore a position in regard to the earth that the late twentieth century would term environmental humility. Humility, a stance that is so complexly enacted in some of Dickinson's religious poems and seems so alien to the proud self-confidence that characterizes much of Whitman's work, might well be one of the most suggestive links between their nature-related poems: from the concern for commonly overlooked creatures to meditations on the vulnerability of the globe, and by way of related formal and stylistic means that include the modification of descriptive and narrative conventions, experiments with perspective and voice, and the respective condensed and expansive qualities of their work, they bring to American poetry a shared but differently inflected notion of environmental humility.

The critical framework within which this study situates itself most directly is that of ecocriticism, both in terms of the field's foundational interest in place, nature writing, and preservationist politics, and in terms of its second- and third-wave turns toward a more diverse set of genres and of science studies, toward questions not only of gender but also of class, and toward nested geographies and planetary perspectives (see Buell, "Emerging Trends"; Slovic, "The Third Wave of Ecocriticism"). Even though ecocriticism—most broadly defined as "the study of the relationship between literature and the physical environment" (Glotfelty xviii)—uses "increasingly discrepant archives and critical models" (Buell, "Emerging Trends" 88), one can still say that its practitioners tend to ask how certain writers imagine the nonhuman world and human-nature interactions at different historical moments, how literary engagements with the environment inform and are informed by changing genre conventions, and how textual expressions of specific ethical positions concerning nature (or the lack thereof) are related to a culture's environmental attitudes and politics. As such, ecocriticism denotes diverse ways of reading that emerge from a set of environmentally oriented questions about literature and the world, as well as related methodological and theoretical debates. For Dickinson and Whitman, whose works are increasingly explored from such green perspectives, an ecocritical comparison in the context of nineteenth-century environmental debates continues to challenge some of the basic premises upon which readings of their poetry have long been based.

Engaging Ecocriticism

One of ecocriticism's most fundamental challenges continues to be how to account for the textual significance of nature as a physical realm without reverting to a naïve understanding of literature's referential dimension. When ecocriticism emerged in the mid-1990s, most critical debates were informed by poststructuralism, and several ecocritics, including Karl Kroeber and Leonard M. Scigaj, defined their interest in "nature as such" in blunt opposition to notions that reality is always socially constructed and mediated by language. Others have worked from within poststructuralist paradigms, emphasizing that the constructivist approach "does not wipe out the possibility of effective political agency, but rather reconfigures such agency 'as a reiterative or rearticulatory practice'" (Mazel xvii). Both stances have pushed the limit of how one can understand the complex of nature-culture relationships and linguistic representation, but they also created antagonisms that take away from what ecocriticism can bring to literary and cultural studies. Yet perhaps this is not so much a question of either/or, of mimesis versus radical constructivism, than one of the willingness to temporarily shift one's critical emphasis for the sake of more fully understanding the role of literature in a culture's views of nature. Lawrence Buell, in particular, has made an early case "for representation in the affirmative sense," focusing "on the recuperation of natural objects and the relation between outer and inner landscapes as primary projects" while stressing that such an "account of the reality of [. . .] fictional realities" does not deny that texts can also be read as an abstract social and political reflection (*Environmental Imagination* 87, 88). Clearly, the recognition that nature is multiply constructed and that human relationships to natural worlds are implicated in texts does not render the literary and critical concern for the referent impossible or irrelevant.

An ecocriticism that discusses literature's environmental resonances without reducing nature's textual presences to mechanisms of alleged representation, and that engages with poststructuralism for its ways of complicating distinctions between nature and culture, real and constructed worlds, seems well suited for reading Dickinson and Whitman because both were concerned with the relationship between (and continuity of) matter and mind, empiricism and human consciousness. Both poets were influenced by the Romantic idea of an organic language that binds symbolic insights subliminally back to the naturescapes from which they were derived, yet they also expressed a sense of alienation from nature's particulars and recurrent doubts regarding the possibility of embracing the earth through language. This study explores the continuities and ruptures between Whitman's claim that "[t]he land and sea, the animals fishes and birds, the sky of heaven and the orbs, the forests mountains and rivers, are not small themes" and his simultaneous insistence that "folks expect of the poet to indicate more than the beauty and dignity which always attach to dumb real objects" (*LG* 621); in the case of Dickinson, it explores the links between ecologically insightful observations such as "Related somehow they may be, / The sedge stands next the sea" and her warning that "nature is a stranger yet" and "those who know her, know her less / The nearer her they get" (Fr1433). How all of these levels work into and play off one another helps to account for Dickinson's and Whitman's particular approaches to the possibilities and limits of nature's representation.

A second aspect of ecocriticism relevant here is the field's interest in literary constructions of nature as historically and culturally specific phenomena. The challenge has to do with approaching the dynamics between literary and environmental histories not in terms of any one-directional "influence" of extraliterary factors, but with an eye to specific implications of a text's nature-oriented language that unfold when it is read in conjunction with related discourses of its time. At the same time it is crucial to reflect upon the ways in which such a historical interest is necessarily informed by twenty-first-century parameters. Such a double perspective that takes nineteenth- and twenty-first-century environmental perspectives into account seems particularly relevant for a green reassessment of Dickinson and Whitman because their frames of reference overlap with a formative moment in the history of modern ecology and environmentalism whose core ideas are still influential, even while some of its premises have recently been questioned and revised.

On the one hand, certain proto-ecological paradigms and environmental perspectives that emerged during Dickinson's and Whitman's time are still at the heart of the science of ecology and of modern environmental politics. In 1864, George Perkins Marsh argued in his popular study *Man and Nature; or, Physical Geography as Modified by Human Action* that "Nature, left undisturbed, so fashions her territory as to give it almost unchanging permanence of form, outline, and proportion, except when shattered by geologic convulsions; and in these comparatively rare cases of derangement, she sets herself at once to repair the superficial damage" (29). Marsh's ideas led to the development of the ecosystem concept (which was discussed for several decades before Arthur Tansley actually coined the term "ecosystem" in 1935) and to the notion that natural systems advance through "ecological succession" toward a fixed "climax" condition, a balanced state of equilibrium (formulated by Frederick E. Clements in the 1920s and 1930s), which in turn have shaped environmentalist perspectives from the 1970s to the present. Keeping in mind that core concepts of ecology, geography, and conservation still prominent today were first spelled out during Dickinson's and Whitman's time makes a contextual interpretation of their nature-oriented poetry highly productive because it allows for historically specific discussions of their poetry's remarkable environmental resonances in their own time and beyond. On the other hand, in the past decades a number of ecologists and environmental historians have called for a revision of core ecological principles that can be traced back to the mid-nineteenth century. Proposing a "disequilibrium" or "disturbance ecology," Daniel Botkin, in particular, has argued that the "concept of a highly structured, ordered, and regulated, steady-state ecological system [. . .] is wrong at local and regional levels" (9) and that we need to account for nature's intrinsic and necessary changeability and messiness (9–11).[1] Whether this approach calls into question the very premises of ecology, of conservation and wilderness management practices, and of related ethical considerations or only shifts its center toward a stronger recognition of unpredictable ruptures as parts of natural systems, it alters the parameters for discussing the environmental implications of Dickinson's and Whitman's work because it makes it difficult to clearly distinguish between environmentally "sensitive" and "precarious" textual positions, both in terms of supposedly stable, harmonious natural systems and in terms of human-made disturbances of such natural environments.

This study reads Dickinson's and Whitman's poetry in relation to a range of nineteenth-century environmental discourses—in particular, the newly specialized sciences, natural history essays, and early preservationist debates—in order to suggest the degree to which they were surrounded by proto-ecological arguments, which in turn offers important clues as to how the language of their poetry engages similar questions. By approaching this historical junction from a twenty-first-century perspective, I hope to be able to assess Dickinson's and Whitman's environmental perceptiveness in their own time without relying on outmoded scientific concepts and environmental strategies (including the idea of nature as a stable, harmonious system in need of protection from change), and to use current ecological insights without judging their work for not addressing issues they could not possibly have been aware of (such as the limitedness of all natural resources and humanity's ability to destroy life on earth irreversibly). But the focus of this study remains on methods of literary studies that do not rely on supposedly objective scientific measures but focus on texts and their analysis without negating literature's ecological and ultimately political dimensions.

A third element of ecocriticism that comes into play here is the field's shift from an early emphasis on "promulgat[ing] environmentally enlightened works" and "exposing stereotypes" in texts where nature figures as a conventional symbol or background for human dramas (Glotfelty xxii–xxiii) to analyses of works that cannot be labeled homo- or ecocentric. This shift also intersects with an increasing ecocritical interest in poetry, a genre that tends to foreground subjectivity and language, suggestiveness and paradox.[2] In this book, I combine an interest in the thematic gestures of Dickinson's and Whitman's nature-oriented poems with the analysis of selected formal and stylistic means whose implications resonate with fresh meaning when considered side by side with scientific publications, nature essays, or conservationist arguments of the time and with each other. Their work is characterized by a suggestive crossover between proto-ecological epistemologies, environmental ethics, and formal innovation, and as such marks a foundational moment in the history of American environmental poetry.

In such a framework, comparing Dickinson and Whitman may seem an obvious choice. The "Belle of Amherst" and the "American Bard" have been linked by reviewers and commentators since the 1890s (see Keller 260) to the point of being perceived as a predictable pair. Yet even though Dickinson herself wrote programmatically that "We see – Comparatively – " (Fr580), there is still only one monograph that focuses on the juxtaposition of two of them (Salska). In spite of their similarities, their differences are so fundamental that they remain difficult candidates for a smooth comparative discussion, especially since reading them as opposites does not get us very far either, invariably highlighting their apparent eccentricities rather than the subtleties of their work. I hope to show here how the exploration of Dickinson's and Whitman's environmental imagination together in the context of their time's intensifying green discussions reveals new similarities and sheds fresh light on those that have been addressed before, while also contributing to the discussion of their different thematic and formal choices. Moreover, such a green comparison offers new perspectives on a number of their best-known poems, while foregrounding some of their supposedly marginal pieces.

Dickinson and Whitman never met in person, and nobody can say for sure whether they read each other's work. Whitman claimed to have never heard of Dickinson, and yet he may have come across her anonymously published poems, particularly those printed in well-known Civil War journals (see Dandurand). Dickinson famously wrote to Higginson in 1862, "You speak of Mr Whitman – I never read his book – but was told that he was disgraceful – " (L261). Yet she often wore a mask when telling Higginson about herself, and a parallel letter in which she commented upon her reading habits to Mrs. Bowles highlights the strategic vagueness of her only Whitman comment: "I never read before what Mr Parker wrote. I heard that he was 'poison.' Then I like poison very well" (L213). Whether Dickinson did know or read Whitman and perhaps even "liked" precisely his "disgracefulness," the *Atlantic Monthly* published his "Bardic Symbols," which later became "As I Ebb'd with the Ocean of Life," in 1860, and the *Springfield Daily Republican* carried excerpts from "As I Ebb'd" and "Song of Myself," framed by derisive articles (Eitner, "Emily Dickinson's Awareness of Whitman" 112–13), bringing some of his poems dramatically close to her world. As such, their poetry can be read as displaced communication between two voices that had a lot to say to each other, albeit not directly. One of the ways in which they indirectly "talk" to one another is through the environmentally oriented discussions of their time, so that ideally, comparing them in this context would allow for readings that grasp the two both with and against each other. This study seeks to demonstrate how, together, Dickinson and Whitman also revolutionized American poetry by formulating different yet related visions of the earth that speak back to the environmental discourses of their time without compromising the idea of poetry as an autonomous imaginative project.

A fourth key feature of ecocriticism that is significant for this study is the field's ongoing emphasis on place as a critical category. Many ecocritics have urged a more vigorous attention to place, parallel to and in conjunction with race, class, and gender (Glotfelty xix), and as "[a] specific resource of environmental imagination," because "neither the imagination of environmental endangerment nor [. . .] of environmental well-being can be properly understood without a closer look at how the imagination of place-connectedness itself works" (Buell, *Writing for an Endangered World* 56). This unremitting interest in place also includes discussions of urbanity and pollution, as well as postcolonial, transnational, and global questions of people's plurilocal affiliations (see Heise), while ecocriticism has become a recognized player in the ongoing investigations of place in American literary and cultural studies (see Buell, "The Timelessness of Place").[3] Such impassioned attention to place adds a new edge to Dickinson's and Whitman's complex and slippery horizontal perspectives because scholarship is far from being in consensus on "the place of place" in these writers. Regarding Dickinson, an earlier generation of scholars has considered "scenelessness" and a "lack of 'outer' situations" (Weisbuch 18) to be one of her central rhetorical strategies. Jane D. Eberwein's important essay "Dickinson's Local, Global, and Cosmic Perspectives" still claims that, "for all her awareness of local and global environments, her truest perspective remained more vertical than horizontal, more attuned to speculations on immortality [. . .] than on Amherst, America, or the wider world opened by friendships and reading" (42); and Maria Farland, while offering a contextual reading, argues that the scenelessless of Dickinson's poetry shows "Dickinson's deliberate departure from a historically specific mode of representing immortality" ("'That Tritest/Brightest Truth'" 369). And yet it has long been noted that Dickinson had a surprisingly keen eye for capturing local natural phenomena, and more recent studies on Dickinson's regionalism, as well as on the links between her poetry and the sciences, have newly foregrounded her remarkably informed investigations of place from the local to the global realm.[4] In Whitman criticism there is a parallel tension between explorations of place as a significant category and its negation. The long-standing interest in Whitman's ambiguous terrestrial dimensions found a relatively recent manifestation in the 2005 issue of the *Mickle Street Review* on "Whitman and Place," where geographically oriented analyses of Whitman's urban poems and Civil War writings stand in an unresolved conflict with the claim that Whitman's poetry is *not* related to actual places (Hubert). More specific place-oriented studies of Whitman range from John Roche's "Democratic Space: The Ecstatic Geography of Walt Whitman and Frank Lloyd Wright" (1988) to M. Jimmie Killingsworth's explicitly ecocritical publications, which particularly emphasize the strength of Whitman's local island poetry (*Walt Whitman and the Earth*) and show his poetry to make room for both abstract, open, imaginary space and historically shaped, specific places ("Nature" 311). An ecocritical analysis of Dickinson's and Whitman's work together highlights that their poems share an interest in imagining the natural world and human-nonhuman relationships as specific to particular places, which makes the intersections between their poetry and the equally place-oriented proto-ecological studies and environmental discourses of their time particularly salient.

In terms of engaging place as a critical category, the following analysis particularly emphasizes the concept of scale, because Dickinson's and Whitman's poems tend to differentiate their platial perspectives along an axis of relative and relational size, negotiating between the microscopic and the global while undermining all-too-stable notions of geographically distinct realms. Geographers have long emphasized how scale functions as a political, social, and ecological construct that shapes human understanding of the world, and how the local, regional, national, and global are distinct realms and yet always intertwined (see Herod 230–37). In ecocriticism, however, while there have been many analyses of textual constructions of nature and human-nature interaction on local, regional, or global levels, only a few have turned to scale as a central parameter or offered in-depth theoretical considerations of the concept. Lawrence Buell was among the first to discuss scale as a relevant ecocritical paradigm (*The Future of Environmental Criticism* 76–96), and Ursula K. Heise, in particular, has reconsidered the environmental implications of local and planetary perspectives in an "eco-cosmopolitan critical project" that aims at moving beyond an "'ethic of proximity' so as to investigate by what means individuals and groups in specific cultural contexts have succeeded in envisioning themselves in similarly concrete fashion as part of the global biosphere" (62). What I am interested in here is how Dickinson's and Whitman's environmentally suggestive poetry engages culturally and historically specific notions of scale while often transcending them at the same time. Where Dickinson locates her creative voice between seeing "New Englandly" and transatlantic worlds (Fr256), Whitman shuttles back and forth between "a leaf of grass" and "the journey-work of the stars" ("Song of Myself"); where her work as a whole spans the distance between the place of individual flowers and "This Bashful Globe of Ours" (Fr677), his explores the dynamics between nature that is "commonest, cheapest, nearest" ("Song of Myself") and "the vast terraqueous globe" ("Passage to India"). Because their overlapping interest in small and large, near and distant naturescapes forms an important common ground both between their respective bodies of work and between their poetry and the time's environmental publications—from botany and nature essays to conservation debates and a new, globally oriented geography—scale works well as a structural, heuristic device that enables a comparative and contextual analysis in ways that keep the integrity of the literary texts intact.

On a different level, the notion of scale—especially if one uses the metaphor of concentric circles[5]—also links their shared concern for particular places to key concepts of their poetic projects at large, that is, Dickinson's emphasis on "circumference" and Whitman's interest in the dynamics between "sympathy" and "pride." When Dickinson claimed that her "Business is Circumference" (L268), she employed what her *Webster's*[6] defined as "the line that bounds a circle" and "the space included in a circle" as an inherently contradictory metaphor for her art. Throughout her poetry, she explores circular shapes and movements not only as symbols for the spirit in movement and religious transcendence, but also as a way of seeing nature on different scales: from seemingly innocuous poems about a butterfly's journey "In purposeless Circumference – " (Fr610), to meditations on the poet's overlapping ties to worlds of "berries," "earths," and "firmaments" (Fr358), she addresses constellations that draw attention to nature's scalar quality while questioning its stability. Whitman declared in his 1855 preface that great poetry always reaches out toward the other in "sympathy" and pulls back toward the self in "pride": "The soul has that measureless pride which consists in never acknowledging any lessons but its own. But it has sympathy as measureless as its pride and the one balances the other and neither can stretch too far while it stretches in company with the other. The inmost secrets of art sleep with the twain" (*LG* 624). As with Dickinson's circumference, this dynamic between gradual expansion and retraction of the self manifests itself with particular power in Whitman's nature-related poems, which makes the notion of scale so productive for an ecocritical comparison. In "Starting from Paumanok," the speaker moves from his birthplace to Manhattan, "southern Savannas," and California to "strike up for a New World," only to turn back inward and regard "underfoot the divine soil"; and "Song of Myself" begins with "a spear of summer grass," swiftly pushes out to woods and oceans, and then turns back to the grass. This swinging back and forth between nearby natural phenomena and faraway geographies as essentially one movement, and the resulting tensions among places and among different kinds of "sense of place," are central aspects of Dickinson's and Whitman's environmental imagination. One of the things I hope to show is how both of them use and revise geographical modes of grasping nature and people's ties to the living world of which they are a part.

Finally, this study links up with ecocriticism's vested interest in the ethical implications of literary constructions of the environment. These ethical debates have initially revolved mainly around the merits of ecocentrism, usually understood in binary opposition to anthropocentrism. Yet while the question as to whether nature's well-being should be considered in moral terms or nature exists mainly for human benefit has much to add to the understanding of textual constructions of nature and human-nature interaction, the apparent binary opposition between ecocentrism and anthropocentrism seems especially detrimental to an analysis of literature that is not primarily interested in formulating an environmental ethics but approaches the nonhuman world as part of other ontological concerns. Ecocentrism may emerge directly from the environmental poetry of Gary Snyder and, in different ways, from Thoreau's later prose, but it does not figure as a dominant stance in Dickinson's and Whitman's work. However, to therefore simply charge the latter with anthropocentrism does little for us either, since anthropocentrism is not irreconcilable with deep environmental sensibilities.

This study instead explores the tensions between Dickinson's and Whitman's poetic interest in human concerns (and the human mind) and in the natural world through the notion of humility, a concept that was especially multivalent in the mid-nineteenth century and deserves more attention in ecocriticism and environmental ethics—also because it offers a way to discuss the dynamics between eco- and anthropocentric positions without engaging their seemingly binary opposition. Dickinson and Whitman often express reverence and even concern for nature in ways that expand the notion of community beyond the human realm; such an attitude suggests a moral accountability toward nature that forms a basis for environmental ethics in the broadest sense, without necessarily choosing between anthropo- and ecocentrism. In particular, Whitman's "absorbing" journeys across the American continent and beyond, a key poetic means by which to constitute the national poet, are interspersed with sincere moments of caution and doubt during which the speaker recognizes natural details and their value in difference. As such, the speaker's sense of self is inspired by and leads back to an intense awareness of natural systems and his ambiguous impact upon them. Such moments find a compelling correspondence in Dickinson's poetry, whose speakers regularly question or forestall poses of superiority and control, not only by way of identifying with small natural creatures considered appropriate topics for nineteenth-century women poets, but also by checking their human sense of self against nature's imposing powers. I argue here that both poets, in spite of their preoccupation with the powers of the human mind, keep expressing a sense of affinity and awe in relation to nature, and perceive themselves as potentially erring and indeed responsible for their limited insights in terms of how to relate to nature, twin strategies that are ethically resonant insofar as they recast the notion of humility as an environmentally meaningful concept.

In mid-nineteenth century America, the concept of humility came laden with religious and gender-related connotations. According to the 1847 *Webster's*, *humility* simply means "freedom from pride and arrogance; humbleness of mind; a modest estimate of one's own worth." Yet Martin Farquhar Tupper's *Proverbial Philosophy* (1838), a popular collection of moralizing prose poems that may have inspired Whitman to organize his 1856 *Leaves of Grass* according to topics (Reynolds, *Walt Whitman's America* 353–54), contains a piece, "Of Humility," that points to the term's ideological complexity.[7] Tupper writes that "HUMILITY mainly becometh the converse of man with his Maker / But oftentimes it seemeth out of place in the intercourse of man with man" (56), suggesting that male humility is acceptable as a religious stance but otherwise out of step with the assertion of "masculine sentiments" (56). As a supposedly distinctly female virtue, it was also a defining quality for Victorian women: "Humility is the softening shadow before the stature of Excellence, / And lieth lowly on the ground, beloved and lovely as the violet: / Humility is the fair-haired maid, that calleth Worth her brother, / the gentle silent nurse, that fostereth infant virtues" (57). This "queen among the graces" (57), then, sits squarely between the performance of conventional Christian piety and binary Victorian gender norms, which would, it seems, make it a difficult concept for anyone to embrace. And yet, as Shira Wolosky writes in her discussion of modesty, a nineteenth-century synonym for humility:

> Modesty emerges [. . .] both as a barrier to be negotiated and as an avenue to self-expression, as a challenge, but also a medium, for female representation. [. . .] As part of nineteenth-century female self-definition, modest representations may genuinely assert feminine values often critical of the broader society, as part of an authentic voice for an historically constituted female identity. ("Poetry and Public Discourse" 163–64)

Like modesty, humility held a considerable assertive and subversive potential, not only for representations of gender but also for negotiating the speaker's subject position in relation to nature as an autonomous and complex living environment. Much of this came together in the time's green discourses, from natural history essays that also offered moral instruction to botany books infused with religious fervor and specifically geared toward female readers. Almira H. Lincoln's *Familiar Lectures on Botany* (1829), for instance, which Dickinson knew well, suggests humility as a stance toward plants' often overlooked features: "[L]et us rather, with humility acknowledge that this blindness must be owing to the limited nature of our own faculties. It would be impious for us to imagine that all the works which we cannot comprehend, of God are useless" (64). This ideological richness also informs Dickinson's and Whitman's poetry, where humility as a stance toward nature remains charged with religious and gender-related overtones.[8] As such, Dickinson and Whitman reconceptualize human-nature relationships in terms of an environmental humility that does not undo their overriding interest in human concerns; after all, "humble" derives from Latin *humilis*, "supposed to be from *humus*, the earth, or its root" (Webster, *Dictionary* [1847]), and "human" derives from *homo*, which itself is derived from *humus* (see Relph 162). Humble and human share the same root: the earth.

Humility has never been an environmentalist buzzword, and that it seems inherently unsuited for such a status may well be one of its strengths. In ecocriticism, the concept does not yet play a significant role, either. One exception is Josh Aaron Weinstein's Ph.D. dissertation, which defines "ecological humility" as an awareness of our nonhierarchical interconnectedness with other beings and provides an extended, insightful overview of humility in Christian, Jewish, and Eastern religions. His analyses include a chapter on Whitman's "Children of Adam" poems, which focuses on "Whitman's understanding of sexuality and sexual desire as involving the same ideas of complex interrelation and harmonic organization as that which is entailed in the ecological," and explores how sexuality in Whitman's poetry serves as an important link between humans and nature's energy flows, "reflect[ing] the working out of an ecological theory of sexuality" (139).[9] Environmental philosophers, however, have for quite some time considered humility as a concept that is crucial for redirecting the vexed human ways of being in the world—including Aldo Leopold's claim in *Sand County Almanac* (1949) that the "[a]bility to see the cultural value of wilderness boils down, in the last analysis, to a question of intellectual humility" (200), and his acknowledgment that even the land ethic he proposes "cannot prevent the alteration, management, and use of [natural] 'resources,' but it does affirm their right to continued existence, and, at least in spots, their continued existence in a natural state" (204).[10] When geographer Edward Relph coined the term "environmental humility" in *Place and Placelessness* (1976), he defined it as a way of "work[ing] with environments and circumstances rather than trying to manipulate and dominate them," and emphasized its "benefit of restraint" in terms of "the willingness to leave places alone and to allow them to be maintained and modified by the people who live in them" (162). For Relph, environmental humility means that "man is not at the centre, but understood to be a part of a continuum of nature and culture in which human beings both influence and are influenced by settings" (163); it depends on "the responsibility for protecting and guarding environments as they are in themselves, and with neither domination nor subservience" (164). As such, environmental humility can be called a non-anthropocentric stance that does not, however, endorse radical ecocentrism; as Relph puts it, going back to bare subsistence levels "would be neither comfortable nor desirable" (164). More recently, Robert Gibson has taken the idea further toward the recognition of people's prevailing uncertainty and ignorance concerning the natural world. For Gibson, ecological thinking requires "an attitude of environmental humility" in the face of human failure "to respect the complexity and vulnerability of the environment, and to appreciate the limits of human knowledge and understanding" (158, 173). Environmental humility, then, involves the willingness to let go of the notion of complete manipulation and control of nature, and the admittance of our limited knowledge of natural processes. It is based on the simultaneous perception of human beings as interconnected, dependent parts of nature and as existing outside and separate from it, especially in terms of understanding, controlling, and destroying the nonhuman world. I argue here that one hundred fifty years ago, when America's collective reverence for nature was at an all-time peak while at the same time the subjugation and exploitation of nature reached unprecedented dimensions, Dickinson's and Whitman's poems were pointing toward such a stance. As they imaginatively engage the conflicting implications of America's relationship to the natural environment, their poems explore a range of responses to the world that can be read as expressions of humility toward the earth—a seemingly innocuous position whose environmental implications were as radical in the nineteenth century as they are now.

Previous Research: Dickinson, Whitman, and the Natural World

Scholarly interest in the environmental implications of Dickinson's and Whitman's work has emerged only in the last decades, and their poetry has never been compared from an ecologically informed perspective. However, there is a long tradition of critical studies on nature in each of their poetic oeuvres. Analyses of nature in Whitman's poetry go back a particularly long way. The works by John Burroughs, which James Perrin Warren reevaluated as ecocriticism *avant la lettre* (*John Burroughs and the Place of Nature* 42–72), are an important starting point here: Burroughs's *Notes on Walt Whitman, as Poet and Person* (1867), co-authored by Whitman, stressed that "true art" arises from "a passionate identity and affiliation with Nature," unlike poetry that merely uses nature for tropes (38, 47); his *Birds and Poets* (1877) concluded with a chapter on nature's presence in Whitman's work; and *Whitman: A Study* (1896) celebrated Whitman's democratic spirit in conjunction with his poetics of open-air life, nature, and real things (266, 274). Several decades later, Norman Foerster's *Nature in American Literature* (1923) praised Whitman as an influential nature writer, emphasizing the role the body and the senses played in his reverie for the land. Since the 1970s, critics have read Whitman's poetry in more explicitly environmental terms. Cecelia Tichi's important *New World, New Earth: Environmental Reform in American Literature from the Puritans through Whitman* (1979), in particular, placed Whitman in the context of nineteenth-century conservationism as a progressive, utilitarian, anthropocentric movement, maintaining that his "New Earth" was the aesthetic and imaginative culmination of the American environmental reform ideal (206, 224). Gay Wilson Allen's "How Emerson, Thoreau, and Whitman Viewed the Frontier" (1980) linked "Song of the Redwood Tree" to Whitman's views of America's West, the emerging environmental crisis, and the science of ecology, while Eric Wilson argued in *Romantic Turbulence: Chaos, Ecology, and American Space* (2000) that the 1855 "Song of Myself" replaced the idea of nature as an orderly whole with the notion of a rhizome and itself represents an evolving ecosystem (119), and Lawrence Buell briefly discussed Whitman as an urban flaneur (*Writing for an Endangered World* 2001).[11]

Three more-recent monographs are especially relevant here. M. Jimmie Killingsworth's *Walt Whitman and the Earth: A Study in Ecopoetics* (2004) focuses on the tensions in Whitman's nature-oriented poetry and argues that it "embodies the kinds of conflicted experience and language that continually crop up in the discourse of political ecology" (9–10). This first sustained environmental reading of Whitman's work elegantly combines the ecocritical interest in place with thing theory and ecological communication, offering detailed and nuanced readings that revisit several key themes in Whitman criticism, including urbanization and the Civil War, Whitman and the (aging) body, and Whitman as an island poet. In particular, Killingsworth engages the differences between Whitman's pre- and post–Civil War work as the shift from an individual, bodily relationship to nature to increasingly abstract "globalizing" poems that stretch to the point of "overextension." Moving in a different direction, Angus Fletcher's *New Theory for American Poetry: Democracy, the Environment, and the Future of Imagination* (2004) traces all of America's environmental poetry back to Whitman; according to Fletcher, Whitman coined a distinct "Whitman phrase" whose suspended grammar and "unprecedented descriptive technique" (2) invite readers to perceive their own world more intensely, a phrase that is at the core of the American "environment-poem" which neither just describes nor "analytically represents" the world but *is* an environment (9). George Handley's *New World Poetics: Nature and the Adamic Imagination of Whitman, Neruda, and Walcott* (2007) sheds fresh light on the eco-ethical duality and chronological development of Whitman's nature-related poetry by arguing that Whitman "seeks a balance between nature and culture" (148), mainly through a "poetics of oblivion" (143) that destabilizes the distinction between the two, and that instead of seeking a "translation of nature's meaning or of history's truths [. . .] acknowledges the appropriateness of both remaining opaque" (141). Finally, several recent essays have also explored Whitman from an ecocritical perspective.[12] Taking these important contributions as a point of departure, my study emphasizes nineteenth-century environmental debates as a significant component of the larger culture Whitman embraced so enthusiastically, and uses these debates as a suggestive framework for discussing his views of nature on different scales, as well as their eco-ethical implications. Such an emphasis draws attention to a specific set of Whitman's poems and new thematic clusters (such as his use of the child perspective in his representations of nature's minutiae) and enables a fresh comparison with Dickinson's poetry that shows both poets to be distant "partners" in a venture that brings them to renewed currency today.

Critics have been more reluctant to explore the environmental relevance of Dickinson's work. Dickinson's "resistance to politicize her topics overtly, combined with the tendency to personalize experience" (Strysick 58) long seemed to run counter to historical and cultural-political interpretations, and her fascination with how "everyday events and objects are italicized into symbols, appearances rush toward essences" (Weisbuch 2) has made the field highly sensitive to what might appear to be a positivistic argument. However, a number of critics have for several decades now linked Dickinson's work to such historical phenomena as nineteenth-century women's culture and literature (Bennett, Miller, Petrino), New England religion (Eberwein, Oliver), Victorian culture (St. Armand), the Civil War (Wolosky), and class and social history (Erkkila, Mitchell, Murray), demonstrating that context-oriented readings do not conflict with the recognition of Dickinson's formal innovations and dense metaphoricity. Indeed, Cristanne Miller's *Reading in Time: Emily Dickinson in the Nineteenth Century* has recently shown how deeply the celebrated formal and stylistic features of her art were embedded in the literary and broader textual cultures of her time. The new collection *Emily Dickinson in Context* (2013) further testifies to contextual readings of Dickinson as a highly productive approach. This ongoing recontextualization of Dickinson has opened up new possibilities for exploring links between the imaginative realm of her poetry and the natural environment, and especially for a comparison with Walt Whitman, the poet who is commonly regarded as most responsive to nineteenth-century cultural changes.

Paralleling the situation in Whitman studies, Dickinson's poems about the natural environment have long played a major role in Dickinson scholarship. As early as 1960, Charles Anderson's chapters on "The Outer World" in *Emily Dickinson's Poetry: Stairway of Surprise* stressed that Dickinson was interested in capturing the limited possibility of knowing nature without fully negating its physical reality, and pointed to her fascination with neglected natural forms. Coming from a different direction, Albert Gelpi's *Emily Dickinson: The Mind of the Poet* (1965) argued that Dickinson's view of the world derived much from the traditional Puritan view of nature as God's grace (86), and emphasized that while she did share with Emerson and Thoreau a view of nature as the externalization of the soul, she reveled in her own (sometimes destructive) power over nature. And Rebecca Patterson's insightful geography chapter in *Emily Dickinson's Imagery* (1979) read Dickinson's diverse topographical references not in scientific or technical terms, but as highly effective metaphors, which the poet used in ways that were both unique and very common in her time. Richard E. Brantley's more recent *Experience and Faith: The Late-Romantic Imagination of Emily Dickinson* (2004), which focuses on the contexts of evangelicalism and empiricism, includes a chapter on Dickinson's "religion of nature" as informed by her "naturalized imagination" and her "poetic faith" (80). Robin Peel's *Emily Dickinson and the Hill of Science* (2010) finds her "alert" to the conflicts caused by seeing nature as God's creation, a "law unto itself" and realm of beauty (288), and argues that her poems are thematically and epistemologically responsive to the debates of her time in the fields of botany, geology, geography, astronomy, optics, and Darwinism. Interestingly, Sabine Sielke's essay on Dickinson and the natural sciences not only stresses that "her take on science is critical and engaged rather than positivist and affirmative," but also reengages earlier arguments about Dickinson as primarily a poet of perception; according to Sielke, she was interested in cognition, while nature, by comparison, was "a crucial, yet not primary concern of Dickinson's poetics" (237, 239). Other studies have linked Dickinson's nature poems to her time's passion for flowers and gardens: Elizabeth Petrino's *Emily Dickinson and Her Contemporaries: Women's Verse in America, 1820–1885* (1998) rereads her poetry against the period's "language of flowers," while Domhnall Mitchell's *Emily Dickinson: Monarch of Perception* (2000) discusses the poet's love of flowers as part of a genteel preoccupation with gardening and horticulture, and Judith Farr's *The Gardens of Emily Dickinson* (2004) links horticulture, painting, and the poet's actual gardens to poems as imaginative, paradisiacal gardens. Coming from a different direction, Adam Sweeting's *Beneath the Second Sun: A Cultural History of Indian Summer* (2003) reads several of Dickinson's nature poems against New England's socioliterary contexts; Rosemary Scanlon McTier's *"An Insect View of Its Plain": Insects, Nature and God in Thoreau, Dickinson and Muir* (2013) provides a useful overview of nineteenth-century entomology and discusses a large number of Dickinson's poems, demonstrating that insects were one of the poet's major thematic concerns.

Finally, a number of groundbreaking studies have linked Dickinson's poetry to gendered views of nature. Joanne Feit Diehl's *Dickinson and the Romantic Imagination* (1981) argues that Dickinson "rejects an Emersonian nature which educates man" and imagines "the world as a deceptive text that cannot be read right" (9–10); Wendy Martin's *An American Triptych: Anne Bradstreet, Emily Dickinson, Adrienne Rich* (1984) links Dickinson's focus on nature's interconnection and emphatic representation to her relationships with other women; Paula Bennett's *Emily Dickinson: Woman Poet* (1990) claims that nature presented for Dickinson "a women-centered and materially-based alternative to established religion" (20) and a space of beauty and healing (90); and Mary Loeffelholz's *Dickinson and the Boundaries of Feminist Theory* (1991) argues that Dickinson was searching for a language of nature as a "language of female desire" (8). None of these crucial studies, however, are centrally concerned with environmental issues. This has begun to change, especially with Rachel Stein's important *Shifting the Ground: American Women Writers' Revision of Nature, Gender, and*

Race (1997), which argues that Dickinson challenges both the notion of nature's conquest and transcendentalist ideas of nature as "feminized 'not me'" (20), yet the focus is more on how Dickinson's poetic revisions conceptually empower women than on the implications of such a move for the role of nature. There is no ecocritical monograph on Dickinson, however, and as in Whitman studies, Dickinson's poetry has not been consistently read in the context of the proto-ecological discourses that make the mid-nineteenth century a watershed moment in America's cultural history. Quite recently, several ecocritical essays have begun to move in this direction, negotiating Dickinson's dense metaphoricity with her keen interest in the natural sciences and in specific natural phenomena and places, also in terms of her poetry's ethical implications.[13]

The only study devoted exclusively to a comparison of Whitman and Dickinson is still Agnieszka Salska's *Walt Whitman and Emily Dickinson: Poetry of the Central Consciousness* (1985). As far as nature is concerned, Salska links both poets to Emersonian notions and argues that Whitman readily "gave his loyalty to the external, physical world" (21), mediating between nature and self and rejoicing in the organic qualities of language, while Dickinson's poetics of rupture and doubt considered nature as an experiment, exposing the limitations of language (15). Daneen Wardrop's *Word, Birth, and Culture: The Poetry of Poe, Whitman, and Dickinson* (2002) is also relevant here, as it discusses how both poets combine a concern for the female and the limits of poetic language with nature-related issues. And Maurice Gonnaud's essay "Nature, Apocalypse or Experiment: Emerson's Double Lineage in American Poetry" (1979) argues that Whitman responds to "a mysterious pull from the objects themselves," while Dickinson searches for the universal in particulars (131–33). My own "'Earth Adhering to Their Roots': Dickinson, Whitman, and the Ecology of Bookmaking" (2008) discusses the similarities between Dickinson's herbarium and Whitman's 1855 edition of *Leaves* as books that engage the natural environment both scientifically and symbolically; my "Sounding Together: Walt Whitman, Emily Dickinson and the Ocean of Organic Life" (2008) compares the environmental implications of their sea poetry.

Drawing from this rich body of analyses of Dickinson's and Whitman's poetry in connection to other cultural forces at work at that time, my own study explores their peculiar responsiveness to the natural world in the context of the developing environmental awareness in the United States, emphasizing both the historical-political and ethical significance of how the human subject relates to his or her environment. This approach seeks to close a gap in the discussions of Whitman as a political poet (an argument put forward by Betsy Erkkila, without, however, considering his views of nature as inherently political) and Dickinson as a feminist nature writer (argued by Rachel Stein). An ecocritical reading of Whitman and Dickinson that is both historicized and comparative thus enables the recovery of key elements in their poetic voices that are vital to the understanding of their work as a whole. In particular, I hope that the following chapters reveal that the geographies of human-nature interaction are not ancillary to their work but operate at the center of their respective poetic projects, that the engagement with environmental discourses is a defining focus of their art both as subject matter and in terms of their formal and stylistic choices, and that their embrace of humility toward nature revolutionized the possibilities of American poetry as an eco-ethical expression.

Contours of This Study

The four parts of this book discuss the notable correspondences between Dickinson's and Whitman's poetry and their culture's environmental discourses by focusing on four geographical scales. Both poets had a keen eye for how scale shapes the human perception and treatment of nature, at a moment when proto-ecological discussions also explored this junction. The following chapters show how on the micro, local, regional, and global level Dickinson's and Whitman's nature-related poems intersect in specific ways with evolving environmental debates and with each other, and how from noticing "a leaf of grass" ("Song of Myself") to envisioning "the general Earth" (Fr1226), both poets use parallel modes of poetic expression that talk back to botany and the new geography, natural history essays, and conservationist arguments. The distinction between these scales is of course not absolute, especially since Dickinson and Whitman were so interested in the paradoxical simultaneity of the minute and the cosmic and kept pushing the metonymic possibilities of linking the local and the global. Nor do I mean to suggest that certain poetic modes operate solely on one particular scale: they transcend any clear-cut boundaries and tend to matter in Dickinson's and Whitman's work as a whole. My point here is rather that specific poetic strategies move into the foreground and are particularly prominent on certain scales, and that attention to this junction enables a productive comparison between their bodies of work in the context of their culture's shifting environmental sensibilities. At the same time, the formal and stylistic features that Dickinson and Whitman engage in their conceptualizations of nature and human-nature relationships invariably point beyond the environmental debates of their time, not only because they let geographical scales imaginatively overlap and slide into each other (ecological scientists and environmentalists explore these relations as well), but also because on each scale and as a whole they confront the ineffability of nature. What is at stake for them is nothing less than trying to forge a poetic language "proportionate to Nature" ("Song of the Redwood-Tree") that neither assumes complete control over nature nor undoes their own poetic voices—a dilemma that, considered from a twenty-first-century perspective, anticipates the impossibility of an ecocentric stance on the level of language.

Part 1, "Noticing Small Worlds," investigates how Dickinson's and Whitman's poetry about the "matchless Earth" (L347) evolves similarly from a persistent attention to the smallest natural phenomena. Their repeated acts of noticing what has long been overlooked in nature precisely because it is small echo the proto-ecological sciences' new empirical interest in individual species, albeit by use of very different means. As they fuse perspectives informed by botany, ornithology, and chemistry, Dickinson's many condensed, ruptured poems and Whitman's recurrent lines on birds, flowers, and insects develop related ways of granting nature's minutiae an autonomous presence and overall significance. But rather than reveling in nature's details as an end in itself, both tackle the epistemological limits of nature, especially on the smallest scale. From different perspectives, Dickinson and Whitman express a sense of humility that stems not only from the sheer act of noticing the smallest creatures beneath one's feet, but also from their identification with the small, which is counteracted by the realization of nature's unspeakable otherness.

Part 2, "Describing Local Lands," explores how Dickinson and Whitman treat nearby natural places as familiar systems that resemble natural households. Ecologically speaking, these poems talk about the nonhuman world on the ecosystem level (*avant la lettre*), much as descriptive biogeographers and popular nature essays did with their detailed renditions of fields, forests, shorelines, and swamps. What moves into the foreground here is how Dickinson's and Whitman's portraits of their imaginative "native lands" (Fr178) engage the mode of description as an environmentally relevant textual practice, adding depth to their local sense of place. As they pay attention to the intricate workings of a seemingly average stretch of land that effaces the human ego of the speaker, they devise descriptive modes that minimize and destabilize the notion of mastery that is part even of this perhaps most humble linguistic practice.

Part 3, "Narrating the Regions," turns to Dickinson's and Whitman's regional imagination, to the ways in which their poems concern themselves with nature's place in larger cultural communities. When they write about nature as an economic resource and people's modes of working the land, Dickinson's snapshots of New England and Whitman's northeastern, western, and southern passages and poems test the possibilities and limits of living sustainably with the nonhuman environment in a culture increasingly characterized by industrialism. When conservationist and preservationist arguments relied on urgent stories about nature's devastation to shake up the country, Dickinson and Whitman too used certain narrative strategies in their poems, recurring to some of their culture's defining stories of civilization and wilderness, dominion and stewardship. Yet while many of their contemporaries developed imposing strategies for nature's alternative management, Dickinson's and Whitman's poems responded to the dilemma of environmental exploitation and protection in ways that bypass the narrative urge to offer solutions. At the same time as they acknowledge the eco-ethical conflicts inherent in modern culture, they express a sense of environmental humility not only in the face of the excesses of human mastery and control, but also by acknowledging the impossibility of using nature innocently.

Finally, part 4, "Envisioning the Earth," explores what happens when Dickinson and Whitman turn to the largest geographical scale, the one that is, in the twenty-first century, often seen as the ultimate test of any environmental expression, since a global awareness is what is both most direly needed in the face of a global environmental crisis and most difficult to achieve. Dickinson and Whitman try to envision the earth as a living globe and planetary place in ways that point beyond transcendental wholes and toward imagining an empirical grasp of the world, as unattainable as such a perspective may be. As they see the earth as a "terrestrial Ball" (Fr1) and "vast Rondure, swimming in space" ("Passage to India") they link the notion of the earth as biosphere back to the most immediate earth at our feet, the soil, directing our attention to the ways in which respect for large natural systems, but also grand and often colonizing schemes of global control, remain related to views of minutest nature. Moreover, they try to make global nature—something beyond a nineteenth-century speaker's actual experience—palpable by imagining it as metaphorically and conceptually related not only to smaller scales but also to "us humans," envisioning quasi-personal relationships with all of this earth. This constitutes another connection between their poetry and the ideas of the fountainheads of global ecology such as Alexander von Humboldt, who similarly mediated between empiricism and the imagination. As for them, for Whitman and Dickinson a global view of life on earth, and of a personal, accountable relationship with it, was both elevating and humbling, since it dramatized people's relative insignificance and ultimately threatened to elude their imagination.

1 · Noticing Small Worlds

In the 1840s Emily Dickinson began work on her first book, a collection of pressed plants preserved in a special herbarium. While keeping a herbarium was a common pastime for mid-nineteenth-century middle-class women, Dickinson's collection differs from those of her contemporaries in quantity and quality. With its more than four hundred flowers, mosses, algae, and tree blossoms, it pays attention to nature's minutiae more extensively than most of the era's amateur herbaria, whose average number of specimens would be about one hundred. The largely accurate Latin names (see Angelo 170) are exceptional for an amateur herbarium, indicating a thorough knowledge of the Linnaean taxonomy. Yet her herbarium also omits information about when and where the plants were collected, leaves specimens unnamed toward the end, does not sort them according to the traditional Linnaean classes, and almost never presents the flowers' roots, the most important parts of a plant in terms of identification. Her carefully crafted herbarium, then, surprises the reader with provocative arrangements that pay as much attention to the flowers' unique morphology and botanical order as to their metaphorical suggestiveness and composition on the page, yet elides crucial gestures of controlling the material, linking the act of noticing nature's details to questions of artistic representation and the limits of human knowledge.

Only a few years later, in 1855, Walt Whitman published the first edition of *Leaves of Grass*, a slim volume whose cover suggested that whatever was inside the book was linked most vitally to nature, especially nature's smallest incarnations. While similar designs were not uncommon at the time, as Jerome Loving and others have pointed out (*Walt Whitman: The Song of Himself* 179), Whitman's cover superseded those of his contemporaries in crucial ways. Compared to Sara Willis Parton's *Fern Leaves from Fanny Fern's Portfolio* (1853), which features stylized golden floral ornaments and a title whose first words turn into vines, while the center is claimed by what looks like paper and writing utensils,[1] Whitman's cover pushes an almost palpable referent into the foreground, drawing attention to a cluster of plant-letter morphs so laden with tiny leaves and roots they seem to literally grow out of the dark green base. They not only look weedy, almost moldy, in ways that Victorians would have found unsettling, and even unattractive; they also radically emphasize nature's smallest, habitually overlooked elements. The phrasing, too, differs from popular book titles of the 1840s and 1850s, suggesting a more specific and smaller vegetation than *Gathered Leaves*, *Fresh Leaves from Western Woods*, *Autumn Leaves*, or *Stray Leaves from the Book of Nature* (see Loving 179). Also, the choice of "leaves" over "blades" of grass talks back to the era's scientific discourses (see Reynolds, *Walt Whitman's America* 241), especially chemistry and botany. If the 1855 *Leaves of Grass* suggested the creation of poetic language as an organic process, it was also a "book of nature" probing the possibilities and limitations of imaginatively lifting the most humble, neglected natural phenomena onto the page without completely controlling their presence.

Dickinson's collection of plants and the cover of Whitman's first volume of poetry already embody the passionate attention to nature's minute details that both would sustain throughout their poetic projects. Clearly, nature's smallest incarnations have a different presence and function in their poetry—Dickinson kept turning Victorian associations of white women with flowers and birds into ambivalent expressions of female autonomy, while Whitman embraced the grass as a multivalent symbol for American democracy and its new, uninhibited language. It is my argument here, however, that for all these differences, their poems also share a deep concern with paying attention to small nature, and that this shared interest expresses itself in related ways that attain fresh eco-ethical resonances when their works are read in the contexts of their time's environmental discussions. Specifically, I hope to show that a key feature of this shared concern lies in what I call their frequent acts of noticing previously overlooked, supposedly minor flora and fauna, which echo but also revise the ways in which the proto-ecological sciences, in particular, were also turning toward nature's minutiae. In Dickinson's and Whitman's poetry, these acts of "noticing"—which the mid-nineteenth-century *Webster's* defined as observing or seeing in the sense of "to regard, to treat with attention and civilities"—matter both thematically and aesthetically, and always involve a potentially eco-ethical change of mind.

It was during Dickinson's and Whitman's most productive years that the field of natural history split into several new disciplines, many of them with sub-branches specializing in the study of nature's smallest phenomena. These "new" sciences, including biology, chemistry, geology, and the new geography, are now understood as proto-ecological because they combined the empirical study of individual organisms with a novel understanding of these organisms' connectivity and interdependence in relation to their biotic and abiotic environment. Botanists, for example, developed tools for cataloguing and systematizing plants and dealt with issues later addressed by the science of ecology; what they discussed under the rubric of plant geography included the role of the environment in determining geographical distribution, and what they described as plant formation soon took on a new relevance when Frederic Clements coined the term "plant community" and provided an important basis for the analyses of ecosystems. Even Charles Darwin's theory of evolution—which was based on older developmental theories about the links between nature's diversity and environmental factors and, among other things, generated "the organismal side" of the community concept (Allen and Hoekstra 130)—received one of its most crucial inspirations from botany and herbarium studies (see Kohn et al.). Another branch of biology, ornithology, was also linked to the advent of ecology, as the study of birds on the Galápagos Islands provided Darwin with a unique opportunity to grasp the role of geographic isolation in the emergence of new species (Bowler 300). Finally, nineteenth-century chemistry developed new integrative models of understanding nature's minute processes, which soon fostered the emergence of an ecological paradigm; Justus Liebig's *Organic Chemistry in Its Application to Agriculture and Physiology* (1840), in particular, argued that the analysis of a plant's mineral needs leads to a more precise understanding of what nourishment it requires than vague ideas about humus. In spite of their growing specialization, these sciences still overlapped significantly, especially in the works of the era's great generalists such as Alexander von Humboldt, whose *Cosmos* combined perspectives from chemistry, botany, geology, and astronomy, and who was both one of the last representatives of the old holism and the preeminent modern ecologist before Darwin. When in 1866 the Darwinist Ernst Häckel coined the term "oecology" and defined it as "the science of the relations of living organisms to the external world, their habitat, customs, energies, parasites, etc." (Worster, *Nature's Economy* 192), this was based on a broad shift toward the study of nature's relationships, especially in terms of very small organisms and phenomena.

This does not mean that the specialized sciences were "ecological" in the modern, prescriptive sense of the term, that is, interested in promoting respect for nature's systems or arguing for its protection, especially from anthropogenic changes. The sciences were part of both the problem and the solution, as they provided the knowledge that also fostered nature's exploitation; paradoxically, ecology itself "began as a science devoted to understanding natural relationships for the purpose of improving our ability to control them" (Bowler 1–2) and was linked to ideas of environmental reform that saw the transformation and "improvement" of nature as a basis for social progress. And yet a modern environmental awareness also depends on the sciences; as Edward O. Wilson has put it succinctly, we must understand nature well in order to move from appropriation to a responsible, caring relationship (*Future of Life* 131). In this sense, the mid-nineteenth century was a foundational moment in the development of a modern environmental consciousness, whose novel understanding of nature as a web of interactive systems hinged upon an investment in the study of nature's smallest elements.

These developments in the proto-ecological sciences and their eco-ethical implications were promulgated by popular lectures and nature essays and linked to emerging conservationist arguments, which in turn were rooted in utilitarian ideals of environmental reform. The complex, sometimes contradictory relationships among these intensifying environmental perspectives find a particularly powerful expression in the writings of George Perkins Marsh, the amateur scientist now widely recognized as a pioneer of modern environmental ethics. Fascinatingly, his *Man and Nature; or, Physical Geography as Modified by Human Action* (1864), which sold 100,000 copies in a few months (Merchant, *Columbia Guide* 127) and inspired the American government to set up the Forestry Commission (Bowler 319), was especially adamant in urging his compatriots to be more attentive to nature's "Minute Organisms":

> [I]f man is destined to inhabit the earth much longer, and to advance in natural knowledge with the rapidity which has marked his progress in physical science for the last two or three centuries, he will learn to put a wiser estimate on the works of creation, and will derive not only great instruction from studying the ways of nature in her obscurest, humblest walks, but great material advantage. (112)

This passage shows that mid-nineteenth-century environmentalist and eco-ethical concerns, and indeed the sense of an impending crisis of global dimensions, were significantly based upon a critique of "man's" ignorance and disregard of minute organisms, even as all of these ideas grew out of utilitarian visions of nature's improved management (see Bowler 319).

This new perception of nature's minutiae forms a crucial context for reading Dickinson's and Whitman's poetry. When Dickinson boasted in an early letter that "I have four studies. They are Mental Philosophy, Geology, Latin, and Botany. How large they sound" (L6), she identified two fields (botany and geology) important to proto-ecological theories. According to Richard Sewall, Almira H. Lincoln's *Familiar Lectures on Botany* may well have been "one of the most important of [Dickinson's] school books" (351). Like many women of a similar background, Dickinson stayed in touch with scientific discussions through her readings of *Harper's New Monthly*, *Scribner's Monthly*, and especially the *Atlantic Monthly*, which carried reviews of Humboldt's *Cosmos* and Darwin's *Origin of Species*, Agassiz's *Contributions to the Natural History of the United States of America* and Marsh's *Man and Nature*, next to discussions of Liebig's discoveries in chemistry and countless nature essays about birds, flowers, and insects.

Whitman came in contact with these debates through slightly different channels but with similar emphases. To make up for his limited formal education, Whitman forged, in Ed Folsom and Kenneth M. Price's words, a "rough and informal curriculum" that included chemistry, botany, and geography (4). He was interested in the latest science books, leading journals, and public science lectures (attending, for instance, a lecture by Harvard biologist and Darwin opponent Louis Agassiz in 1868; see Beaver 107), and his collection of clippings from magazines and newspapers included scientific publications on botany and "Scenes on the Ocean Floor" (*Complete Writings*, 7:70, 95). While it would be too facile to say that Dickinson's and Whitman's geographical and intellectual closeness to the era's debates about nature's supposedly minor elements translates directly into clearly identifiable proto-ecological sensibilities in their poetry, these interlocking discourses were part of the culture from which their poetry emerged.

As both poets talk back to the era's scientific publications, with their specialized terminology and nomenclature, as well as to the popular, often moralistic natural history essays, they develop an environmentally suggestive poetics of the small that hinges upon repeated acts of noticing minor natural phenomena, which their poems not only talk about but also perform. The environmental significance of these gestures has to do with the very frequency with which both of them insist on paying attention to nature's most inconspicuous elements and making room for "estimating" them in their own right; it also involves the short, condensed quality of Dickinson's poems and Whitman's individual lines, which attends to the problem of the sheer mass of physiological details that such an interest in "small nature" entails; and it emerges from a speaking position characterized by recurrent but unstable moments of awareness rather than lasting knowledge or control. Overall, such noticing goes hand in hand with a profoundly humbling change of mind that begins with seeing what is beneath one's feet and leads to the realization that even the most unassuming embrace of nature's small creatures in many short micromoments risks their conceptual domination, while the re-inscription of their otherness increases the sense of nature's alterity and is therefore no viable solution either. Instead of lapsing into silence, however, Dickinson and Whitman keep engaging this paradox, carving out a language that seeks to speak about weeds, insects, and birds in nonappropriative ways. The following two chapters read their approaches to nature's small worlds as different but related strategies of environmental intervention: both poets participate in the era's increasing proto-ecological awareness of nature's minutiae through an aesthetic and ethical urgency of their own, an urgency that, paradoxically, derives much of its power from the particular humility it entails.

1

"Turns unperceived beneath – our feet"

Dickinson's Frequent Acts of Noticing Small Nature

From her earliest poems about America's most familiar flora and fauna to later philosophical and epistemological meditations that seem to leave all earthly concerns behind, Dickinson's poetic language emerges from an interest in flowers and birds, grasses and insects, and many of her imaginary journeys to the mind's circumference remain grounded in the "Minuter landscape[s]" (Fr964) by which they were inspired. The poet who described herself as "Daisy" and "small, like the Wren," who habitually sent single blooms to friends and relatives and whose letters gave vivid accounts of so many birds, was seldom more passionately involved with the world than when noticing the singularity and immediacy of nature's smallest incarnations.

Dickinson's fascination with the small is among the best-known features of her work, yet one that has been eyed with skepticism. Alfred Habegger, for instance, expressed relief that after 1862, the poet "dropp[ed] her too frequent bees and birds" for "a sublime perspective that utterly changed the scale" (439). While it is true that "bees and birds" figure less prominently in Dickinson's later work, they never vanish completely, as poems such as "Quite Empty, quite at rest" (Fr1632), "Upon his Saddle sprung a Bird" (Fr1663), and "The Jay his Castanet has struck" (Fr1670) inform us. Moreover, Habegger's comment shows what happens when Dickinson's poems are measured against Romanticism's interest in sublime experiences evoked by larger phenomena, a preference many critics share. Several feminist critics, however, have stressed the autonomy and power of Dickinson's small creatures (see Eberwein, *Strategies of Limitation* 169, 170), thus providing an important foundation for environmental revaluations of her small-nature poetics. In this chapter I argue that placing Dickinson's poems about small organisms in the context of her culture's growing interest in these phenomena further challenges notions about their comparative insignificance. Specifically, I hope to show that her repeated acts of noticing America's supposedly minor flora and fauna resonate as complex eco-ethical gestures whose green implications have much to do with how they talk back to the environmental publications of her time—in their thematic focus, formal and stylistic features, and, especially, through a speaking position that recasts Victorian sentimental conventions as gestures of environmental humility.

Noticing the Small

The following little-discussed poem from 1865, in which the speaker anthropomorphizes worms and a bird to formulate a seemingly simple analogy, exemplifies the ways in which Dickinson responds to her era's emerging concern for nature's small creatures:

> Our little Kinsmen – after Rain
> In plenty may be seen,
> A Pink and Pulpy multitude
> The tepid Ground upon.
>
> A needless life, it seemed to me
> Until a little Bird
> As to a Hospitality
> Advanced and breakfasted –
>
> As I of He, so God of Me
> I pondered, may have judged,
> And left the little Angle Worm
> With Modesties enlarged. (Fr932)

In three short stanzas, the spectacle of an unspecified "Pink and Pulpy multitude" becomes recognizable as a particular kind of earthworm, whose name "Angle Worm" not only strengthens the poem's perhaps predictable religious connotations but also denotes a particular species. Considering that zoologists (most notably Jean-Baptiste Lamarck, a forerunner of Häckel and Darwin) were only beginning to sort out Linnaeus's initial subdivisions of invertebrates, and classification was slow since many did not regard insects and worms worthy of study, Dickinson's reference to a specific worm without overburdening the poem with scientific terminology echoes this interest in the intricacies of supposedly inferior natural phenomena while keeping a distance from the controlling gestures of biological classification. Moreover, the speaker understands an apparently "tepid," dull spot as teeming with vitality, and what "seemed" to be "a needless life" turns out to have its place in a larger ecological scheme that would now be called a food chain, all of which can be linked to the time's novel interest in the interconnectedness of vegetation, birds, and insects. Marsh's first edition of *Man and Nature*, for instance, emphasizes that most birds live on insects and worms rather than human crops, and in a short section on the "Utility of Insects and Worms" suggests that these underestimated creatures might be significant and even worth protecting:

> Some enthusiastic entomologist will, perhaps, by and by discover that insects and worms are as essential as the larger organisms to the proper working of the great terraqueous machine, and we shall have as eloquent pleas in defence [*sic*] of the mosquito, and perhaps even of the tzetze-fly, as Toussenel and Michelet have framed in behalf of the bird. (88)

In the 1870 edition of his study, he was more definite on this subject:

> But the action of the creeping and swarming things of the earth, though *often passed unnoticed, is not without important effects in the general economy of nature*. The geographical importance of insects proper, as well as of worms, depends principally on their connection with vegetable life as agents of its fecundation, and of its destruction. (128; emphasis added)

Dickinson's innocuous poem indirectly participates in shifting her culture's attention to "nature's economy" toward the most undervalued species, probing their environmental significance when it was still widely ignored even among naturalists. In this context, some of her stylistic choices—the dash in the first line that links the worm's appearance to rainy weather, and the perplexing first lines of the last stanza, whose reduced syntax and parallel structures result in ambiguous relationships between subject and object and between clauses—also become environmentally meaningful as they highlight nature's multiple and dynamic interrelatedness that may be difficult to discern.

As such, the poem not only talks about but also performs the act of noticing undervalued creatures and emphasizes the change of mind involved in such a shift of perspective, investing conventional concepts of religious revelation and Victorian virtues with fresh ecological meaning. How the speaker considers wriggling worms as her "Kinsmen," how she combines sentimental views of "little" creatures with a quasi-scientific interest in small species whose physiognomy is less cute than stark, and how she implies that inattentive humans are a potentially destructive factor for what lives precariously at their feet, all push the limits of Victorian sensibilities and those of the time's proto-ecological science alike. The poem's apparently plain moral, then (human existence is no more relevant than that of worms, but part of larger webs of significance; the poet depends on seemingly minor elements of her environment for nourishment as the bird does on worms), expressed in a deceptively small format and three seemingly straightforward sentences, involves a number of provocative insights, and culminates in humility as an eco-ethical perspective. The ironic recognition of the empowerment that comes with realized modesty ("with Modesties enlarged") makes the poem ecologically even more intriguing because it addresses the inherently paradoxical character of such an ethical stance. Again, the cultural context highlights such implications. In his late prose piece "Huckleberries" (1862), Thoreau warned precisely of the condescending attitude that may be part of such attention to nature's minutiae: "Many public speakers are accustomed, as I think foolishly, to talk about what they call *little things* in a patronizing way sometimes, advising, perhaps, that they be not wholly neglected [. . .] but Pliny said, *In minimis Natura praestat*—Nature excels in the least things" (468). Where Thoreau's extended essays and public lectures, personal in tone but also learned and often didactic, always struggled with this downside of the new fascination with nature's "little things," Dickinson expresses a similar concern in a short, innocuous poem that itself poses as a "little thing," and whose speaker performs the humble gesture of noticing a minor natural phenomenon with an ironic distance that mocks the grand tone of the enlightened nature lover, thus sidestepping the hubris that always lurks on the other side of humility.

In a number of other poems, Dickinson's speakers similarly perform acts of noticing what is habitually disregarded, combining sentimental and religious perspectives with scientific ways of seeing in ways that talk back to the evolving environmental discourses of the day while also keeping their distance. For instance, her famous "The Spider as an Artist" (Fr1373) is about a defiant act of paying respectful attention to the "Neglected Son of Genius" that is habitually destroyed, charging religious morals ("in a Christian Land"), especially the notion of being the guardian of the weak ("I take thee by the Hand – "), with green overtones without claiming an exhaustive knowledge of the species. Also, the observant speaker in "The Bat is dun, with wrinkled Wings– " (Fr1408) stresses that this songless, "fallow" animal is worthy of "praise" and that his "Eccentricities" are actually "Beneficent," indirectly alluding to the evolving understanding of the complex relationships in nature's living systems. And in "The Jay his Castanet has struck" (Fr1670), the speaker warns that whoever "ignores" the voice of the bird that signals the coming of Fall "Is impudent to nature," again investing conventional moral considerations with environmental meaning. Other poems, in which the call to notice nature's minutiae is less explicit, include poem Fr1395, which evokes "The Butterfly's Numidian Gown / With spots of Burnish roasted on" as aptly functional "proof against the Sun," so that the exotic butterfly on a clover not only resonates as a symbol of the soul but comes alive as a migrating species. Similarly, the well-known "A Bird came down the Walk" (Fr359) takes minute account of the robin's characteristic movement and physiognomy in a local situation before releasing it by way of a beautifully condensed image of its flight into the sky—not so much dangerously distorting natural truths, as E. Miller Budick claimed (61), but exploring them through a combination of sentimental conventions and natural history information that increases the poem's symbolic and environmental correspondences. And her famous twin hummingbird poems, "Within my Garden, Rides a Bird" (Fr370) and "A Route of Evanescence" (Fr1489), sketch this tiny, elusive bird's physiognomy, movement, and color through its effect not only on the human soul but also on the natural environment. As specific life-forms in their characteristic environments, all of these creatures attain the status of subjects that are worthy of ethical consideration. In such poems, a quasi-scientific interest and formulaic Victorian modesty yield a complex position of environmental humility that starts from the sheer willingness to notice small, even miniscule creatures and culminates in the realization that their life is as inherently valuable as our own. Dickinson's fine eye for relationships among small natural phenomena, and between them and people, echoes her time's evolving scientific, proto-ecological interests, while the poems' shortness and their reliance on just a few physical features and scientific terms also revise the script of contemporaneous science writing that displayed a wealth of details and reveled in the resulting classifications. As such, they point the way toward a stance that today, in the face of a global environmental crisis largely caused by human hubris, is at the heart of many green arguments—the respectful recognition of nature's often overlooked phenomena that is informed by but not limited to the scientific understanding of their complex position in the world and the appreciation of their use value, and that includes the humble awareness of our own limited knowledge. As Edward O. Wilson suggests in his ecological manifesto *The Future of Life*: "The creature at your feet dismissed as a bug or a weed is a creation in and of itself. It has a name, a million-year history, and a place in the world. [. . .] The ethical value substantiated by close examination of its biology is that the life forms around us are too old, too complex, and potentially too useful to be carelessly discarded" (131).

• • •

Dickinson's more or less explicit calls to notice the small in nature are reinforced by two characteristics of her oeuvre as a whole: the sheer *number* of poems that make small natural phenomena their primary subject, and her way of presenting natural history *detail*—two poetic strategies I discuss in general here before showing how they play out in Dickinson's flower and riddle poems. First, her poetry is so thickly lined with small life-forms that quantity itself becomes a forceful statement. Her four hundred poems on flowers and flower parts—unusual "even for her flower-obsessed period," as Paula Bennett puts it ("Flowers" 116)—together with her many poems about birds, insects, and other creatures that were often not part of the genteel imagination, comprise a passionate gesture of noticing small natural beings that undermines standard notions of their insignificance. In these many poems together, Dickinson urges attention to and indeed childlike astonishment at what received "adult" knowledge degrades to a place of insignificance. Such attentiveness promulgates not only the comprehension of basic ecological processes, but the humbling insight that nothing is too small to merit poetic recognition.

Considering the cultural context helps to see the degree to which the sheer mass of Dickinson's poems about flowers, birds, and bees constitutes an environmentally relevant gesture. Back then, professionals and amateurs became increasingly interested in the vast numbers of small life-forms, amassing data in huge quantities. Thoreau, for example, studied plants by the hundreds, even thousands: "He began collecting, drying, labeling, and classifying botanical specimens until in a period of ten years he was able to locate more than eight hundred of the twelve hundred known species of Middlesex County"; his herbarium contained more than one thousand specimens (Harding, qtd. in Walls, *Seeing New Worlds* 136). The publications of the time generally stressed that understanding the multitude and diversity of nature's undervalued phenomena was requisite for grasping the complex web of life—a cultural climate to which Dickinson's countless small nature poems seem to respond. While some of these poems are certainly related to a Romantic interest in the ugly or abject, overall they echo and amplify the time's attention to nature's minutiae as valuable in their own right. This also sheds fresh light on their role in Dickinson's work as a whole. Rather than "too frequent," these hundreds of poems can be read as a numerically appropriate response to the unfathomable quantities of small natural phenomena; rather than embarrassing moments in which the poet of the mind's "circumference" lapses back to naïve and limited perspectives, they constitute critical elements of her oeuvre that keep grounding the imagination in the humbling attention to the smallest natural phenomena and insist on their significance as objects worthy of poetic scrutiny.

Second, Dickinson's approach to physiological detail also contributes to the environmental impetus of her poems about flowers, birds, and similar phenomena. It has often been noted that these poems are particularly rich in detail and that this eye for detail is grounded in her familiarity with Victorian painting and the time's decorative arts (Farr, "Dickinson and the Visual Arts"),[1] but critics have so far said little about the proto-ecological literacy such poems are grounded in and convey. In Dickinson's poems, detail matters environmentally because it gives prominence to nature's physical existence as noteworthy in itself, in its actuality and material presence, not just as a route to transcendence.

Again, it is helpful to consider that around midcentury, scientific attention to previously unknown details was a key aspect of such newly specialized fields as chemistry, botany, and plant geography, particularly by way of taxonomy, the often undervalued science of hierarchical classification. Yet taxonomy is all about systematics based on minute details and a proto-ecological "dynamic science, dedicated to exploring the causes of relationships and similarities among organisms" (Gould 98). Dickinson's botany book, for example, included hundreds of entries, between two and twelve lines long, on the details and preferred habitat of individual plants, such as this one on the barren sedge: "spikelets in fives, sessile, approximate: fruit ovate, acuminate or somewhat beaked, 2-cleft, 3-sided-compressed, scabrous at the margin; equaling the ovate acutish scale. 8 i. Wet" (Lincoln 279). Her poems, whose condensed form and elliptic phrases resemble the staccato entries of botanical, ornithological, and entomological handbooks, doubled this interest back to her culture, deploying precise and intriguing physiological details as indices of why small nonhuman phenomena matter. Yet because they never present more than a handful of physiological features and the relationships between individual elements often remain ambiguous, Dickinson's poems manage to be informed by precise knowledge without suggesting complete understanding and conceptual control of the objects at hand. This is crucial insofar as attention to small natural details, while it can question the superiority of human concerns, does not necessitate a speaking position grounded in environmental humility, since it may also serve to quantify and thus control such entities. As poems, her condensed but epistemologically open snapshots of so many flowers and birds are legible as nuanced comments on her time's humble attention to the "lowest" creatures, which always threatens to flip over into scientific hubris.

Flower Poems

The green overtones of Dickinson's frequent and detailed attention to nature's minutiae are clearly evident in her flower poems, which respond not only to the time's sentimental language of flowers but also to botany's proto-ecological microperspectives. Midcentury botanists sought to accurately describe plant forms and structures, created systematic plant catalogues, and developed new principles of taxonomy; these efforts to understand plants in their natural surroundings formed a basis for the later formulation of ecological concepts such as plant families, natural distribution and adaptation, and ecosystems. The fact that during Dickinson's time botany was considered "peculiarly adapted to females" because "the objects of investigation are beautiful and delicate" (Lincoln 12) infused popular botany books with substantial doses of sentimental allusions, yet it also allowed women to use the field as an entryway into science (see Baym, *American Women of Letters* 20–22). In this context, Dickinson's poetic syntheses of scientifically inspired observations and sentimental conventions not only complicate Victorian floral discourses "on change, mortality, and the afterlife" (Petrino 160), they also talk back to her culture's proto-ecological interest in plant physiology and plant geography. In particular, her flower poems deploy the sentimental trope of personification in ways that complicate the eco-ethical implications of paying passionate attention to botanical details "which had perhaps remained *unnoticed*" (Lincoln 12; emphasis added).[2]

Personification is a trope that grants the phenomena it perceives considerable autonomy and agency rather than constructing them as mere objects that exist for humankind to explore and use, and yet it has troubled environmental critics because of its inherent paradox. If personification "allows us to use our knowledge about ourselves to maximal effect, to use insights about ourselves to help us comprehend such things as forces of nature" (Lakoff and Turner 72), it also reinforces the human urge to understand things on our own terms, potentially encouraging self-absorption and abuse of the other. Lawrence Buell, however, claims that the trope is ultimately more of an asset than a liability for literary representations of the environment, especially if it is based on information (*Environmental Imagination* 180–218). Personifications in Dickinson's flower poems tend to be grounded in information, but only to such a degree and presented in such an elliptical format that they do not foster visions of understanding and control. On this basis, they engage personification in ways that draw the speaker toward an emotionally charged attention to small nature in place, imagining human-nature relationships that include ethical considerations.

The poem Dickinson once signed "Arbutus" is an excellent example of her combination of attention to certain natural details with intense anthropomorphism in ways that invoke the possibility of an ethical stance:

Pink – small – and punctual –
Aromatic – low –
Covert in April –
Candid in May –

Dear to the Moss –
Known to the Knoll –
Next to the Robin
In every human Soul –

Bold little Beauty –
Bedecked with thee
Nature forswears –
Antiquity – (Fr1357)

Because the arbutus was "emblematic of the flower cult of the young Amherst circle," Charles Anderson has read this poem as an example for Dickinson's failure to control her sentimental mode (99); not minding the poem's sentimentality, Elizabeth Petrino has argued that it "celebrates the arbutus for its human virtues of humility and constancy" and boldness (150). What I would stress here is that the plant's symbolic humility is also transferred to the speaker's attitude toward the "little" flower, and that this gesture is enabled by the combination of a certain amount of botanical detail with the sentimental trope of personification, all in a poem whose lines are short to the point of canceling the very act of speaking (or writing poetry).

The poem offers a condensed botanical portrait that, at least structurally, echoes the entry on the arbutus in *Familiar Lectures on Botany*, especially if one replaces Lincoln's colons with Dickinsonian dashes: "stem creeping : branches and petioles very hirsute : leaves cordate-orvoate, entire : corolla cylindric" (286). Of course, the poem also forgoes the field's technical nomenclature; instead, it grasps the flower's color, size, exquisite scent, time of bloom, and mode of growing "low" by way of synthesizing scientific observation and the sentimental personification of flowers as women. This strategy was in itself not alien to botanical books, which habitually used personification (see Buell, *Environmental Imagination* 490n20) and even included poems that performed the same move (Lincoln's *Lectures on Botany*, for instance, opens and ends with a poem, and includes another one on the succession of flowers by Charlotte Smith). In Dickinson's botanically informed poem, the personification of the flower as a humble woman and the speaker's identification with it strengthen its botanical suggestiveness but undermine any scientific pose of mastery. Moreover, this move amplifies the speaker's humbling awareness of this delicate and vulnerable species in place. "Female" humility as a mode of approaching small flowers was part of the time's environmentally sensitive debates—Lincoln's botany handbook, for instance, talks about the way flowers of mosses are easily overlooked: "You have learned, it is to be hoped, so much humility, as to see that all that God has made is important, and that our ignorance of the uses of natural production, is not a proof of his want of wisdom, but of our blindness" (189). In Dickinson's poem about the act of noticing a mosslike plant, humility is presented less as a stance toward God's creation than as one with which to approach the plant itself.

In other Dickinson poems, the personification of flowers strongly suggests a metaphorical reading, yet their informed references to natural history details also let them function as invitations to notice nature for its own sake—as in this example:

There is a flower that Bees prefer –
And Butterflies – desire –
To gain the Purple Democrat
The Humming Bird – aspire –

And Whatsoever Insect pass –
A Honey bear away
Proportioned to his several dearth
And her – capacity –

Her face be rounder than the Moon
And ruddier than the Gown
Or Orchis in the Pasture –
Or Rhododendron – worn –

She doth not wait for June –
Before the World be Green –
Her sturdy little Countenance
Against the Wind – be seen –

Contending with the Grass –
Near Kinsman to Herself –
For Privilege of Sod and Sun –
Sweet Litigants for Life –

And when the Hills be full –
And newer fashions blow –
Doth not retract a single spice
For pang of jealousy –

Her Public – be the Noon –
Her Providence – the Sun –
Her Progress – by the Bee – proclaimed –
In sovereign – Swerveless Tune –

The Bravest – of the Host –
Surrendering – the last –
Nor even of Defeat – aware –
What cancelled by the Frost – (Fr642)

This floral allegory about an unassuming, open-handed person cannot be reduced to the botanical information it is grounded in, yet its dramaturgy expresses a genuine fascination with the interaction of different life-forms around this common species that is part of its meaning. As the poem draws the reader's attention toward insects and birds attracted by the clover's nectar, to its shape, color, and long time of blooming, its preference for meager soil and competition for nutrition within the ecosystem, it fuses the perspectives of plant morphology, biogeography, and comparative anatomy ("ruddier" than "Orchis" or "Rhododendron") and talks about local adaptation ("sturdy" smallness) and a balanced system ("proportioned" to "capacity") in ways that further amplify the quasi-ecological tint of this microcosmic sketch. Informed by botany's basic principles, but relying only on a limited number of details and replacing technical terms with sentimental, anthropomorphizing ideas, it does not assume a serious scientific position, and yet it can be said to point the way from nineteenth-century plant geography toward a notion of community in which mutual responsibilities matter. Much later, ecology would base its theories on notions of ecosystems as communities, and environmental ethics would push for a radical revaluation of human-nature interaction under such terms. Dickinson's informed interest in the details of one flower's microcosm, in conjunction with the empathy that comes from her embrace of personification, participates in her culture's moves in such a direction.

Other flower poems that combine botanical knowledge with the sentimental trope of personification in ways that foster close attention to and possibly ethical concern for the most common plants include, for instance, "The Dandelion's pallid Tube" (Fr1565), which opens with a reference to what Lincoln's *Familiar Lectures on Botany* describes as "[t]he lower hollow cylinder of a monopetalous corolla" (327) and personifies the flower and its environment through the claim that it "Astonishes the Grass," inspiring a similar astonishment in the reader; the second stanza renders the appearance of "a signal Bud" as an act of will, suggesting respect for a common flower. Similarly, "The Gentian has a parched Corolla – / Like azure dried" (Fr1458) also alludes to Lincoln's botany book ("Corolla, or Crown, is that part of the flower which is most remarkable for the liveliness of its colours, the delicacy of its substance, and the sweetness of its perfume"; 75), yet Dickinson's way of combining classification with a rhetoric of gentleness ("As Casual as Rain / And as Benign – "), friendship, and remembering turns sentimental patterns of female behavior, at least potentially, into a blueprint for relating to a delicate flower.

A variation on Dickinson's repeated acts of noticing nature's small phenomena is offered by several poems that express a sense of guilt over *not* paying attention, as in the following example:

It bloomed and dropt, a Single Noon –
The Flower – distinct and Red –

I, passing, thought another Noon
Another in it's stead

Will equal glow, and thought no more
But came another Day
To find the Species disappeared –
The Same Locality –

The Sun in place – no other fraud
On Nature's perfect Sum –
Had I but lingered Yesterday –
Was my retrieveless blame –

Much Flowers of this and further Zones
Have perished in my Hands
For seeking it's Resemblance –
But unapproached it stands –

The single Flower of the Earth
That I, in passing by
Unconscious was – Great Nature's Face
Passed infinite by Me – (Fr843)

Rebecca Patterson has argued that the poem evokes a "red rose of love" which the speaker failed to "pluck" (48), while Judith Farr stresses that the poem is probably about a daylily, which, however, has several flowers (*Gardens of Emily Dickinson* 135), concluding that the poem is not realistic but "seeks to describe a mysterious event and an equally exquisite punishment that avenges mysteriously primitive powers that deserve more respect that has been accorded them" (*Gardens of Emily Dickinson* 136). While such symbolic transferrals are clearly implied, the speaker's "retrieveless blame" over having missed a *flower* is part of the poem's meaning. Again, the account of one "Species'" color and mode of briefly growing in a certain "Zone" is subtly informed by the language of botany and plant geography, yet emphasizes the ethics of paying attention, if only in its absence.

A number of other poems address the juncture between noticing easily overlooked plants and a feeble sense of human power and control this may involve, especially when the flowers are collected. In "So bashful when I spied her!" (Fr70), the coy speaker plucks a "struggling, blushing" flower, and in "Who robbed the Woods – " (Fr57), the forest's "trinkets" are "scanned," "grasped," and carried away. In an environmental context, these early poems, which might be brushed aside as inconsequential or cute, express certain qualms over the ways in which such attention turns out to have a destructive impact. In these deceptively simple poems, childlike ease and moral urgency put considerable pressure on each other: the first speaker suggests she has "robbed the Dingle" and "betrayed the Dell – ," while the second is concerned about the betrayal of "robbing" the "trusting Woods," opening spaces for environmental interpretations of the speaker's ambivalent gestures of concern. Finally, the poem "Except to Heaven, she is nought" (Fr173) turns the Christian tenet that all beings are included in God's grace into a parable about a "superfluous" flower-as-woman who is noticed by no one but the bees, winds, and butterflies "on the Acre." The poem ends with a sentimental but no less urgent call not to "Take her from the Lawn"—a plea that works both in the context of the inevitable end of summer that Dickinson was so concerned with because it tested her faith, and as a reference to mindless human destruction. At a time when botanists were beginning to discuss the disappearance of flowers in particular places but did not yet connect this phenomenon to human action (explaining it instead by the "traveling" of plants to other places, as did Higginson in his essay "The Procession of the Flowers," which Dickinson knew well), and when not even the ethical treatment of domestic animals found a general consensus, Dickinson's scientifically informed yet unassuming flower poems transfer the traditional Victorian ideal of (female) humility and care from interpersonal behavior to human ways of treating small, insentient beings, thus participating, however ambiguously, in a general broadening of imaginative possibilities that would eventually lead to a serious consideration of moral accountability toward "The most unworthy Flower" (Fr741).

Riddle Poems

Riddle poems are another manifestation of the ways in which Dickinson kept talking back to her time's evolving environmental debates by enacting moments of noticing small natural phenomena that were taken for granted. Like her flower poems, her riddle poems are an integral part of nineteenth-century culture, and in an early study (1969), Dolores Lucas began to explain Dickinson's conscious use of the literary riddle to talk "ambiguously" about "family relationships, nature, nineteenth-century progress, God and death" (131). More specifically, her riddle poems about small nature also echo and revise the conventions of scientific and popular discourses, but in different ways than her flower poems. For one, the genre's question-answer dynamic loosely resembles the structure of scientific inquiry and includes natural history information, yet scientific visions of knowledge and control are destabilized because riddles depend on the innovative, defamiliarizing presentation of detail and play with the option of often remaining unsolved. Dickinson's poems thus amplify the epistemological critique implied in her characteristic combination of dashes, ellipses, slippery subject-object relations, and nonrecoverable deletions. Second, the playful, sometimes mocking tone of her riddle poems undermines not only the sciences' air of seriousness but also the speaker's implied critique, as well as the sense of achievement that may come with answering the riddle's question, thus suggesting a complex stance of humility in terms of understanding nature's smallest creatures. And third, since riddles constitute a genre suggestive of childhood and often evoke a child's voice, these poems reassess not conventional female perspectives but a child's viewpoint—itself a prime sentimental interest of Victorian culture—as an environmentally resonant poetic perspective. Dickinson's child voice has troubled critics almost as much as her frequent focus on nature's small creatures, as another comment by Charles Anderson indicates: "[T]he 'fanciful' for its own sake remained a troublesome aspect of her own temperament throughout maturity, as witnessed by the game of playing 'little girl' that she indulged in to the very end of her life. [. . .] How could this childish habit be overcome, or turned to poetic advantage?" (97). After Lucas discussed the child speaker in Dickinson's poetry as a coping strategy to deal with her ostensible fear of God, nature, and her father, one that enabled playful innocence and anonymity as well as the freedom of direct assault (22), feminist critics have further explored the empowering aspects of this child persona. Jane D. Eberwein, for instance, has shown how Dickinson uses "mimesis to reverse [the] thrust toward adulthood in an attempt to retain the abundant options" of childhood (*Strategies of Limitation* 96), and Cristanne Miller has argued that Dickinson subversively uses "the exaggeratedly feminine mask of perpetual childhood" as one of her key "disguises in the bid for power" (*A Poet's Grammar* 167). The liberating impetus of the child voice also plays a role in Dickinson's riddles about small nature, as it enables the speaker to approach the nonhuman environment in ways largely unrestrained by the norms of adult imagination and, to a degree, of Victorian associations of white middle-class women with (small) nature, pointing toward environmental humility without perpetuating stereotypical notions of women's servility. At the same time this juncture also gives a new twist to the paradoxical empowerment that the pose of a child—conventionally characterized by limited social and political power, limited access to accepted forms of knowledge, and occasional self-doubt—holds for a female poet facing not only small nature but masculine realms of power and knowledge as well.

In "You'll know Her – by Her Foot" (Fr604), for instance, the riddle format is crucial for how the features of a common bird are being noticed without the suggestion of conceptual mastery:

> You'll know Her – by Her Foot –
> The smallest Gamboge Hand
> With Fingers – where the Toes should be –
> Would more affront the sand –
>
> Than this Quaint Creature's Boot –
> Adjusted by a stem –
> Without a Button – I c'd vouch –
> Unto a Velvet Limb –
>
> You'll know Her – by Her Vest –
> Tight fitting – Orange – Brown –
> Inside a Jacket duller –
> She wore when she was born –
>
> Her Cap is small – and snug –
> Constructed for the Winds –
> She'd pass for Barehead – short way off –
> But as she closer stands –
>
> So finer 'tis than Wool –
> You cannot feel the seam –
> Nor is it Clasped unto of Band –
> Nor held opon – of Brim –
>
> You'll know Her – by Her Voice –
> At first – a doubtful Tone –
> A sweet endeavor – but as March
> To April – hurries on –
>
> She squanders on your Head
> Such Arguments of Pearl –
> You beg the Robin in your Brain
> To keep the other – still –

The childlike wonder does not inhibit attention to natural detail; to the contrary—the speaker is intensely alive to the world around her, and by withholding the bird's name invites readers to imaginatively zoom in on a robin's specific features. Interestingly, the speaker personifies the bird as a finely dressed woman, harking back to sentimental conventions, yet several of the metaphors mockingly employed here instead of ornithological terms defy conventional standards of female beauty (a seemingly bareheaded "Quaint Creature" with a foot resembling a gumlike hand, and a loud, unceasing voice). This teasing but precise rendition amplifies the environmentally relevant attention to often overlooked creatures that was part of both the Victorian identification of women with birds and the evolving scientific discourses, but subverts the sentimental rhetoric of the former and the interest in classification of the latter. From such an angle, the poem's surprising ending does not necessarily reintroduce Dickinson as primarily a poet of the mind, but it can be read as a comment on the challenges involved in fully fronting natural particulars that may not quite match our preconceived notions.

Reading the poem against nineteenth-century ornithological discourses strengthens its eco-ethical resonances. Throughout the century, amateur birdwatchers provided countless specimens and surveys for field naturalists who generated massive ornithological information that would soon span the continent (Bowler 252, 317), while nature essays combined this specialized knowledge with moral discussions, often urging the humble recognition that even with the most extensive collections of data, nature's complex systems will be difficult to explain. Susan Fenimore Cooper's *Rural Hours* (1850), in particular, interspersed detailed accounts of birds with critical comments on the time's prevailing anthropocentrism ("the birds seem to have collected there for our special amusement; but in reality, were attracted there, no doubt, by some insects from the water"; 40) and notions of intellectual mastery ("it is tantalizing not to be able to settle the question, [. . .] it is quite possible that the strangers may have been some other variety"; 40–41). Indeed, Cooper explicitly suggests a stance of humility, admonishing amateurs and professionals alike: "Learned ornithologists, with a bird in the hand, have sometimes made great mistakes on such matters, and, of course, unlearned people should be very modest in expressing an opinion, especially where, instead of one bird in the hand, they can only point to two in a bush" (60). Dickinson participates in these discourses insofar as she, too, values detailed observation of usually overlooked species and echoes the joys of imaginative control ("You'll know

Her" is repeated three times), yet also playfully destabilizes the urge to classify a bird and move on. If the twentieth-century classic *Silent Spring* utilizes a distinctly female speaking position to show "that adequate seeing and feeling are more important than the ability to label and categorize the environment" (Norwood 757), Dickinson's poem formulates a similar position, which may be all the more radical when it concerns the most common species.

One of Dickinson's best-known poems, published anonymously under the title "The Snake" in 1866, complicates the riddle routine and the humbling gestures it implies. What begins as an innocent game reminiscent of "You'll know Her – by Her Foot – " turns into a complex meditation on human relationships with the earth's less approachable co-inhabitants:

A narrow Fellow in the Grass
Occasionally rides –
You may have met Him? Did you not
His notice instant is –

The Grass divides as with a Comb –
A spotted Shaft is seen,
And then it closes at your Feet
And opens further on –

He likes a Boggy Acre –
A Floor too cool for Corn –
But when a Boy and Barefoot
I more than once at Noon

Have passed I thought a Whip Lash
Unbraiding in the Sun
When stooping to secure it
It wrinkled And was gone –

Several of Nature's People
I know and they know me
I feel for them a transport
Of Cordiality

But never met this Fellow
Attended or alone
Without a tighter Breathing
And Zero at the Bone. (Fr1096)

Here, too, the formulaic withholding of the object's identity intensifies the attention to an ostensibly minor spectacle, and the sentimental personification that pushes against scientific nomenclature enables such a precise rendition of natural detail that Samuel Bowles exclaimed, "How did that girl ever know that a boggy field wasn't good for corn?" (see Habegger 160). But as this poem enacts the process of noticing that riddles are all about—condensed in the phrase "His notice instant is"—the script is significantly altered. Instead of playfully leading readers closer to understanding what is meant, this poem repeats the misunderstanding of the "Fellow" as "Whip Lash" and offers an unsettling solution in which the animal turns out to be potentially dangerous to the vulnerable, "Barefoot" speaker. Ultimately the "Fellow" that seemed so familiar cannot be "secured," neither physically nor conceptually.[3]

The child perspective, too, is complicated. The curious crossover of age and gender highlights how the child voice frees Dickinson's green imagination not only from the conceptual restrictions of the adult mind but, specifically, from the limiting associations of women with nature. That the poem focuses on the experience and perspective of a boy has led critics to argue that Dickinson formulates a critique of the spatial restrictions girls had to face, but a boy is not only the opposite of a girl, and different from a man, he is also not a woman, which allows Dickinson to explore realms that were considered inappropriate for women and girls. In an environmental context, the child perspective here strengthens the significance of the imaginary encounter as an immediate human-nature interaction because it is inspired by curiosity about the actual world, and marred by misreading nature's signs and by the urge, however playful, to control it (further emphasized by the image of the "Whip Lash"). The boy-child perspective also prevents this poem from functioning solely as a parable about the place of girls or women in Victorian culture or as a biblical narrative about seduction; the poem precisely does not succumb to the era's habitual disparagement of snakes as a biblical evil nor to the related view of snakes as pests; rather, it echoes the perspective of Cooper's *Rural Hours*, which includes accounts of usually harmless snakes that "occasionally cross [one's] path" while the speaker maintains a respectful distance (54). The boy in "A narrow Fellow in the Grass," too, humbly notices a snake's characteristic features with an air of anxious respect that grants one of nature's smaller beings the autonomy of an elusive fellow creature.

A third poem that is significant in this context is not in itself a riddle poem, but it comes close to formulating a principle of unassuming childlike attention to the often overlooked spectacles "beneath – our feet" that is at the heart of many of Dickinson's small nature poems:[4]

> Dew – is the Freshet in the Grass –
> 'Tis many a tiny Mill
> Turns unperceived beneath – our feet
> And Artisan lies still –
>
> We spy the Forests and the Hills
> The Tents to Nature's Show
> Mistake the Outside for the in
> And mention what we saw.
>
> Could Commentators on the Sign
> Of Nature's Caravan
> Obtain "admission" as a Child
> Some Wednesday Afternoon. (Fr1102)

In an early discussion of this poem in a version without the first stanza, Charles Anderson reads the child perspective as a metonym for our general human ignorance, claiming that in the face of nature's mysteries "man must remain forever a child incapable of growing up to true knowledge," especially since nature may be but a colorful façade without "essential meaning" (84). I believe that the child perspective has a different function here, especially when the first stanza is included, where the speaker notices usually "unperceived" drops that cover grass on cool mornings and evenings and considers them as a dynamic agent comparable to a river turning "many a tiny Mill." When New England was covered with extensive systems of river-powered textile mills, and even Emerson's essay "Water" (1834) viewed the element in thoroughly appropriative ways (see Walls, *Emerson's Life in Science* 94), Dickinson echoes this utilitarian perspective ("Artisan") without, however, pressing the water into human service, understanding it instead as part of nature's self-sufficient micro-economy. Her speaker goes on to mock people's preference for sizeable "Forests" and "Hills," and the hypocrisy involved; but even though she, too, views a natural process as an inspiring spectacle and "comments" on it, the dew here does not primarily matter as a sublime apparition that takes the imagination elsewhere but remains grounded in its natural context. Finally, the poem suggests what it may take to notice such phenomena: the perspective of "a Child" who approaches the world with a creative openness, relish for detail, and a gesture that resembles the act of entering a "Tent" whose "Show" consists of infinitesimal drops close to the ground. Getting "admission" to such a tent requires either a small size or the willingness to momentarily relinquish one's larger stature by bowing—in short, a gesture of humility.

Reading this poem next to Cooper's *Rural Hours* highlights the intricate ways in which Dickinson's focus on a child's perspective, expressed by way of a completely regular rhythm and set of half rhymes, responds to the time's green discourses. When Cooper refers to female modesty as a prerequisite for seeing nature's "little events" (3) and mentions the gesture of bowing or bending low, she tends to remain within the framework of female modesty and domesticity, as in this characteristic passage: "[A] meadow is a delicate embroidery in colors, which you must examine closely to understand all its merits; the nearer you are, the better. *One must bend over the grass* to find the blue violet in May, the red strawberry in June" (76; emphasis added). Dickinson's poem, by contrast, divorces this stance from restrictive notions of femininity, recurring instead to the equally sentimental Victorian notion of supposedly innocent children with their supposedly privileged access to nature, and thus turning it into an eco-ethical strategy available to everyone; that she talks about dew rather than flowers or birds further de-genders and radicalizes this gesture.

If, as Paul Crumbley writes, "representation of childhood became an important tool in [Dickinson's] critique of nineteenth-century American culture" (44), she used this tool not only to challenge familial power structures and biblical ideologies, but also to foster her contemporaries' emerging interest in nature's small phenomena as valuable in their own right. Indeed, Edith Cobb argues in *The Ecology of Imagination in Childhood* that the most striking experience of childhood is "an acute pleasure in the incoming flux of minutiae—the mosaic of immediate sensory experience of the natural world," and that the child's "willing acceptance and enjoyment of the muck and mire of life" has the "power of creating mutual relations with the total environment" (87, 31). This attentiveness to and indiscriminate "acceptance" of nature's smallest features marks an environmentally noteworthy stance because of its focus on unbiased perception rather than arrogance, mutuality rather than control, and humility rather than condescension. At a time when American culture was just developing a conscience and vocabulary for approaching nature's microcosms from a less anthropocentric perspective, Dickinson's use of a child's perspective brings in precisely these elements, with an environmental humility that functions as a cultural intervention.

Identification and Dissociation

Apart from her focus on flowers and her embrace of the riddle pattern and its characteristic child perspective, Dickinson's recurrent acts of noticing nature's microcosms often involve relationships between the speaker and nonhuman nature that are shaped by dual gestures of identification and dissociation. Her speakers frequently draw attention to nature's inconspicuous aspects by identifying with them, by getting closer to nature to the point of becoming it, and almost as frequently dissociate themselves from the small creatures they encounter, recognizing nature's ultimate otherness. Environmentally speaking, both moves have complex implications: identification, seeing the other through the self, reaffirms the human as the ultimate reference point for viewing nature, while dissociation highlights nature's alterity, and potentially also its domination. While deep ecologists have embraced identification as "a spontaneous, non-rational, but not irrational, process through which *the interest or interests of another being are reacted to as our own interest or interests*" to which there is no alternative (Naess 261), environmental philosopher Val Plumwood has warned that identification leads toward merger and holism, calling instead for the "recognition of both continuity and difference; [which] means acknowledging the other as neither alien to and discontinuous from self nor assimilated to or an extension of self" (6). In ecocriticism, M. Jimmie Killingsworth's study on ecopoetics is particularly relevant here; he argues that identification is "at the heart of both environmental rhetoric and ecopoetics, [as it] is traditionally associated with overcoming division in a setting of discord and domination [. . .] but also includes the kinds of appeals associated with the lover, the peacemaker, and the apostle" (*Whitman and the Earth* 5). Interestingly, Edward Relph has discussed the imaginative capacity to see the world with the eyes of the other, to "transpose ourselves into the lives of others [. . .] so that we can see matters from their point of view and realise the effects of our action for them" (163), as a defining principle of environmental humility—a stance that, I would argue, Dickinson's repeated identification with nature's smallest creatures explores in a radical form, while her equally frequent gestures of dissociation point the other way.

Dickinson's frequent identification with small plants, animals, and inanimate phenomena is a specific expression of her passion for personification and a major characteristic of her work. To my knowledge, the only environmentally oriented analysis of this strategy comes from Rachel Stein, who shows that for Dickinson's speakers, identification with a feminized nature re-imagined as an "omnipotent, powerful, defiantly playful and uncontainably mysterious subject" was a key strategy for subverting woman's and nature's secondary social status (23–24). What I want to emphasize is that Dickinson's identification with *small* natural creatures has specific environmental implications. While it certainly does imbue speaker and nature with subversive power, it also entails a relative *de*-centering of the speaker's subject position. It is an imaginative move that undermines the Romantic urge to speak the self through nature and brings with it a momentary relinquishment of the utilitarianism that so dominated America's view of nature in the nineteenth century, a utilitarianism that also pervaded the environmental debates of the time and the transcendentalist desire to identify with nature to speak the self.

The poem "The Grass so little has to do – " (Fr379) is one of the strongest examples of this dynamic:

The Grass so little has to do –
A Sphere of simple Green –
With only Butterflies to brood
And Bees, to entertain –

And stir all day to pretty tunes
The Breezes fetch along –
And hold the Sunshine, in it's lap
And bow to everything,

And thread the Dews, all night, like Pearl,
And make itself so fine
A Duchess were too common
For such a noticing,

And even when it die, to pass
In odors so divine –
As lowly spices, laid to sleep –
Or Spikenards perishing –

And then to dwell in Sovreign Barns,
And dream the Days away,
The Grass so little has to do,
I wish I were a Hay –

This speaker's yearning for identity with the personified grass intensifies the act of noticing nature's smallest phenomena I have discussed here. Fueled by the speaker's desire for leading a similar life, the poem draws attention to a "little" and "simple" plant, adding one detail to the next so that the abstract "sphere" of green is recast as a species that lives in its distinct micro-environment. As the poem moves from the interaction between the grass and elusive "Butterflies," "Bees," "Breezes," and "Sunshine" toward its transformation into fine-smelling hay, the poem also situates the grass progressively more in place: the allusion to "spikenards" evokes "numerous widely different plants" (Webster, *Dictionary* [1847]), especially the *Aralia racemosa* (Lincoln 274), an herbal wildflower that grows near the edges of woods; by letting the hay "dwell" "in Sovreign Barns," the speaker integrates it into New England's agricultural economy, where hay serves as food for cattle.

In this context, the identificatory allusions to Victorian womanhood strengthen the attention to the grass as a species. The poem's references to emblems of female beauty such as pearls point to some of the plant's characteristic features; the evocation of an upper-class woman's busy yet strangely eventless life also traces the grass's life cycle; and the speaker's yearning for a divine life-in-death accentuates its role as "herbage," "the plants which constitute the food of cattle and other beasts" (Webster, *Dictionary* [1847]), containing the energy that ensures survival during the winter. Whether this identification subversively empowers grass and speaker by way of its allusions to aristocratic refinement or suggests that the conventional life of a lady meant death to Dickinson, as Wendy Barker has proposed (89), it performs an environmentally crucial act of noticing a minor plant as a self-sufficient agent, a perspective most contemporaries would not have been ready for—including the "Duchess" in the third stanza who, paradoxically, "were too common / For such a noticing – ."

Moreover, the speaker's identification with the grass destabilizes the difference in size and power from which humans derive their sense of superiority. The speaker who identifies with a plant that "bows" to everything and resembles "lowly" spices imaginatively adopts these humbling gestures for herself, as a way of interacting not only with other people but potentially also with nature. Fascinatingly, the child's perspective is reentered here by an adult speaker who seeks to regain some of that ability to recognize nature's details by light-heartedly identifying with it, all the way down to the final, fanciful death wish, whose alliteration and harmony (and a final "Hay" that also sounds like "hey") suggest a childlike luckiness.[5]

It is the poem's enactment of the grass's death that dramatizes an environmentally suggestive de-centering of human authority without, however, wholly negating the speaker's subjectivity. The speaker explicitly identifies with the "Hay" and yearns to "perish" with it, but it is a death that brings a new form of life. Much like spices, hay achieves its characteristic quality after the death of the plant; indeed, the hay's existence in "Barns" evokes death not as pointing to an afterlife, as in conventional religion, but as part of ecological processes that circle material existence back into the natural economy, emphasizing organic cycles that precede and constitute the basis of human economy in the form of agriculture. Imaginatively joining this circular movement of matter and life, which is underscored by the repetition of the first line in the last stanza and by the smooth alliteration of the last line, the speaker does not so much yield her autonomous identity (she retains it, stressing against the rules of common grammar that she wishes she were "a Hay") as abandon her culture's visions of control and utilitarianism, which dominated interaction with nature even on the smallest scales. Instead of aligning herself with New England's agrarianism, she identifies with the hay in ways that foster the recognition of the plant's self-contained life in its characteristic microsystem and larger natural cycles.

This peculiar dynamic can be seen in a number of other poems about nature's small creatures. Apart from "Except to Heaven, she is nought," which I discussed above, it also informs "I was a Phoebe – nothing more – " (Fr1009), where the speaker's identification with the bird includes images of fitting "into place" (rather than forcibly shaping it), of dwelling "low," and of making "a little print" proportionate to its size, which resonates with modern notions of sustainability and living lightly on the earth. And in "Where I am not afraid to go" (Fr986), the speaker muses about the death of her "Flower" in ways that make separation of flower and speaker impossible, and also draws an ethical imperative from this identification, explicitly urging readers to transfer the principles of human interaction to the flower: "Who was not Enemy of Me / Will gentle be, to Her." Dickinson's environmentally suggestive attention to inconspicuous natural elements, then, is intensified by gestures of identification, because this identification with small life-forms, often in their transience, invokes nonutilitarian relationships based on the momentary relinquishment of human mastery.

So instead of unfortunate lapses into pathetic fallacy, Dickinson's identification with small plants and animals serves as a mode of noticing nature's inconspicuous features as significant presences and communicates an ethical, noninstrumental responsiveness to nature.

Yet for all her gestures of identifying with small natural creatures, Dickinson's work maintains their otherness and distance. This admission of difference is an important expression of her acts of noticing "small nature" and of recasting formulaic poses of female submissiveness as environmentally resonant gestures. So far, her speaker's frequent dissociation from nature has mostly been looked at in terms of skepticism. Christopher Benfey's important *Emily Dickinson and the Problem of Others* (1984) reinvigorated this debate by arguing that Dickinson was concerned "with the ways in which the human body and the natural landscape express or withhold their meanings" (4), yet sought to provide an answer to skepticism by linking knowledge of others and of nature to "nearness" (6). Approached from an environmental perspective, Dickinson's concern with the limits to our knowledge of the world also works as a counterforce to her urge to get closer to nature by way of identification. This keeps her poetry not only in a mode of continued curiosity but grounded in the awareness that full understanding of even the smallest creatures is impossible.

There are several well-known Dickinson poems about small flora and fauna in which such dissociation from nature goes hand in hand with a distrust of science as a means of attaining spiritual truths. These poems include her early "Arcturus is the Other name" (Fr117), whose childlike speaker finds her naïve, "old-fashioned" approach to flowers, birds, and butterflies spoiled by the rational epistemology of botany and entomology, casting the amateur scientist as "A monster with a glass." Similarly, in "Split the Lark – and you'll find the Music – " (Fr905), the speaker records the "Scarlet Experiment" that fails to get a doubting scientist closer to the essential meaning of the bird's song. Apart from these much-discussed poems, lesser-known poems such as "How soft a Caterpillar steps – " (Fr1523) demonstrate how her speakers' withdrawal from small creatures fosters a poetic recognition of nature's autonomy and a momentary de-emphasis of human concerns that further contribute to the green resonance of her work.

How soft a Caterpillar steps –
I find one on my Hand
From such a Velvet world it came –

Such plushes at command
It's soundless travels just arrest
My slow – terrestrial eye –
Intent opon it's own career –
What use has it for me –

Repeating the basic move of the earlier, more playful "A Fuzzy Fellow, without feet" (Fr171), in which the childlike speaker traces a caterpillar's physiognomy only to mockingly exclaim, "By me! But who am I, / To tell the pretty secret / Of the Butterfly!," this speaker notices a small creature by way of dissociating herself from it. The recognition of a caterpillar in its sensual immediacy does not lead to familiarity and closeness, but provokes the realization that this presumably approachable creature will always retain its otherness. The image of a visitor from another "world" invites readings of the soon-to-be butterfly as a symbol for the soul; but the alertness to the animal's physical presence and the culminating question regarding its "use" suggest that it also matters as a biological entity, which cannot be reduced to an outward projection of the speaker's sense of self. The way in which the "it" in the last line refers to both the caterpillar and the speaker's "slow – terrestrial eye" even implies a couched critique of transcendentalism's obsession with the perceiving human consciousness, since such a self-absorbed perspective leaves little room for a recognition of the phenomenon at hand. The unanswered final question, and the opposition between the animal's "command" of its own body and the speaker's lack of "command" of the animal, further indicate that the perspective of utilitarianism does not work here. Even as the speaker's concern with nature's "use" suggests an interest in nature as a resource, the poem ultimately presents it as an autonomous sphere.

A similar dynamic characterizes the poem "Those cattle smaller than a Bee" (Fr1393), whose speaker finds humans "Unqualified to judge" flies, as well as "How fits his Umber Coat" (Fr1414), whose speaker finds human wisdom "undone" by the intricate construction of a chestnut, and "A narrow Fellow in the Grass" (Fr1096), whose way of destabilizing human authority I discussed earlier. Most intriguing in this respect is perhaps "Flowers, well if anybody" (Fr95), in which the speaker challenges "anybody" to "define – / Half a transport – half a trouble – / with which flowers humble men." Even though the speaker can be seen to identify with the fathomless flowers, and paradoxically offers "all the Daisies / Which opon the hillside blow" to the person who might solve their riddle, as if being in control, she is mainly taken by humankind's *in*ability to grasp nature, casting herself as "a simple breast" bound to realize that the nearest, apparently simplest flowers "Have a system of aesthetics – Far superior to [hers]." Dickinson's skepticism toward the knowability of small nonhuman beings thus translates into a recognition of nature's difference that accompanies her most exultant statements of identity and which, together with her gestures of identifying with nature, contributes to her work's green overtones.

Not despite but because she often feels she cannot fully grasp these phenomena, they assume a self-directed place in the world of her poetry. It is the baffling complexity and heterogeneity that make her cast nature's microcosms in such detail, while her prevailing reluctance and doubt about their meaning induce her to question an instrumental perspective. In Dickinson's work, dissociation from ostensibly minor beings works as a check against the uncritical assumption of identity with the earth that threatens to incorporate the other into the self, see it as a mere extension of the self, and deny its autonomous existence and intrinsic value. If, as Val Plumwood argues, "the ecological self must be able to recognize both the otherness of nature and its continuity with the human self [and] this project does not require any sort of identity, merger, or loss of boundaries between self and other" (160), the self that Dickinson carves out in her small-scale nature poetry can be called "ecological" precisely because it contends with the limits of perceiving and connecting to the nonhuman world.

This eco-ethical impetus hinges in part on the objects' very smallness. As Dickinson's work amply suggests, it is on this scale that the gap between the human sense of mastery and our actual lack of awareness of the natural world is the greatest, and it is here that both identification with nature and the realization of its irreducible otherness have the most deeply humbling effects. In this implicit critique of humankind's assumed superiority, Dickinson finds an unexpected ally in Whitman—unexpected because Dickinson works from within Victorian associations of white middle-class women with small natural creatures and with gestures of refined submissiveness, while Whitman imagines his representative male singer to proudly incarnate the entire American continent. Yet even though, as Joanne Krieg has written, "in the case of Whitman and Dickinson the lines of connection are so slight as to be hardly even tenuous" (400), their respective poetic engagements with nature's minute life-forms meet in a number of ways, which is what the next chapter is about.

2

"What is the Grass?"

Whitman's Originating Moment of Noticing Small Nature

Leaves of Grass is in many ways the extensive celebration of a large, democratic self that corresponds with the vastness of the American continent. Yet there is only one thing Whitman saw fit to serve as a title, an innocuous weed that most contemporaries would not have deemed worth a second look. Whitman's evocative choice of title relates his book to nature by way of a distinctly small life-form—a powerful reminder that his poetry, for all its continental and global aspirations, was centrally concerned with nature's minutest aspects.

Compared to Dickinson's hundreds of poems that focus on one flower or bird, Whitman's *Leaves of Grass* includes only a handful of more extended sections about America's lesser flora and fauna. Usually, his speaker seems to merely glance at weeds, shells, and insects before moving on. So strong is the pull toward larger realms that Gay Wilson Allen actually de-emphasized Whitman's choice of a small plant for the title: "Although the key symbol of *Leaves of Grass* is botanical, the grass 'sprouting alike in broad zones and narrow zones,' the aesthetic dimension most often employed by Whitman in his poems is space" ("The Influence of Space in the American Imagination" 329). Moreover, the eclectic mix of arbutus and morning-glory, salt weed and sage, beetles and gnats suggests a transcendentalist belief in the world's unity in diversity, and it may appear counterintuitive to single out something so thoroughly woven into his overall project, let alone emphasize its physical over its spiritual meanings.

Yet if one follows the title's lead and looks more closely at Whitman's views of "[t]he leaves and flowers of the commonest weeds" ("Song of Joys"), his references to minor natural phenomena, which usually last only a line or two but sometimes continue over several passages, constitute a poetics of the small that has wide-ranging environmental implications. Indeed, if the line is the primary unit of Whitman's poetry, as Folsom and Price argue in *Re-Scripting Walt Whitman* (32), such a reading does not go against the integrity of *Leaves of Grass* as one carefully structured unit—to the contrary. Considering all of these micromoments together reveals that they form a basic feature of Whitman's environmental imagination that matters in the book as a whole, precisely because they are tucked away in a few lines here and there.

On this scale the comparison with his genteel Amherst contemporary, who was trained in botany and fluent in sentimental floral discourses, is particularly productive because it helps to tease out what would otherwise remain obscure, including the fact that Whitman's work does involve a distinct approach to small life-forms. This chapter identifies and discusses suggestive similarities and differences in the ways in which Dickinson's and Whitman's poems respond to their time's proto-ecological debates. Specifically, I hope to show that where the environmental resonance of Dickinson's "small nature" poetry emerges largely from the frequency with which she notices details of these life-forms, each in a separate poem, Whitman's work achieves a similar effect through the interplay of essentially one key passage and a large number of short references that perpetuate this original momentum throughout *Leaves of Grass*. Moreover, Whitman's poetry employs similar but differently inflected strategies in his approach to the wealth of available natural history details and the epistemological control they imply, his use of the child's perspective, and the modes of identification with and dissociation from small natural phenomena. Nevertheless, a particular tension arises from the fact that Whitman works an interest in nature's minutiae into a project that is invested in discourses of individual and national expansiveness, and whose central male persona is "a kosmos," "No sentimentalist," and "no more modest than immodest" (1855 "Song of Myself")—unlike Dickinson, who comes to this discussion by way of the revision of a prescribed female interest in small matters, sentiment, and modesty. Still, his more conflicted perspective on nature's innocuous objects intersects with Dickinson's outlook in significant ways, not the least of which is the commitment to an environmental humility that hinges upon repeated acts of noticing these objects in their smallness.

Noticing Small Nature: An Originating Moment

There is one passage that gives nature's microlevels a prominent position in Whitman's work as a whole, an originating moment to which all other "small nature" references in *Leaves of Grass* are indirectly linked. After the title of the book has drawn attention to the inconspicuous plant, section 6 of "Song of Myself" develops an entire poetic program from the encounter between poet, reader, child, and grass:

> A child said *What is the grass?*
> fetching it to me with full hands;
> How could I answer the child? I do not know what it is any more than he.
> I guess it must be the flag of my disposition, out of hopeful green stuff woven.
>
> Or I guess it is the handkerchief of the Lord,
> A scented gift and remembrancer designedly dropt,
> Bearing the owner's name someway in the corners, that we may see and remark, and say *Whose?*
>
> Or I guess the grass is itself a child, the produced babe of the vegetation.
>
> Or I guess it is a uniform hieroglyphic,
> And it means, Sprouting alike in broad zones and narrow zones,
> Growing among black folks as among white,
> Kanuck, Tuckahoe, Congressman, Cuff, I give them the same, I receive them the same.
>
> And now it seems to me the beautiful uncut hair of graves.
>
> Tenderly will I use you curling grass,
> It may be you transpire from the breasts of young men,
> It may be if I had known them I would have loved them,
> It may be you are from old people, or from offspring taken soon out of their mothers' laps,
> And here you are the mothers' laps.
>
> This grass is very dark to be from the white heads of old mothers,
> Darker than the colorless beards of old men,
> Dark to come from under the faint red roofs of mouths. (*LG* 30–31)

This passage is usually read as the expression of an epistemology that is inseparable from the evolving relationship between poet and reader. But does the grass that is "fetched" so joyfully in the beginning of the section fully dissolve into the "drift of significances suggested by a simple word" (Larson 474)? M. Jimmie Killingsworth emphasizes how the suggested meanings of the grass link "individual lives and regional or racial types [. . .], people and nature, heaven and earth, human language and 'substantive words'" without claiming interpretive authority and without "overwhelming the integrity of individual things" (*Walt Whitman and the Earth*

34–35); and Paul Outka has suggested that the grass links nature and nation, becomes the speaker's identity, a "child" of a "vegetative" God "metaphorically linked to the child/reader" and a construction of hieroglyphic language (45–46). While I agree with Killingsworth's and Outka's emphasis on the grass's double presence as both trope and plant, I would argue that the era's interest in small flora and fauna invites an even closer look at the actual plant and the human-nature relationships that are part of this poem's play of tropes. The passage combines several environmentally resonant moves: the reluctant embrace of botanical, chemical, and geographical perspectives, which increases the presence and significance of the grass itself without fully endorsing the gestures of mastery that also played into these discourses; the child's perspective, which engages sentimental ideas about children's privileged access to nature as a potentially green perspective up and against related notions of women's supposedly appropriate interest in nature's small things; and the riddling quality of this section, which not only strengthens the idea of unassuming, childlike attention to small nature's implications but also an interest in understanding nature while playfully destabilizing this very notion. All of these moves imply gestures of environmental humility that, in different but related ways, also characterize Dickinson's poems about nature on the smallest scale.

The section's initial, seemingly naïve question about the grass, and the preliminary answer "I do not know what it is any more than he," immediately identify the speaker's frame of mind with that of the asking child while also retaining the plant's difference, thus accessing the child's perspective as an implicit critique of learned adult discourses about natural phenomena at our feet. At the same time, the section opens with an in-your-face encounter with the plant, fetched "with full hands." This physical immediacy is strengthened by its echo of section 5, in which the speaker invited his soul and the reader to "Loaf with [him] on the grass," and which culminated in an earthy communion in which the male body becomes indistinguishable from a microcosm of small flora and fauna: "And limitless are leaves stiff or drooping in the fields, / And brown ants in the little wells beneath them, / And mossy scabs of the worm fence, heap'd stones, elder, mullein and poke-weed" (*LG* 29–30). The opening gesture of section 6 evolves from this imaginary encounter with "elder, mullein and poke-weed," retroactively increasing their significance as botanically specific rather than symbolic plants, and turning this momentum into an expansive list of associations in which the actual grass is never far away.

This botanical presence spills over into the speaker's first "guess" that the grass might be understood as the "flag" of his "disposition," which, apart from the natural-national link Outka has suggested, also evokes the showy leaves of large grass species, especially the calamus, or sweet flag. In the botany-obsessed nineteenth century, the short reference would easily come to life as the 1–4-foot-high green "flag" that grows in swamps and along riverbanks, and whose 2–4-inch fleshy flower spike held such powerful "manly" associations for Whitman. Yet where Lincoln's botany book explains, "spike protruding from the side of a sword-form leaf-like scape. Water or wet. Root strongly aromatic" (271), Whitman evokes the plant by just one allusive term, yet one specific enough to fold out into a botanical image. This mode of noticing "small nature," which echoes but keeps its distance from the scientific discourses of the time, parallels and even radicalizes Dickinson's way of inviting such humbling attention to commonly overlooked plants by way of very few details.

The suggestion that the grass could be "the handkerchief of the Lord" seems wholly removed from earthly concerns, but its evocation of fine scents and delicate fabrics, as well as its emphasis on looking closely so "that we may see," both recall the outlook of botany as a field of study "particularly adapted to females" (Lincoln 12), and, more specifically, Susan Fenimore Cooper's view of a meadow as "a delicate embroidery in colors which you must examine closely to understand all its merits" (76), both of which embrace standard notions of female modesty as a nature-oriented gesture. Whitman's speaker, too, seems to bend down "to the owner's name someway in the corners," as one would in order to see the tiny flowers of grasses—a humbling gesture in regard to an unexpectedly complex weed that in his case, however, unsettles the gesture's gender connotations.

This dynamic continues into the third "guess," that "the grass is itself a child, the produced babe of the vegetation," which suggests that even such a widespread plant deserves being treated gently, with parental (especially motherly) tenderness. Where Killingsworth has convincingly argued that the poet is "using the grass symbol 'tenderly'" (*Walt Whitman and the Earth* 34), this promise of tenderness also applies to the grass itself. The poem evokes an ethic of care here that Thoreau often implied when he extended human interest to small, nonhuman creatures and that Susan F. Cooper linked to the sentimental context of women's floral discourses; in the twentieth century, it has become a core concern for deep ecology and certain branches of ecofeminism.[1] Similar to the move Dickinson performs in poems whose speaker is either male or a not clearly gendered child, Whitman's speaker, for whom a quasi-parental concern for small plants was less culturally sanctioned (but also less precarious) than for women, also extends familial ethics toward nature's minutiae in ways that echo but undermine the Victorian association between attention to small natural phenomena and restrictive views of femininity.

At the same time, "the produced babe of the vegetation" also alludes to the proto-ecological sciences. It evokes the concept of "the economy of nature," used then for ecological processes through which matter is endlessly (re-)produced, circling back to life through death. This idea gains momentum throughout section 6, as the speaker perceives the grass to be growing "from the breasts of young men" and muses that "The smallest sprout shows there is really no death." Whitman here condenses and anticipates the notion that natural matter gives life through decay, and, as Killingsworth has pointed out, the "faith that human beings participate in the perennial renewal of life" which poems such as "This Compost" explore in greater detail (*Walt Whitman and the Earth* 34). Moreover, this unassuming phrase also refers to the evolving field of chemistry. While critics have shown how Justus von Liebig's discoveries in organic chemistry influenced Whitman,[2] this also adds to the environmental richness of this passage because chemistry's insights soon contributed to ecological notions of energy flow and food chains. Finally, the botanical term "vegetation" connects with the poem's following two lines on the grass "Sprouting in broad zones and narrow zones," using a rhetoric that was prominent, for instance, in the works of botanist, geographer, and meteorologist Alexander von Humboldt, whom Whitman knew and admired. Humboldt was not only an "ecologist before the term" (Ashworth 187–88) but also "the real founder of botanical geography" (Bowler 272), who divided mountains, plains, and entire regions into different "zones" of vegetation, wrote much about the ability of plants to grow in a wide range of low and narrow zones (see Ette 162), and used drawings and tables to show "what proportion of the population in any zone was made up of grasses or any other major type of plant" (Bowler 273). In other words, Whitman's terminology and perspective take up concepts from plant geography and historical biogeography, fields whose study of spatial patterns of plant distribution in conjunction with climate and historical changes in the land fed into the emerging science of ecology (see Bowler 272–80). Yet his lines never privilege scientific terms and the superior perspective they tend to signify, thus avoiding implied gestures of control in ways that resemble Dickinson's mode of echoing yet destabilizing the time's botanical discourses.

This is not changed by the fact that Whitman finds the grass "Growing among black folks as among white." To the contrary, the notion of geographical zones may have become popular, Bowler explains,

> because it could be understood as a biological equivalent of the nations of humanity [. . .] Humboldt himself had shown an interest in the native inhabitants of the regions he visited, and his views on how the environment affects plants and animals may have been influenced by his studies of the ways in which human societies adapted to local conditions. (273)

In Whitman's lines, too, the grass's relevance as a plant that is adapted to specific geographical conditions and its symbolic resonance in terms of race and ethnicity mutually reinforce each other.

Whitman's section about the grass as a symbol of life and death, or life *in* death, does not stop with the lines that evoke the hair of men and women. After several attempts to "translate the hints," the poet proclaims that "to die is different from what any one supposed, and luckier," an ending that has baffled many critics and that is not part of Killingsworth's and Outka's arguments. If one reads Whitman together with Dickinson, however, this "lucky" last line recalls the fanciful death wish at the end of "The Grass so little has to do – " (Fr379), which I discussed in the previous chapter. Dickinson's easygoing identification with "a Hay" that dreams "in Sovereign Barns" suggests that the perplexing lightness with which Whitman's speaker concludes his meditation about grass and death derives from a similar trust in organic cycles, a "hopeful" perspective that considers the composting of matter as a "natural" alternative to resurrection.[3] And although Whitman's speaker does not identify with the grass as clearly as Dickinson's, the interplay highlights that he, too, seems to fade out of the section with it, in death that leads to life. As both speakers merge with the grass—the "Lowly spices, lain to sleep – " (Fr379); "The smallest sprout [that] shows there is really no death"—they engage in a corresponding relinquishment of nature's linguistic and implied physical control. In Whitman's case, this has been present all through the section in the awareness that it will remain impossible to grasp the meaning of such a simple weed, culminating in a joyful embrace of identity with, rather than above, "the smallest sprout." Here, Dickinson's allusions to the grass as a "common" and "lowly" plant that "bows," and the way in which notions of stereotypical female modesty slide into humility as a quality played out in relation to nature, reveal that Whitman's speaker enacts a comparable gesture that is perhaps more radical since it is performed by a male persona.

The interplay between the two poems also accentuates the role of the child's voice, which Dickinson's poem accesses and which initiates Whitman's meditation on the grass. The unusual tenor of the final line—"And to die is different from what any one supposed, and luckier"—circles back to the innocent opening question, so that the child's seeming naïveté frames the entire section. Whitman, like Dickinson in several poems, expresses an attentiveness to nature's small life-forms that is initiated and fed by a child's undiscriminating curiosity, and ready to relate to the minutest elements in ways that are not yet marred by Victorian gender norms, including the traditional link between Euro-American masculinity and the domination of nature. That a domineering stance is absent from this section has much to do with Whitman's embrace of the child perspective—a dynamic that also informs such environmentally powerful poems as "There Was a Child Went Forth," which I discuss later in this chapter and which finds a dimmer echo in his views of nature on larger scales.

Section 6 of "Song of Myself," then, functions as an extended act of noticing a small natural phenomenon in its complexity, whose manifold evocations of humility come from the momentary shift of attention away from the supposed superiority of the male poet's mind (initiated by the child's question and culminating in the evocation of a common death that unites all living matter), from the way in which these lines evoke but never privilege the terminology and perspectives of the evolving sciences, and from its riddling quality, underscored by the rhythmically repeated "I guess"es and "may-be"s. This defining moment in *Leaves of Grass* expresses a green poetics of the small that Whitman already alluded to in an early draft of "Song of Myself," which included the line "I am the poet of little things and of babes" (qtd. in Folsom and Price 36). Its erasure points to the tension that the devotion to the small would create in his work, a tension that has to do with connotations of restraint and pettiness contrary to his ideal of "a poetry with cosmic and dynamic features of magnitude and limitlessness" ("A Backward Glance"). And yet Whitman embraced precisely this orientation in a central passage of "Song of Myself" and kept returning to "little things" throughout his work, a commitment that points to an investment in issues similar to those that concerned Dickinson.

Reaffirming the Small

Leaves of Grass is studded with short references to small nature that recall and amplify the environmental implications of section 6 in "Song of Myself." Apart from this section, Whitman wrote only a few unified passages about small natural phenomena, and fewer short poems about flowers or birds. The comparative insignificance of most of these poems underscores that it is largely through the interplay between section 6 of "Song of Myself" and many much shorter moments that Whitman expresses his views of nature's microlevels. For instance, the short poems "Unseen Buds," "The First Dandelion," and "My Canary Bird" may superficially resemble Dickinson's compact snapshots, yet they add little to the presence of nature's minutiae in Whitman's work. And the pompous "Soon Shall the Winter's Foil Be Here," which explicitly calls upon the reader to pay attention to the details of spring—"Thou shalt perceive the simple shows, the delicate miracles of earth, / Dandelions, clover, the emerald grass, the early scents and flowers, / The arbutus under foot, the willow's yellow-green, the blossoming plum and cherry" (*LG* 444)—engages a conventional moralistic rhetoric that limits its green potential. It is from cursory glances at plants, birds, and beetles, and the ways in which they thematically and stylistically respond to the time's proto-ecological discussions, that the strength of Whitman's references to small creatures derives.

As in Dickinson's case, the frequency with which Whitman pays attention to the smallest flora and fauna already intersects with the time's scientific interests. Between 1840 and 1860, dozens of volumes of regionally specific botany manuals appeared, journals published scientific and amateur discoveries (Reveal and Pringle 172–73), and "the collection of masses of information on the numbers of plants to be found in any area" enabled groundbreaking publications such as Humboldt's tables of species distribution in certain zones (Bowler 273). Whitman's poetic interest in "little things" echoes this fascination, and where Dickinson's short, elliptic poems outwardly resemble the condensed taxonomic information of botany handbooks such as Lincoln's, with their clusters of two or three words divided by colons, his catalogues recall passages from Lincoln's and similar scientific publications that summarized the "Natural Orders of Linnaeus":

> 2. Piperitae. Pepper and its relatives. In crowded spikes; as Indian-turnip, sweet-flag. *Tonics and stomachics.*

3. Calamariae. Reed-like grasses, with culms without joints; as cat-tail, sedge. *Coarse cattle fodder.*
4. Grimina. The proper grasses with jointed culms; as Wheat, Rye, Oats, Timothy-grass, Arrow-head. *Tonics and rough cattle fodder.* (Lincoln 35)

Yet this superficial resemblance also highlights how few scientific details Whitman's individual free verse lines actually present. His reluctant embrace of detail can be read as an expression of the desire to understand nature's smallest particles without reveling in notions of scientific mastery. Moreover, again resembling Dickinson, the eco-ethical impetus of his poetry about small natural worlds is reinforced by the speaker's struggle against his own oblivion that is implicit in these repeated acts of noticing and sometimes made explicit in moments of regret—a critique of the human ignorance and arrogance that underlie much mindless environmental destruction, and a humbling insight that is part of the poet's democratic relationship with his readers.

"Song of Myself" includes more than a dozen short passages about small natural elements that signal such an unassuming interest in supposedly negligible phenomena. In section 1, the first thing the poet mentions apart from himself, his soul, and the reader is grass, and the famous line "I lean and loafe at my ease observing a spear of summer grass" prefigures section 6 in the evocation of grass as a palpable plant and in the implication that all his songs evolve from such attention to small nature. Moreover, the line captures an easygoing amateur interest that nods toward botanical observation but bypasses its preoccupation with an overabundance of scientific details, while the gesture of leaning or bending down suggests a humble turn toward the small that does not entail a relinquishment of one's own sense of self—the same dynamic that is at the heart of so many Dickinson poems about nature's minutiae.

In section 2, a catalogue of the world's "perfumes" includes "The sniff of green leaves and dry leaves, and of the shore and dark-color'd sea-rocks, and of hay in the barn" (*LG* 27). Sandwiched between "the passing of blood and air through my lungs" and" The sound of the belch'd words of my voice loos'd to the eddies of the wind," this line anticipates the symbolic link Whitman establishes in section 6 between grass and poetic language ("a uniform hieroglyphic"), breathing and speaking (the "uttering tongues" that "come from the roofs of mouths"), and the human body's materiality in life and death; at the same time, it captures the elusive yet distinct presence of small natural phenomena that are not just generic but made tangible here at transitional moments in their life cycles.

Section 9 again evokes the grass, giving several lines over to its colorful, heavy physicality:

> The big doors of the country barn stand open and ready,
> The dried grass of the harvest-time loads the slow-drawn wagon,
> The clear light plays on the brown gray and green intertinged,
> The armfuls are pack'd to the sagging mow.
> I am there, I help, I came stretch'd atop of the load,
> I felt its soft jolts, one leg reclined on the other,
> I jump from the cross-beams and seize the clover and timothy,
> And roll head over heels and tangle my hair full of wisps. (*LG* 32–33)

It is noteworthy here that the speaker, as he celebrates thick loads of hay and especially the "clover and timothy" that form the basis for this agricultural economy, moves downward from his elevated position, his superiority in difference, to immerse himself in "wisps" of hay and herbs. As such, he calls attention to the grass's beauty and botanical diversity as much as its economic significance, filling the spaces imaginatively opened by the promise of section 6 to use "the produced babe of the vegetation" "tenderly."

In section 13, after the poet gazes at a black man on his dray, he extends his inclusive reach to horses, oxen, and small fauna and flora. Here the innocuous line "to niches aside and junior bending, not a person or object missing" (*LG* 35) suggests small "niches" he notices somewhere on the side, and while a niche primarily meant "[a] cavity, hollow, or recess, within the thickness of a wall" (Webster, *Dictionary* [1847]) before it became an ecological term for the role of a species in a local ecosystem (see Bowler 529), Whitman's phrase denotes the usually unrecognized ("aside") and inferior ("junior") place of certain elements in the landscape. The casual mention of "person or object," however, is disconcerting, as it seems to align a black man with objects, horses, or oxen; this link between biogeographical and racialist discourses, which was part of proto-ecological publications especially through Louis Agassiz's publications, is not fully compensated by the fact that two lines earlier the poet himself had joined the team of horses, and that the passage's crossover of interpretive possibilities also works the other way around, denoting the animals listed in the following lines as "persons" rather than "objects."

As section 13 unfolds, there is a twist in how the poet comes to notice nature's particulars, subtly referring back to the child's question "*What is the grass?*"

Oxen that rattle the yoke and chain or halt in the leafy shade, what is that
you express in your eyes?
It seems to me more than all the print I have read in my life.
My tread scares the wood-drake and wood-duck on my distant and day-long
ramble,
They rise together, they slowly circle around.
I believe in those wing'd purposes,
And acknowledge red, yellow, white, playing within me,
And consider green and violet and the tufted crown intentional,
And do not call the tortoise unworthy because she is not something else,
And the jay in the woods never studied the gamut, yet trills pretty well to me,
And the look of the bay mare shames silliness out of me. (*LG* 35–36)

Unlike the micromoments I have discussed so far, the speaker is now startled into recognition after being *in*attentive. He is made to notice "the wood-drake and wood duck" by the birds themselves (who fly up as a pair, as is characteristic of this species) after he disrupted their habitat, and in hindsight professes to "acknowledge" and "consider" what lies beneath his feet. And while the subsequent list of colors certainly matters as a transcendental expression of the poet's insight regarding the universe's unity in diversity, it also does just that, acknowledging and considering the ornithological details of this North American species—especially the drake's yellow, burgundy, green, and iridescent purple plumage and his black, red, yellow, and white bill. It is as if these shy, solitary birds who prefer undisturbed wetlands and forest (much like the wood thrush in "When Lilacs Last in the Dooryard Bloom'd") impel the speaker to revise his carelessness and to formulate his remarkable pledge: "And [I] do not call the tortoise unworthy because she is not something else, / And the jay in the woods never studied the gamut, yet trills pretty well to me" (*LG* 36). In section 6, where a child initiated his attention to the grass, the speaker's own inattentiveness remained implicit; now, the poet himself notices the smaller life-forms around him and expands upon this insight. Indirectly passing judgment on his earlier thoughtless disruption of a natural habitat, these lines imply the potential revision of action as well.

The impulse spills over into section 14, where the speaker turns to another bird and critically reviews his culture's negligence of such phenomena:

The wild gander leads his flock through the cool night, Ya-honk he says, and
sounds it down to me like an invitation,
The pert may suppose it meaningless, but I listening close,

Find its purpose and place up there toward the wintry sky.
The sharp-hoof'd moose of the north, the cat on the house-sill, the chickadee,
    the prairie-dog,
The litter of the grunting sow as they tug at her teats,
The brood of the turkey-hen and she with her half-spread wings,
I see in them and myself the same old law.
The press of my foot to the earth springs a hundred affections,
They scorn the best I can do to relate them. (*LG* 36)

It is as if Whitman transforms the somewhat rough awakening of the speaker's attention by panicking ducks in section 13 into a gentle invitation extended by traveling geese to someone ready to pay attention. Here, the poet who briefly focuses on cat and chickadee, "The litter of the grunting sow as they tug at her teats, / The brood of the turkey-hen and she with her half spread wings," sets himself apart from the "pert" who "suppose it meaningless" and articulates a remarkable credo of environmental alertness and responsiveness. When he muses, "I see in them and myself the same old law. / The press of my foot to the earth springs a hundred affections, / They scorn the best I can do to relate them," he takes the proto-Darwinian recognition of the basic resemblance between "man" and other creatures further, toward a touching profession of an "affectionate" relationship with the earth below his feet, an imaginary mutuality between two potentially equal players that points beyond the human-centered concern for his own (lack of) attention. Moreover, he realizes that despite his yearning for mutuality, nature's self sufficient creatures do not depend on his compassionate outreach. That is, while the poet moves from "pride" to "sympathy," as suggested in the 1855 preface, *nature* now expresses contempt and pride. While any attempt to breach the gap between humankind and nature must remain futile, as even most deep ecologists would acknowledge, the idea of nature's smaller creatures scorning the earth-bound poet is perhaps the ultimate expression of environmental humility. Compared to Dickinson's poetry, which also includes moments of human inattentiveness followed by remorse ("It bloomed and dropt, a Single Noon – " [Fr843]), and of reaching out to small creatures who do not respond ("A Bird came down the Walk – " [Fr359]), Whitman's sense of being scorned by nature seems even more unsettling because it refers to a proudly masculine bard.

As Whitman's speaker moves on to celebrate his thoughts as "the thoughts of all men in all ages and lands" in section 17, he points to "the grass that grows wherever the land is and the water is" (*LG* 40), grounding his imagination by way of drawing attention to the plant that has for many pages now (indeed, beginning with the cover of the book) served as more than a symbol. Again he strengthens its presence as the smallest geographical pole of his art, just as "the common air that bathes the globe" marks the largest, in a language that is specific and yet undogmatic. Similarly, in section 23, the often-cited "Hurrah for positive science! long live exact demonstration!" is followed by the bizarre line "Fetch stonecrop mixt with cedar and branches of lilac," another example of Whitman's references to small nature that allude to the sciences but leave out excessive details, an empirically based earth-writing that suggests awareness but not control. As the editors of the Norton edition have pointed out, stonecrop, cedar, and lilac symbolically suggest ancient modes of healing, graveyards and comfort, love and male comradeship (*LG* 45n9), yet the manner of fetching and mixing branches here and there, especially after alluding to science's "exact" observation and expression, also implies that the positivistic sciences should retain some of the fresh, sensual attention to nature that precedes its detailed study. The rich texture of this line, with its spontaneous, joyful fascination that matters more than adherence to botanical names, and with its rather messy "fetching," again refers back to section 6, the child's gesture now taken up by the poet-speaker himself.

In section 24, "Walt Whitman, a kosmos, of Manhattan the son" calls himself "No more modest than immodest" and declares that "Whoever degrades another degrades me, / And whatever is done or said returns at last to me." In the context of the time's new scientific attention to small nature, these comments about egalitarian relationships are general enough to also refer to "modest" or "degraded" aspects of nature, recalling Dickinson's sentimental "Where I am not afraid to go" (Fr986), in which she identifies with a dying flower and claims "Who was not Enemy of Me / Will gentle be, to Her." Another five lines later he perceives "many long dumb voices" to express themselves through him, including what seems most "trivial" and "despised" in nature, such as "beetles rolling balls of dung." This, too, is a surprisingly Dickinsonian moment, transgressing the limits of Victorian sensibilities, as Whitman's 1855 book cover had promised; enfolded in the rolling alliteration and steady trochaic rhythm of the phrase is the unconventional attention to natural details of the most "degraded" kind, noticed by a speaker whose ideal of modesty includes an environmentally oriented humility. In the same section, after celebrating his body by way of associations that blur the line between his physiognomy and small natural phenomena ("Root of wash'd sweet-flag! timorous pond-snipe! Nest of duplicate eggs!"), the speaker notices another plant: "That I walk up my stoop, I pause to consider if it really be, / A morning-glory at my window satisfies me more than the metaphysics of books" (*LG* 47). Compared to Dickinson's botanical poems, Whitman's references are much more reduced, also in terms of botanical detail, and yet they enact a similar refusal to view flowers as pure symbols, a crucial prerequisite for the formulation of an ethical stance toward small nature.

One of the most powerful instances of Whitman's occasional attention to nature's minutiae comes in section 31:

> I believe a leaf of grass is no less than the journey-work of the stars,
> And the pismire is equally perfect, and a grain of sand, and the egg of the
> wren,
> And the tree-toad is a chef-d'oeuvre for the highest,
> And the running blackberry would adorn the parlors of heaven,
> And the narrowest hinge in my hand puts to scorn all machinery,
> And the cow crunching with depress'd head surpasses any statue,
> And a mouse is miracle enough to stagger sextillions of infidels. (*LG* 51–52)

If this is a proclamation of faith in the divine unity of reality designed to shake the "infidels," it is also a metapoetical credo that comes as close to answering the child's question in section 6 as Whitman would, a preliminary answer that carries on and develops the green overtones of the poem's recurring micromoments. As in so many other lines about small natural phenomena, the specificity of its natural references pushes against their function as mere symbols of democratic inclusiveness or emblems of a divine order. Moreover, the passage seems constructed as an argument against habitual ignorance and hypocrisy, emphasizing that "a leaf of grass is *no less than* [emphasis added] the journey-work of the stars." The speaker's sensitivity no longer depends on the revision of his ignorance but has become part of his outlook, so that the image of the cow with a bowed head can be read as a gesture of humility, putting considerable pressure on the pride suggested by the manmade statue to which it is compared. This dynamic subtly echoes the discursive comments with which environmentally sensitive scientists like Humboldt addressed readers as responsible co-inhabitants of the earth, as Aaron Sachs explains:

> [T]hroughout his writings, he emphasized the importance of even the most frail and finespun filaments in the web of life, those "phenomena which

> naturalists have hitherto singularly neglected." "Our imagination," he explained, "is struck only by what is great; but the lover of natural philosophy should reflect equally on little things." After his experience on the Orinoco, Humboldt was not exactly imbued with sympathy for mosquitoes, yet he felt compelled to remind prejudiced Europeans that even "these noxious insects [. . .], in spite of their minute size, act an important part in the economy of nature." (129–30)

Whitman's passage suggests a corresponding willingness to let oneself be "staggered" into a humbling acknowledgment of small nature's "equally perfect" presence.

The lines that immediately follow, however, complicate this radically egalitarian stance toward small nature:

> I find I incorporate gneiss, coal, long-threaded moss, fruits, grains, esculent
> roots,
> And am stucco'd with quadrupeds and birds all over,
> And have distanced what is behind me for good reasons,
> But call any thing back again when I desire it. (*LG* 52)

Several small life-forms seem to function mainly as contributions, even as they retain a living presence, and the speaker claims to be in control and evokes an image of himself as the crown of creation, although it is impossible to draw a line between his body and the creatures he "incorporates." Yet this curiously vital statue also unsettles this image of human achievement because it suggests the poet's absolute dependency on smaller life-forms (take them away and he dissolves), thus pushing against the hubris of seeing all development culminate in the human form and consciousness. On a different level, the passage also suggests a diverse ecosystem, organic cycles (it mentions edible fruits, grains, and roots, as well as a fossil consisting of decomposed vegetation), and, as Whitman's earliest critics have shown, the historical process of evolution.[4] Whether the lines anticipate Darwinian theories of natural selection, as Beaver has argued, or draw from earlier models such as Lamarck's or Chambers's notion of transmutation (see Bowler 189, 293), all of these fed into the evolving environmental sciences, and the passage offers a stunningly beautiful allegory for the diversity of smaller organisms that was at the heart of nineteenth-century development theories.

In section 33, with its extended nature catalogue, grand continental scenes are interspersed with weeds, hummingbirds, and cobwebs, solidifying the impression that this speaker, who seldom stops long enough to look too closely at nature's microcosms, never loses sight of them completely. As his imagination moves from places "Where the quail is whistling betwixt the woods and the wheat-lot, / Where the bat flies in the Seventh-month eve, where the great goldbug drops through the dark," to the vulnerable "pale-green eggs in the dented sand," and to places "Where the mocking-bird sounds his delicious gurgles, cackles, screams, weeps" (*LG* 54–55), he keeps perceiving small natural phenomena as parts of larger systems, while his notion of "Coming home with the silent and dark-cheek'd bush-boy, / (behind me he rides at the drape of the day,) / Far from the settlements studying the print of animals' feet, or the moccasin print" (*LG* 56) harks back to a child's awe and curiosity, this time possibly implying a black or Native American child.

When the poet claims toward the end of "Song of Myself" that "The nearest gnat is an explanation, and a drop or motion of waves a key" (*LG* 74), and wonders, "I hear you whispering there O stars of heaven, / O suns – O grass of graves – O perpetual transfers and promotions, / If you do not say any thing how can I say any thing?" (*LG* 76), he once more refers to small natural phenomena as autonomous presences on whom he depends, echoing section 6 through both the allusion to "the grass of graves" and his ultimate inability to speak nature. This dynamic also characterizes the final section, in which he feels provoked by a bird to reconsider his ability to give answers: "The spotted hawk swoops by and accuses me, he complains of my gab and my loitering" (*LG* 77). Although he does not exactly yield to the "criticism" but identifies with the bird's wild power—"I too am not a bit tamed, I too am untranslatable, / I sound my barbaric yawp over the roofs of the world"—he grants the animal a presence as a specific manifestation of "untranslatable" nature, while he himself prepares to imaginatively perform his own death. As the poet's voice and material body dissolve into the air and ground, his poem undermines the notion of its own culmination. Instead, the speaker's downward motion suggests an organic transformation into the grass and ground from which his song grew in the first place—"I bequeath myself to the dirt to grow from the grass I love, / If you want me again look for me under your boot-soles" (*LG* 77)—an act of dying into the organic cycle that, one last time, reaches back to section 6, but now includes the poet's own body in a "lucky" embrace of death. The poet whose voice emerged from the grass returns to it; after many encounters with weeds, insects, and birds, in which he continually moved back and forth between pride and sympathy, he concludes his song by expressing the hope that his readers will pay similar attention not only to his poetry but also to the small nature that inspired it.

Such humble turns to nature's usually overlooked minutiae are woven through the entire book. In the 1892 edition, "Beginning My Studies" establishes "The least insect or animal" as one of the starting points of Whitman's poetry, and much later, "Miracles" marvels at "honey-bees busy around the hive of a summer forenoon, / Or animals feeding in the fields, / Or birds, or the wonderfulness of insects in the air" (*LG* 327). Glimpses of small flora and fauna run through "Starting from Paumanok," "Out of the Cradle Endlessly Rocking," "As I Ebb'd with the Ocean of Life," "When Lilacs Last in the Dooryard Bloom'd," and "O Magnet-South," where they feed into evocations of life in particular landscapes and regions. In the "Drum-Taps" section, the speaker notices how the "priceless blood reddens the grass" ("The Wound-Dresser") and embraces the plant not only as a symbol but also as a noteworthy part of the American landscape: "Covering all my lands – all my seashores lining! [. . .] Ah my silvery beauty – ah my woolly white and crimson!" ("Delicate Cluster"). Each of these micromoments offers just enough detail to echo the proto-ecological insights of the sciences, while leaving enough "free margins" to aid in the "enjoyment" of these phenomena and resonate as an ethical encouragement to notice what has been neglected. Their submersion in catalogues of more forcefully visible entities or abstract ideas does not diminish the physical immediacy of minute natural objects, but gives them a specific place in his overall scheme, one that is only seemingly marginal. The way in which weeds, birds, and "the wonderfulness of insects in the air" ("Miracles") briefly come up in sections on the body, language, the sciences, and war turns them into the largely oblique but ubiquitous foundation not only of nature's systems but of everything Whitman celebrates in his work, including poetry itself. Moreover, the way in which the attention to the small repeatedly gives way to wider angles accounts for the simultaneous embeddedness of these phenomena in places proportioned to their small size and in local, regional, and even global contexts. This movement between and among scales undermines the notion of one separate microperspective, at a time when the sciences struggled with the implications of fragmented knowledge and too little synthesis.

These scattered micromoments, then, do not suggest that the speaker is paying mere lip service to small creatures as being "equally perfect." While one could question Whitman's dedication here, just as critics of his democratic inclusiveness have complained that his egalitarian concern stretches quite thin, this analogy also works the other way around. That he keeps coming back to weeds and insects just often enough so as not to lose sight of them testifies to an ongoing struggle to notice in nature what most contemporaries would not deem worthy of attention. Like Dickinson, Whitman occasionally makes this dynamic explicit, when the speaker has to remind himself not to overlook or mindlessly disrupt intricate microsystems, or is alerted by a child or by nature, while it is also structurally part of the repeated, short acts of noting small nature themselves.

Identification and Dissociation

Much like Dickinson, Whitman often approaches mosses, weeds, and birds by way of the dual modes of identification and dissociation. In his important study *Walt Whitman and the Earth*, Killingsworth distinguishes "incomplete identification" and "turning away" as critical elements of Whitman's ecopoetics, especially in the first three editions of *Leaves of Grass*, arguing that Whitman uses "incomplete identification" to associate natural phenomena "with the human body" without reducing them "to human meanings" (33) and "turns away" from nature as a strategy to express nature's difference and the impossibility of assuming identity with it (19–23). What I suggest here is that identification and dissociation develop a particular force in Whitman's small nature poetics, and that the context of mid-nineteenth-century proto-ecological discourses and the comparison with Dickinson further accentuate how these two modes function in his work. With different but related formal means, the tentative "poet of little things and of babes," too, struggled with the possibilities and limitations of granting nature's microsystems an autonomous textual presence.

Whitman's imaginative identification with nature has often been linked to his representations of the body and sexuality as integral parts of the natural world, as well as to his inclusive ideal of American democracy. In terms of his small nature poetics, these two are related insofar as his identification with minute natural phenomena often absorbs them into his own self and body, while also giving them a place in the new American idiom. Such incorporation radicalizes the inclusion of the other in the self in ways that put pressure on identification as an environmentally wholesome practice; as Plumwood stresses, incorporation, in which "the other is recognized only to the extent that it is assimilated to the self" (52), is a key feature of Cartesian dualism that casts the other as a subordinate entity to be controlled. Yet such incorporation, for all its colonizing implications, also involves attention to nature's undervalued presences and indicates, with particular emotional and sensual force, the dependency that binds the speaker to "the commonest weeds by the road" (*LG* 150).

"There Was a Child Went Forth," often considered to be one of Whitman's best poems, exemplifies this dynamic. Here is the opening passage:

> There was a child went forth every day,
> And the first object he look'd upon, that object he became,
> And that object became part of him for the day or a certain part of the day,
> Or for many years or stretching cycles of years.
> And grass and white and red morning-glories, and white and red clover, and
> the song of the phoebe-bird,
> The early lilacs became part of this child,
> And the Third-month lambs and the sow's pink-faint litter, and the mare's
> foal and the cow's calf,
> And the noisy brood of the barnyard or by the mire of the pond-side,
> And the fish suspending themselves so curiously below there, and the
> beautiful curious liquid,
> And the water-plants with their graceful flat heads, all became part of him.
> The field-sprouts of Fourth-month and Fifth-month became part of him,
> Winter-grain sprouts and those of the light-yellow corn, and the esculent
> roots of the garden,
> And the apple-trees cover'd with blossoms and the fruit afterward, and
> wood-berries, and the commonest weeds by the road [. . .]. (*LG* 306–7)

The poem goes on to survey gradually larger geographies, ending with "The horizon's edge, the flying sea-crow, the fragrance of salt marsh and shore mud"; it is often read as a piece on the poet's psychological development, or the "the sources of poetry" (Black 353). Yet the relationship between the human subject and the world is perhaps not as blameless as Whitman implied when he called the poem "the most innocent thing [he] ever did" (qtd. in Aspiz, "There Was a Child Went Forth" 714). Alan Trachtenberg has pointed out that the poem, while it signals "hope of unity at the site of difference and conflict," also exemplifies Whitman's "way of subduing and containing recalcitrant particulars within his dream of an American oneness" (170). Intent upon the emergence of this child's voice, the poem casts small natural particulars as symbolic correspondents (see Aspiz, "There Was a Child Went Forth" 714) and figuratively identifies them with the child's differentiating sense perception. As all other elements become "part of" the child, they mainly serve the constitution of its growing self.

At the same time, however, the way in which identification plays out in this poem also communicates an interest in nature, especially its smaller elements, and suggests that human existence depends on its natural environment in an existential way—a perspective that was new and radical in the mid-nineteenth century, as the writings of Humboldt and Marsh suggest. This has to do with how the lyrical identification with nature here is modified by the third-person child perspective. Without actually assuming the child's voice, the speaker accesses his curiosity and unconditional embrace of nature, which begins on a small scale and from there absorbs the world. In this childlike mode, the speaker expresses a fascination with how external objects "became part of" the human self and emphasizes the physical presence of a whole range of minor natural entities in communication with a larger whole, which does not eclipse but transcends the symbolic import of these small entities. Transfixed by this process of identification, the speaker casts these phenomena as integral parts of a specific landscape, turning them from objects of human self-constitution into self-sustained subjects, even as they are imaginatively absorbed into the human self. Moreover, this self, the child's being human, is itself lost in the process; it is a child that becomes indistinguishable from the world around it. Ultimately, the speaker appropriates this projected child's ability in order to achieve the complete loss of self that drives the poem and generates a sense of humility toward small natural phenomena that midcentury environmental thinkers were just beginning to consider.

The poem's environmental resonance in terms of small nature, then, stems in part from its presentation of specific natural phenomena, including many small ones, by way of a vision of complete identification. The colonizing effects of this imaginary incorporation are balanced not only by the attention it pays to natural objects and by the way it presents human subjectivity as dependent on these objects, but also by the speaker's reliance on a child's perspective. Whitman here links standard Romantic notions of supposedly innocent children to an identification that contributes to the powerful presence of small nature in the poem, while also visualizing the human and the nonhuman as essentially and perennially indistinguishable. Deploying the child in the third person enables the speaker to become wholly attentive to small nature without automatically feeding into the ever-expanding sense of masculine, potentially destructive pride.

The speaker can thus evoke a (perhaps utopian) human identity with the earth based on a self that, even though it "will always go forth every day," remains part of "the fragrance of salt marsh and shore mud" with which the poem ends.

Other passages and poems in which Whitman's speaker conceives of his body as being one with nature's smallest creatures similarly serve the constitution of the male speaker's supreme sense of self, while also expressing his physical and historical dependence that undermines such anthropocentrism. Section 5 of "Song of Myself" presents the poet's male body as a collage of nature's minutiae, yet while the image of "leaves stiff or drooping in the fields, / And brown ants in the little wells beneath them, / And mossy scabs of the worm fence, heap'd stones, elder, mullein and poke-weed" integrates the environment into his anthropomorphic system of thought, nature's particles retain a sovereign presence. Likewise, in section 31, "gneiss, coal, long-threaded moss, fruits, grains, esculent roots" give definition to the poet, who derives legitimacy from being one with the earth, while the "incorporating" embrace of lesser flora and fauna also communicates their complexity and a sense of human dependency. The image of the poet's body lushly overgrown with small plants and animals to the point of fading into them also harks back to the theme of life folding into death through nature's cycles, further destabilizing the notion of human superiority.

As in Dickinson's work, then, Whitman's identification with the "commonest, cheapest, nearest, easiest" (*LG* 36), including the "commonest" nonhuman life-forms, contributes to his poetry's green overtones. But it does so in a more conflicted way, since he leans further toward their radical incorporation into the speaker, and also because he tends to approach the world from a social position of masculine power. As such, his poetry prefigures a paradox that has become a point of contention in twentieth- and twenty-first-century environmentalism, where deep ecologists have promulgated identification as a source of ecocentrism without being able to evade the charge of ultimately empowering the human self. "There is a process of ever-widening identification and ever-narrowing alienation," writes deep ecologist Arne Naess, "which widens the self. The self is as comprehensive as the totality of our identifications. [. . .] Our Self is that with which we identify" (261). Just as Naess and others have found it difficult to make the argument that they are interested in an alternative self that depends on the self-realization of everyone and everything,

Whitman's identification with nature's obscure creatures is faced with the impossibility of such a move. In this sense, the image of the child who forever becomes what he sees also embodies the ultimate inability of the poet to leave behind his subjectivizing perspective and thus his anthropocentrism, even in the most "innocent" identification with nature's smallest elements. And yet, identification as a poetic strategy also effectively intervenes in the destructive relations between an expanding capitalist culture and the natural world—it just sits more uneasily when pronounced by a self-declared representative proponent of such a culture than by a female poet who uses it as a complexly subversive strategy. In Whitman's poetry, these moments of identification do suggest a radical turn toward depreciated natural phenomena, a turn that often implies the realization of their utter fragility and marvelous intricacy. This realization, together with the particular sense of kinship and dependence which identification can evoke, seems to preclude a utilitarian view of nature. Instead, it invites an ethical responsiveness to the environment, momentarily relinquishing human self-sufficiency, and indeed mastery over nature. In Whitman, this ethical responsiveness is again projected most powerfully through the figure and perspective of the child.

One key way of countering the troublesome aspects of identification as an environmentally oriented discursive practice is by reinstating the distance between the human self and nature. As Jhan Hochman has phrased it, we need to know "not only how to 'become' nature, how to attempt a merging with the real or imagined subjectivity of a plant, animal, or mineral, of air, water, earth and fire; [we] also need to pull back and grant these beings and entities unromanticized difference, an autonomy apart from humans" (192). In the previous chapter I argued that Dickinson's poetry about small natural elements derives much of its environmental suggestiveness from the way her speaker both identifies with and distances herself from such small creatures. The comparison highlights how Whitman's embrace of small nonhuman life-forms is occasionally ruptured by instances of doubt as well, and while such instances tend to be more subtextual, they keep Whitman's speaker from embracing too fully a mode that tries to possess the other by becoming it.

One instance of hesitation and withdrawal that disrupts Whitman's all-encompassing identifications occurs in the second half of "There Was a Child Went Forth," when the catalogue of natural objects that "became part of the child" is briefly interrupted:

> Affection that will not be gainsay'd, the sense of what is real, the thought if after all it should prove unreal,
> The doubts of day-time and the doubts of night-time, the curious whether and how,
> Whether that which appears so is so, or is it all flashes and specks? (*LG* 307)

The speaker here questions the child's ecstatic becoming what he sees and dissociates himself from everything he has so hopefully incorporated into his younger self. In the 1855 version of the poem, the second line included the phrase "received with wonder or pity or love or dread," giving this element of doubt greater thematic prominence, but even in the final version its residual presence is part of Whitman's poetic project.

Such disrupting instances of doubt remain comparatively sparse in Whitman's poetry, but they still unsettle his louder assertions of identity with the earth. When, for example, the speaker admits at the beginning of section 6 of "Song of Myself" that he doesn't know what the grass is, he indirectly pulls back from the blurring of grasses into his male body at the end of section 5, subtly granting them the difference and autonomy that is so crucial for an ecological outlook. In this respect, the poem "A Noiseless Patient Spider" reads like a metapoetic commentary on such dissociation from nature, staging paradoxically both a moment of identification with a small creature and the loss of touch with the natural world of which the creature is a symbol:

> A noiseless patient spider,
> I mark'd where on a little promontory it stood isolated,
> Mark'd how to explore the vacant vast surrounding,
> It launch'd forth filament, filament, filament, out of itself,
> Ever unreeling them, ever tirelessly speeding them.
>
> And you O my soul where you stand,
> Surrounded, detached, in measureless oceans of space,
> Ceaselessly musing, venturing, throwing, seeking the spheres to connect them,
> Till the bridge you will need be form'd, till the ductile anchor hold,
> Till the gossamer thread you fling catch somewhere, O my soul. (*LG* 377)

Killingsworth has read this poem as an exquisite example of how Whitman "dramatizes the difficulty of completing, much less sustaining, the energetic connections that the soul seeks" and as part of "a poetic ecology based on association rather than dominance and complete identification"

(*Walt Whitman and the Earth* 36, 38); he has also shown how the poem moves from actual place into open, lonely space ("Nature" 317). I would emphasize that in this poem, Whitman's habitual process of noticing a tiny creature in place by way of identifying with it becomes something else, because the spider is itself so isolated, "on a little promontory" and unsuccessfully trying to connect to the world. In other words, the speaker's identification with this strangely isolated animal does not bring him any closer to nature but performs the failure to connect to the (natural) environment, structurally underscored by the space between the first and second stanzas. If this is a poem about connections that will not work, this also implies that in some constellations even identification does not suffice to bridge the gap between human self and nature. For all their subtlety, such small dissociating gestures serve as an important counterbalance to the grand all-absorptive reach in Whitman's poetry.

In an early discussion of the ethical implications of Whitman's poetry, Thomas B. Byers charged him with anthropocentrism and with not fully extending democratic equality to nonhuman creatures. Referring to the passage from "Song of Myself" in which Whitman's speaker imaginatively reaches out to a "gigantic beautiful stallion," Byers writes that "admiration and even love for nature [. . .] are based on his utilitarian sense of nature's value as a symbolic means in the project of self-realization. [. . .] For Whitman, nature has no greater value; human self-realization is the project of the universe" (76). While it is true that the speaker here seems to use the horse to absorb his powers and "out-gallop" him, Whitman's many references to smaller creatures complicate Byers's assertion. Throughout *Leaves of Grass,* occasional encounters with minor flora and fauna in their unexpected intricacy do grant them a "greater value" and a presence that cannot be reduced to their metaphorical suggestiveness or utilitarian value. Indeed, the utilitarianism that feeds into much of Whitman's work is conspicuously absent from his nature references on the smallest scale, which is all the more remarkable since even Marsh often took note of nature's "humblest" creatures owing to the "great instruction" and "material advantage" one might derive from them. While Whitman's identification with seemingly negligible weeds and insects does serve the project of "human self-realization," it also destabilizes the sense of human difference and superiority. This is especially the case in conjunction with his occasional admission of doubt regarding his loving embrace of nature. To quote Plumwood again: "Although we may aim for a relationship of mutual enrichment, cooperation and friendship, we may often have to settle for that of respectful but wondering strangers (not necessarily second best)" (139). What speaks from Whitman's small-scale poetry is the recognition that attention to nature can have a deeply sobering effect upon the arrogant presumption that humans can fully understand nature and control their relationships with it. In a sense, all of his studiedly sketchy turns toward nature's neglected minutiae reiterate a thought he had expressed in one of his early notebook entries: "Bring all the art and science of the world, and baffle and humble it with one spear of grass" (qtd. in Lawson 98).

Overall, there are a number of unexpected intersections between Dickinson's and Whitman's approaches to small natural phenomena and their green repercussions in the context of their time and beyond. Their multifaceted dialogue revolves around a shared investment in noticing the minutiae that have long been overlooked and whose ecological significance and vulnerability mid-nineteenth-century environmentalists were just beginning to discuss. With almost the same frequency as Dickinson, Whitman notices what is commonly deemed trite because it is small, talking back to similar proto-ecological debates not despite but because of his more sparing use of botanical or ornithological detail. That he tends to do so in passing is not tantamount to being superficial, especially since his short references often include scientific allusions and a muted ethical urgency. Like Dickinson's poems, his lines and passages write against a culturally condoned myopia that environmental scientists and essayists such as George Perkins Marsh in *Man and Nature* were also criticizing:

> Nature has no unit of magnitude by which she measures her works. Man takes his standards of dimension from himself. [. . .] To a being who instinctively finds the standard of all magnitudes in his own material frame, all objects exceeding his own dimension are absolutely great, all falling short of them absolutely small. Hence we habitually regard the whale and the elephant as essentially large and therefore important creatures, the animalcule as an essentially small and therefore unimportant organism. (111–12)

Dickinson's and Whitman's poems parallel this charge in essence and environmental momentum, while their fine-tuned, evocative language also carries this debate further to face some of its own complexities.

This is especially the case in their common dedication to identification and dissociation. In their work, the notion of kinship fosters the move from a rational statement of concern to an ethical revaluation of human-nonhuman interaction, while the recognition of difference helps to avoid the pitfalls of appropriation that the act of identification involves.

Owing to their disparate speaking positions, as Victorian woman and aspiring male national poet, respectively, they express different aspects of the conflicts involved in such a recognition of small natural phenomena and our dependency on them—in often paradoxical poems and passages whose eco-ethical suggestiveness points beyond what most of their proto-ecological contemporaries would formulate. That Dickinson and Whitman sustain the tension that derives from such a simultaneous commitment to identity and difference makes their poetry so environmentally compelling because this tension points to the core of the human struggle to devise a nondominating relationship to nature, what Plumwood calls "a relationship of non-hierarchical difference" (60).

The most remarkable result of reading Dickinson's and Whitman's work on the microlevel, however, may well lie in their related evocations of humility. Where Dickinson mainly charges Victorian norms of female modesty with green overtones, Whitman's sporadic turns toward nature's minutiae have more to say about the danger of losing sight of them. By doing so, their poetry destabilizes the centrality of the human self profoundly: it does not merely "teach" humility for the moral elevation of the human subject, but also performs it with respect to natural particulars on the smallest scale. This humility requires dissolving the human subject in radical identification and reconfirming human subjecthood, expressed in the act of speaking, on the other side of this dissolution. Just as much of their poetry never relinquishes completely the natural scenes it evokes, their nature-inspired humility continues to matter, in the world of their poems, as a mode of relating to the very natural situations that motivated this stance in the first place.

II · Describing Local Lands

At about the same time that Emily Dickinson signed her letters "Amherst" and regularly referred to northeastern fields and forests in her poetry, Walt Whitman signed a series of early essays for the *New York Sunday Dispatch* "Paumanok" (Genoways 11) and grounded several of his major poems in "Mannahatta's ship-fringed shore" and nearby Long Island. Both poets imagined familiar landscapes and seascapes with a passion that in itself merits a comparison of their work on the local scale—the distance one could easily walk and grasp in a day or even see on a clear day, stretches of land that are in people's everyday "circumference." From an environmental perspective, such a comparison draws attention to another unexpected correspondence between their poetic projects: even though Dickinson alluded mostly to the backlands of the Connecticut River valley, while Whitman wrote much about the sights and sounds of the New York coast, they formulated related visions of people's lives in their immediate natural environments. In particular, they express a common dedication to description as a means of drawing attention to local geographies as specific places and living systems in ways that deflect attention away from the centrality of the perceiving mind—a strategy that overlaps in indirect but telling ways with certain environmental discussions of the day. By way of particular aesthetic choices, Dickinson and Whitman devise very open, suggestive descriptive modes that rely on a small number of descriptive details and experiment with radically minimizing the presence of the speaking subject in favor of the object, turning the inherently unassuming pose of description, with its eco-ethical potential but also with its limitations, into a defining feature of their local poetry.

The environmental resonances of their poems about "native lands" (Fr178) become particularly evident if one considers the shift that occurred in people's relationships with their immediate surroundings at that time. Around midcentury, fields such as botany, geography, geology, and especially biogeography, which emerged in 1858 and is sometimes considered to be the same as ecology (Ball 407–8), studied local natural units primarily by way of detailed descriptions. When Dickinson moved from deceptively simple poems such as "Frequently the woods are pink" (Fr24) to more complex evocations of local systems in "Nature – the Gentlest Mother is" (Fr741) and "Four Trees – opon a solitary Acre" (Fr778), and Whitman composed some of his most powerful poems about intricate landscapes and seascapes, including "Crossing Brooklyn Ferry," "Out of the Cradle Endlessly Rocking," and "As I Ebb'd with the Ocean of Life," "descriptive biogeographers" defined climatic zones and topographical boundaries, and "establish[ed] the complexity of the distribution patterns, [. . .] perhaps attempting to explain them primarily in ecological terms" (Ball 408). Biogeography was also crucial for the development of the ecosystem concept—the idea that biotic and abiotic elements in an area form a dynamic, interdependent, and self-sustaining community—which was discussed for several decades before Arthur Tansley coined the term in 1935. Overall, the field marked a crucial stage in the development of America's early ecological sciences, but also exemplified the limitations of nineteenth-century green thought: in the words of ecologist Jacob Weiner, the tendency to "collect huge amounts of descriptive data without a clear purpose" was among ecology's "youthful follies" (373). In this light, Dickinson's and Whitman's local poetry becomes legible as an indirect response to the time's developing environmental interests; they talk about local naturescapes as living systems by combining descriptive elements with poetic strategies that tackle the problems of quantity and selection of details.

For assessing the environmental import of nature descriptions in their local poetry, the popular nature essays of the time, which combined extended descriptions of natural systems with personal narratives of the enlightened self (see Fritzell 73), are even more relevant. The opening paragraph of Higginson's "Water-Lilies," first published in the *Atlantic Monthly* in 1858, later collected in his *Out-Door Papers* (1863), and probably well known to Dickinson (see Sewall 547; St. Armand 195–96), serves as a good example:

> The inconstant April mornings drop showers or sunbeams over the glistening lake, while far beneath its surface a murky mass disengages itself from the muddy bottom, and rises slowly through the waves. The tasselled alder-branches droop above it; the last year's blackbird's nest swings over it in the

> grape-vine; the newly-opened Hepaticas and Epigaeas on the neighboring bank peer down modestly to look for it; the water-skater (Gerris) pauses on the surface near it, casting on the shallow bottom the odd shadow of his feet, like three pairs of boxing-gloves; the Notonecta, or water-boatman, rows round and round it, sometimes on his breast, sometimes on his back; queer caddis-worms trail their self-made homesteads of leaves or twigs beside it; the Dytiscus, dorbug of the water, blunders clumsily against it; the tadpole wriggles his stupid way to it, and rests upon it, meditating of future frogdom; the passing wild-duck dives and nibbles at it; the mink and musk-rat brush it with their soft fur; the spotted turtle slides over it; the slow larvae of gauzy dragon-flies cling sleepily to its sides and await their change: all these fair or uncouth creatures feel, through the dim waves, the blessed longing of spring; and yet not one of them dreams that within that murky mass there lies a treasure too white and beautiful to be yet intrusted to the waves, and that for many a day that bud must yearn toward the surface, before, aspiring above it, as mortals to heaven, it meets the sunshine with the answering beauty of the Water-Lily. (465)

In this passage, many descriptive details are the basis for the reappraisal of swamps as what would now be called densely alive, diverse ecosystems, at a time when they were still mostly considered a nuisance. With scientific names and the discussion of relations among species couched in the language of Victorian sensibilities, the text mediates between seemingly objective depiction and subjective perception, cultivating a scientifically informed appreciation for a common stretch of land as an interrelated living whole.

John Burroughs, who became America's favorite nature writer during his more than twenty-year-long friendship with Whitman, provided more abstract discussions of this generic convention and its ethical implications, as in the introduction to his *Wake-Robin*:

> The literary naturalist does not take liberties with facts; facts are the flora upon which he lives. The more and the fresher the facts the better. I can do nothing without them, but I must give them my own flavor. [. . .] To interpret Nature is not to improve upon her: it is to draw her out; it is to have an emotional intercourse with her, absorb her, and reproduce her tinged with the colors of the spirit. (xiii)

While Burroughs emphasizes the need for scientifically informed descriptive details as well as a personal style of rendition, the latter must not dominate the former. Today, Burroughs is mainly remembered for his passionate arguments for precise natural history essays that are true to natural phenomena and describe them with "*moderation and self-denial*" rather than being dominated by personal "flavor" ("Real and Sham Natural History" 299; emphasis added). As Bill McKibben puts it, Burroughs's "moderation, his calm observations, and most of all his seductive and accurate descriptions [. . .] should give him a central place in the environmental movement" (18). This tension between, on the one hand, the "mere" description of nature's "facts" and the self-effacing (or humble) pose this stance implies, and, on the other hand, the interest in understanding and interpreting nature and the processes of personal growth involved, makes nature essays a crucial reference point for discussing Dickinson's and Whitman's poetic negotiations between the presentation of self-sustained natural systems and the interest in the human observer as eco-ethically significant choices.

Finally, the dawning conservation ideas of the time, too, evolved in part from an understanding of local natural systems and their fragility. The sense of nature's aesthetic and spiritual significance that played into most descriptive nature essays became a defining theme of the conservation movement, and the impending turn from appreciation to legal protection was prepared by such essays' habitual move from description to implicit or explicit prescription (see Slovic, *Seeking Awareness* 137). Before John Muir's accounts of western landscapes would launch campaigns for their protection, the descriptive essays of writers such as Higginson implicitly called for restraint in people's interactions with nearby nature, as this passage from "Water-Lilies" shows:

> Hither the water-lilies have retreated, to a domain of their own. Darker than these dark waves, there stand in their bosom hundreds of submerged trees, and dismasted roots still upright, spreading their vast, uncouth limbs like enormous spiders beneath the surface. They are remnants of border wars with the axe, vegetable Witheringtons, still fighting on their stumps, but gradually sinking into the soft ooze [. . .]. The present decline in business is clear revenue to the water-lilies, and these waters are higher than usual because the idle factories do not draw them off. (466)

Again, when such wetlands were mainly seen as waste areas, Higginson's detailed description includes a charge against logging and other "business" as a threat to a swamp's delicate flora, an ecopolitical argument that constitutes another important backdrop for discussing the environmental implications of Dickinson's and Whitman's presentations of common stretches of land and their fragile biologies.

Overall, the local landscape descriptions embraced by biogeographers, nature essayists, and early conservationists leaned toward human "moderation and self-denial" (Burroughs), yet remained linked to the urge to master the land, as Robert Sattelmeyer emphasizes:

> The naturalist's role was no less than a new version of Adam's charge in paradise: to name and describe each living thing man was to have dominion over. On a less mythological level, natural history writing provided Americans with an inventory of their riches and a forum for important debate about the relations of man to nature and about the nature of nature itself in the New World. (vii)

These conflicting implications of local nature descriptions also shed new light on some thematic and stylistic features of Dickinson's and Whitman's poetry. In their frequent turns to familiar landscapes, they present just a few details that, however, are richly suggestive in terms of the interactions among natural elements and their ethical implications, responding to their time's interest in local nature with a descriptive openness that makes all the difference.

While "landscape" and "description" figured prominently in nineteenth-century approaches to nature, they are not exactly fashionable categories in current literary criticism, where landscape is often associated with tame or tamed places whose histories of cultivation and domination are glossed over by middle-class pastoral notions, while description is seen to rely on the controversial merits of realistic depiction. The situation is beginning to change, however. In terms of landscape, publications such as W. J. T. Mitchell's collection *Landscape and Power* have critically discussed the concept's entanglements with practices of surveying, (re)organizing, and (often imperially) reshaping the land, while Bonnie Costello's *Shifting Ground: Reinventing Landscape in Modern American Poetry* has shown how twentieth-century landscape poetry records human history in and with the land as often as it participates in its mastery. It is part of my argument here that Dickinson and Whitman already developed poetic modes that deal with the pitfall of conceptual mastery by portraying dynamic local landscapes that retain a remarkable degree of autonomy and dignity, while letting their speakers rethink their position to the point of virtually canceling out their own poetic voice.

In terms of description, two studies have begun to reclaim this basic type of literary discourse as central to American (environmental) literature. Lawrence Buell's *The Environmental Imagination* urges that "the willingness to admit that thick description of the external world can at least sometimes be a strong interest for writers and for readers, even when it also serves ulterior purposes, is particularly crucial in the case of the environmental text" (90); focusing on natural history prose, Buell stresses that "[n]onfictional nature representation, especially, hinges on its ability to convince us that it is more responsive to the physical world's nuances than most people are" (90). The second book, Angus Fletcher's *A New Theory for American Poetry*, includes a reappraisal of descriptive poetry that reengages some of Buell's concerns, arguing that "description in fact is the most important necessary preliminary to Romantic aesthetics" (51):

> When Romantic poetry turned to its involvement with nature, it committed itself to deepening, analyzing, but generally idealizing a practice which the study of nature makes virtually unavoidable, namely, the description of the natural scene. [. . .] By failing to grasp the role of description as the grounding strategy of the Romantic impulse, criticism has been forced into its overestimation of the problems of authorial consciousness and creativity. (24)

Fletcher also claims that certain kinds of verse, from John Clare via Walt Whitman to John Ashbery, display a dynamic descriptive technique that points beyond the mimetic and discursive, and finds that "environment poems," while grounded in nature and science, can supersede environmental prose because they take "environmentalist concerns to a higher level" that transcends narrow political interests (3). So while Buell praises the "representational density" of environmental prose in contrast to poetry's "increasing separation of mind from nature" (199), Fletcher celebrates environment poems precisely for being neither representational nor tied to "laws of consistent logical derivation" (226). Also, where Buell is interested in how texts about real or imagined places direct our attention to environments that exist outside of texts, Fletcher focuses on the poem-as-place, emphasizing the reality of imagined places. And while Buell's embrace of "thick description" as mimetic representation forms the basis for an openly political reappraisal of environmental prose, Fletcher's focus on poems that "are not *about* the environment" but "intended to surround us in exactly the way an actual environment surrounds us" (227) circumvents environmentalism's immediate political concerns. Neither Buell nor

Fletcher, however, considers description in relation to the role it played in nineteenth-century proto-ecological debates. My reading of Dickinson's and Whitman's local poetry, consistently in conjunction with their time's environmental discussions—especially descriptive natural history essays—suggests that an important achievement of their work lies in the development of an open descriptive mode that transcends the binary oppositions that emerge from this critical debate. Their poetry embraces precise detail but also, and perhaps more importantly, the gaps between a landscape's specific elements, and thus avoids definitional certainty; it grants local landscapes agency, especially that of resisting being described and thus understood, while the speakers yield parts of their actual and conceptual control; and it implicitly points toward proto-environmentalist ethics without being prescriptive or normative.

As such, Dickinson's and Whitman's local poetry, for all their thematic and formal differences, also points in a direction that is not often discussed in contemporary literary scholarship. With their peculiar modes of description, they link epistemology to ethics in terms similar to those humanistic geographer Edward Relph suggests:

> Confronted with the recognition that a landscape is comprised of countless elements—such as houses, trees, soil particles, clouds, cars, advertisements and mountains—and involves countless processes, most of which are far more complex and intractable than anything encountered in a physics laboratory, the only sensible option for a geographer is to be *humble*, confess that none of it can be adequately explained and confine all efforts of understanding to *description*. (163; emphasis added)

Dickinson's and Whitman's poems often express a similar sense of humility when faced with a landscape's diverse phenomena, refraining from the more explicitly controlling positions of analysis or valuation and embracing description instead. Environmentally speaking, the merits of this choice do not so much lie in its promise of objective and detailed depiction, but in the ethics of humility it implies. Yet as poets, Dickinson and Whitman also question the power of description itself. Description as I use the word here mainly refers to the desire to bring a sense of familiarity with and appreciation for certain natural phenomena to the page, in a language that faces the challenge, as well as the ultimate impossibility, of relinquishing interpretive control. When Dickinson employs a halting, stumbling language full of dashes, and concludes the minimal portrait of a dynamic acre with trees (Fr778) with a lingering "unknown – ," and when Whitman's speaker, walking a shoreline strewn with organic particles, is overcome by intense doubts as to the point of imaginatively staging his own death ("As I Ebb'd"), the local descriptions involved here precisely do not assume a simple relation between text and world, but constitute one of the most challenging aspects of environmental literature.

3

"The acre gives them – Place – / They – Him – Attention"

Dickinson's Sparse Description

In April 1862, Emily Dickinson responded to Thomas Wentworth Higginson's inquiry about her social environment with a surprising comment on nearby natural phenomena: "You ask of my Companions Hills – Sir – and the Sundown – and a Dog – large as myself, that my Father bought me – They are better than Beings – because they know – but do not tell – and the noise in the Pool, at Noon – excels my Piano" (L261). Dickinson does more here than construct her life and art as intimately connected to the local landscapes around her. If it is true that Dickinson saw Higginson's nature essays as a "firm bond between them," and that her poems were answers to his question as to what literature could do "towards describing one summer day" (see Habegger 453), this letter also responds to the descriptive strategies of his sprawling, often didactic environmental prose by offering a moderate sample of her own descriptive technique. With a few strokes she sketches a local scene that is concise but not strict or hermetic, granting nonhuman beings an active presence while deflecting attention away from her own eloquence precisely at the height of achievement—a strategy she embraces in her poetry in even more radical ways.

The notion that description is central to Dickinson's local poetry has not been too common, perhaps also because landscape description appears to be antithetical to what is perceived as her idiosyncratic genius. An important exception here are discussions that link Dickinson's poetry to nineteenth-century landscape painting; Barton Levi St. Armand, in particular, has stressed that much like the Pre-Raphaelites, Dickinson's poems render nature precisely and retain a high degree of "concreteness behind the elusive symbology" (250), while Judith Farr has discussed how Dickinson's lucid renderings of nature and its spiritual dimensions were inspired by other contemporary painters ("Dickinson and the Visual Arts").[1] But while nineteenth-century painters—and poets such as Dickinson, who sought to emulate and challenge the canvas through language—certainly explored links between nature and the divine, their "pictures" also derive from and refer back to the earth and human interactions with it in ways that express noteworthy environmental sensibilities.[2]

The views of John Ruskin, whom Dickinson once called one of her favorite prose writers (L261) and whose passion for nature was crucial for her style (see St. Armand; Farr), highlight this juncture. Environmental historians have emphasized that for Ruskin, landscape painting was grounded in proto-ecological scientific insights and was itself capable of revealing them: "Ruskin was the first to anatomize and explain the surface form of landscape for the general reader [. . .]. To understand the surface form of landscape—the skin of the Earth—he realized that we must understand its underlying anatomy, in other words, its geological structure and material"; to him, an informed rendering of mountains, for instance, could thus increase people's awareness of nature's intricate web of soil, air, and water (Palmer 830). Moreover, Ruskin celebrated the description not of supposedly wild natural scenes, but of landscapes shaped by human agency, and sought to develop a community's capacity "to look at landscape with awareness of its (imagined) history" (O'Gorman 20), which makes him a forerunner of environmental geographers (Cosgrove 58–62).[3] Interestingly, Ruskin also linked landscape description to a particular subject position, which is rarely explored for its environmental connotations:

> From young artists, in landscape, nothing ought to be tolerated but simple bona fide imitation of nature. [. . .] Their duty is neither to choose, nor compose, nor imagine, nor experimentalize; but to be humble and earnest in following the steps of Nature, and tracing the finger of God. (447)

This passage is sometimes taken as a full embrace of mimesis, or as advice for *aspiring* artists on how to practice their skills because Ruskin wrote elsewhere that great landscape art should precisely not just copy a given scene. Either way, for Ruskin landscape art, whether mimetic renderings or imaginative ones that appear to leave all actual scenes behind, was based on a religiously inflected humility, so that the environmental subtexts of his influential landscape theory derive both from the powerful hold over the spectator that natural systems retain on the canvas and from the artist's implied attitude toward nature, which remains humble even as the painting seems to glory in its superior evocation of the land.

Many of Dickinson's poems about local lands express a similar stance, yet as a poet, she also "chose" and "composed" in distinct ways. To carve out the green connotations of her local art, this chapter reads her landscape poems not against nineteenth-century paintings or Ruskin's theories, but against the time's more explicitly environmental debates, especially the fashionable natural history essays. Next to their detailed, learned, often didactic descriptions, Dickinson's sparse portraits become legible as sensitive responses to a broader cultural turn toward the intricate workings of familiar landscapes that also rewrite certain assumptions about how to relate to the nonhuman world. While most nature essays, even as they embraced the self-effacing mode of description, were centrally about the nature-sensitive speaker's increasing awareness and intent upon enlightening readers, her poems communicate nature's agency while de-emphasizing her own, thus creating a powerful tension between successfully grasping a well-known stretch of land with minimal means and expressing a humble awareness of the poet's ultimate inability to evoke such a common place in all its facets.

Sparse Description

In early 1865, Dickinson wrote a poem that serves as a poignant example of what I call sparse description here. She talks about a nearby natural scene that, for all its symbolic implications, also matters as place, evoking the interaction among its elements with the barest of means and without calling attention to the speaker's understanding or interpretation of the scene:

> An Everywhere of Silver
> With Ropes of Sand
> To keep it from effacing
> The Track called Land – (Fr931)

In one of the few critical commentaries on the poem, Francis V. Madigan stresses that one can trace "the possible symbolic value of the [sea] image even in such descriptive poems as ["An Everywhere of Silver"]," which lies in the "threatening power" of this beautiful, infinite space (40). While Madigan implies that the poem's descriptive quality might defy the habitual critical move from place to symbol, this descriptive edge also constitutes an achievement deserving of further critical attention, especially, but not only, from an environmental perspective.

First of all, the poem highlights that when Dickinson sketches an elusive natural scene that seems on the verge of disintegrating into the symbolic, the few descriptive elements she employs tend also to evoke a distinct place, registering its vivid materiality up and against the prominent pull toward transcendence. This sea may appear like an immaterial sphere without beginning or end, forever threatening to recede into a distance and to take the imagination with it, and yet its silvery thereness never vanishes. Similarly, "Ropes of Sand" metaphorically suggests, according to the mid-nineteenth-century *Webster's*, a "feeble union or tie" or bands "easily broken," but the poem reenters the phrase into a context where it also captures the size and shape of sand at a tidal beach. And while the "Ropes of Sand" symbolically keep the sea from "effacing" the land, and tie it *to* the land, as one would a ship, so as not to "efface" itself, this crossover also captures the give-and-take between both elements as they take turns disappearing but never dissolve completely. Without undoing the symbolic implications that range from ancient mythology (the futile task of weaving ropes of sand) to biblical allusions (the Flood), these minimal descriptive references acknowledge the shore's geography so compellingly that the allure of this translucent realm cannot be separated from its triumphant physicality. The environmental significance of a descriptive style such as this, that mediates between the symbolic and the geographical, becomes particularly apparent if one considers that the mid-nineteenth century witnessed a shift from imagining oceans as a mythical realm to seeing them as a unique place and habitat. The role of this shift for the emergence of an ecological perspective can hardly be overstated: it was during the *Beagle*'s famous sea voyage that Darwin converted "to a dynamic view of the relationship between living things and their environment" and began to understand that the relationship between species and geographical factors was highly sensitive to disturbances (Bowler 299, 244); shortly thereafter, Edward Forbes divided the oceans' fauna into zones by depth (Bowler 275), leading to early ecological discussions of species distribution patterns depending on local variants; and in 1866, Darwin follower Ernst Häckel defined the concept of "oecologie" in the wake of various marine expeditions (Bowler 316). Nature essays brought this shift to larger audiences, relying on extensive descriptions of oceans and seashores as not only mythical but also geographically specific sites; Thoreau's *Cape Cod*, for instance, serialized in *Putnam's Monthly* in 1855 and in the *Atlantic* in 1864, wrote that Cape Cod "is anchored to the heavens, as it were, by a myriad little cables of beach-grass, and, if they should fail, would become a total wreck, and erelong go to the bottom" (164), and characterized the dunes' movement as "a tide of sand impelled by waves and wind, slowly flowing from the sea toward the town" (161). In Dickinson's poem, too, the shore's transcendental possibilities are part of the speaker's perception, but its powerful expression of the land's fragile materiality also echoes and fosters her culture's turn to maritime landscapes as densely alive places.

Dickinson's "An Everywhere of Silver" also shows in an exemplary way how she tends to grasp the character of local places without dominating the scenes with a plethora of descriptive details or subduing them to definitional closure. Her imaginary shoreline comes into view by way of only two or three descriptive elements—color and texture of sea and shore, push and pull of their interaction—which create a sense of letting the place be, of granting it as much ontological sovereignty as may be possible in a text. If description per se refrains most strongly from explanation and explicit interpretation, even as it can never function outside of human signification and understanding, Dickinson's way of reducing description to the bare minimum while withholding any overt interpretive gestures grants the landscape perhaps the highest possible degree of dignified autonomy.

Such a descriptive openness is an environmentally interesting strategy if one considers that the time's proto-ecological sciences, which sought to describe natural systems as complex webs of life, were unable to control the mass of new data. Alexander von Humboldt, for instance, eventually found that his *Cosmos* suffered from the sheer weight of detail (Walls, *Seeing New Worlds* 102), and partially withdrew from the idea of total descriptive control by devising a new form of science writing. Laura Walls explains that as a result, his widely read *Aspects of Nature* (1850) consisted of very short key essays, "gems of kinetic description," each followed by a separate, longer section of details, creating an "open-ended accordion form" (102–3). Dickinson's uncluttered snapshot of a shore can be said to perform a related move. In a culture where scientifically informed nature descriptions were ubiquitous, it participates in (and in a way depends on) a larger intertextual "accordion." Yet her minimalist poem, which could hardly be reduced any further, also takes Humboldt's gesture a step further as it cuts detail almost to the point of canceling speech itself, using nothing but a provocative four by four (and one time, five) rhythmic words to describe the interplay between land and sea.

As such, "An Everywhere of Silver" also shows how Dickinson's sparse description amplifies the unassuming position toward nature that is part of the mode of description itself. Any description of an external object involves a relative de-centering of the human speaker, compared, for instance, to the speaker's position in interpretation or evaluation. In "An Everywhere of Silver," the speaker is absent from the scene, and rather than explicitly interpreting it or commenting upon the process of perception, grants the seashore center stage. The poem's hovering quality—created through its concern with "effacing," the final dash at the end of its sentence fragment, and the interplay of words and empty spaces that creates as many blanks on the page as it fills—also suggests that such poetic description remains slippery even at the high point of achievement and might efface itself at any moment. Paradoxically, traditional signs of poetic control or closure contribute to this elusiveness as this poem's regular rhyme scheme, rhythm, and meter emphasize the inconclusive to-and-fro of the tidal shoreline. At the time, most nature essays and conservationist arguments were, for all their occasional expressions of environmental humility, intent upon moving from description to overt interpretation and prescription. Thoreau's *Cape Cod*, between its long descriptive passages, includes speculations about plants' local distribution, advice about how to grow certain trees, and warnings that along the fertile shores, once "thought to be inexhaustible," various species are declining because they were being harvested too often (27). By contrast, the epistemological indeterminacy of Dickinson's poem precludes the facile deduction of any one practical stance toward the natural world, so that this condensed portrait of a familiar maritime landscape as an intricate place pushes against the urge to fully grasp or define a viable position toward nature, even the most environmentally sensitive one. This is not changed by the paradoxical sense of power that is involved in evoking a natural scene with such seemingly meager elements: the poem may be a marvel of artistic accomplishment, but the glory is the land's.

The Town and Beyond

Most of Dickinson's local poems deal with the woods and fields around her speaker's "native town." Here, too, she combines a reduced form of poetic description that intertwines these places' autonomous vitality (and spiritual import) with speaking positions that negotiate the possibility of an environmentally oriented humility—at the height of natural insight and poetic achievement. The following, early example renders a seasonal forest with minimal descriptive means, yet to complex eco-ethical effects:

Frequently the woods are pink –
Frequently, are brown.
Frequently the hills undress

Behind my native town –
Oft a head is crested
I was wont to see –
And as oft a cranny
Where it used to be –
And the Earth – they tell me
On it's axis turned!
Wonderful Rotation –
By but *twelve* performed! (Fr24)

These references to hills changing their "pink" and "brown" garments may be conventional, but they are also specific, and although the middle lines shift away from place to ponder the cycle of human life and the divine in nature, the personifying trope of a "crested" then bald head also increases the geographical presence of forest-covered hills, while the "crannies," which can refer to small niches or fissures, hint at their unexpected vulnerability. How these gestures take up the time's interest in describing local landscapes can be seen by reading the poem alongside popular nature essays such as Wilson Flagg's "Trees in Assemblages," published in the *Atlantic Monthly* in 1861:

> In the lowland the scarlet and crimson hues of the Maple and the Tupelo predominate, mingled with a superb variety of colors from the shrubbery, whose splendor is always the greatest on the borders of ponds and water-courses, and frequently surpasses that of the trees. As the plain rises into the hill-side, the Ash-trees may be distinguished by their peculiar shades of salmon, mulberry, and purple, and the Hickories by their invariable yellows. The Elm, the Lime, and the Buttonwood are always blemished and rusty: they add no brilliancy to the spectacle, serving only to sober and relieve other parts of the scenery.
>
> When the second period of the Fall of the Leaf has arrived, the woods that were first tinted have mostly become leafless. The grouping of different species is, therefore, very apparent at this time,—some assemblages presenting the denuded appearance of winter, some remaining still green, while the Oaks are the principal attraction, with an intermixture of a few other species, whose foliage has been protected and the development of their hues retarded by some peculiarity of situation. (132)

Dickinson, too, combines attention to the aesthetic and geographical characteristics of a nearby forest, yet without detailing "the superb variety" of colors and species, or emphasizing the "splendor" of the "spectacle." Her short, regular lines, which mirror the rhythmic changes in the land, replace such extended descriptions with a handful of references. Moreover, where the prolific Flagg, author of *Studies in the Field and Forest* (1857), *The Woods and By-Ways of New England* (1872), and *The Birds and Seasons of New England* (1875), sought to "inspire readers with a love of nature and a simplicity of life, confident that the great fallacy of the present age is that of mistaking the increase of national wealth for the advancement of civilization" (qtd. in Lyon 67), her unassuming speaker—probably female, considering her easy reference to pink garments—is more of a learner than teacher, and uses this pose to both enter and doubt the male-dominated sphere of scientific explanation. She may be fascinated by the ways in which contemporary scientists—including Amherst's Edward Hitchcock in his "Religious Lectures on Peculiar Phenomena of the Four Season" (1850)—linked the twelve months to the twelve apostles, and local to cosmic spheres, but her skeptical "they tell me" and the three exclamation marks also imply that no one can verify such a claim. The poem thus foregrounds the seemingly naïve sketch of a familiar place, which does, however, remain full of gaps, much like the forest's "crannies," and lets the land's dynamics imaginatively unfold, unrestricted by elaborate explanations or explicit ethical conclusions. It thus responds to her culture's fascination with nature descriptions that culminated in scientific and moral interpretations by way of a humble speaking position that is less subservient than subversive, as it pays full attention to a familiar landscape yet remains suspicious of the epistemological control such observations may exert.

A poem written the same year, which evokes a different landscape of change, is equally interesting in terms of its descriptive restraint and the human-nature relationship it implies:

> The morns are meeker than they were –
> The nuts are getting brown –
> The berry's cheek is plumper –
> The Rose is out of town.
>
> The maple wears a gayer scarf –
> The field a scarlet gown –
> Lest I sh'd be old fashioned
> I'll put a trinket on. (Fr32)

A quick list of concrete images—two different kinds of fruit, a botanically specific flower and tree, and a colorful field—come together as geographical place here without creating a sense of closure, and the dashes point beyond the simple rhythms of life, captured in two direct sentences. The speaker, who enters the scene only toward the end, appears reluctant to act and interpret at all, and does so mainly to follow nature's lead. Here, too, Dickinson pushes against the descriptive fervor of writers such as Edward Hitchcock, whose nature essays combine rich detail with scientific and religious explanations, as in his description of Amherst in autumn:

> The gay splendor of our forests, as autumn comes on, may seem to some inappropriate, when we consider that it is the precursor of decay and death. But when we remember that the plant still lives, and after a season of inaction will awake to new and more vigorous life, and that the apparent decay is only laying aside a summer robe, because unfit for winter, is it not appropriate that nature should hang out signals of joy, rather than of sorrow? Why should she not descend exultingly, and in her richest dress, into the grave, in hope of so early and so glorious resurrection? ("Religious Lectures"; qtd. in Rotella 34)

Dickinson's poem uses the same imagery of a feminized nature changing clothes, but de-emphasizes the religious connotations so prominent in the naturalist's text. It leaves the focus on the natural changes in a temperate northeastern landscape and on the idea of human adjustment to nature's rhythms. Instead of the prominent moral-religious slant in many of the nature essays of the time, there is only the understated ethics of nondominant interaction with a familiar locale.

This dynamic also characterizes local poems in which Dickinson seems to display rather proudly the force of her artistic vision:

> Blazing in Gold and quenching in Purple
> Leaping like Leopards to the Sky
> Then at the feet of the old Horizon
> Laying her Spotted Face to die
> Stooping as low as the Otter's Window
> Touching the Roof and tinting the Barn
> Kissing her Bonnet to the Meadow
> And the Juggler of Day is gone (Fr321)

Several critics have read the poem as an example of Dickinson's peculiar brand of idealism; E. Miller Budick, in particular, finds that the poem tries "not simply to describe day and sunset in the most graphic terms available, but to sketch out [. . .] the idealist configuration of reality in which dissolution follows emanation" (6). Stressing the poem's feminist implications, Rachel Stein has argued that it "describe[s] nature as an irrepressible, uncontainable, and ultimately unknowable female whose freedom questions normative Victorian social boundaries" (47), as a "public, active, lower-class, carnivalesque performer" (48). I would point out that the poem's cultural force also has to do with its refusal to let go of the phenomenal world, with its interest in the dynamics of familiar landscapes of home that matter geographically as well as symbolically and aesthetically. Although the evening light flares up into the sky, the poem grounds the imagination softly in place: the "feet of the old horizon" and the "spotted" quality of the light evoke the land without so much as mentioning it; allusions to the area's natural and cultural history by way of "Roof," "Barn," and "Meadow" add depth to the poem's sense of place; and the "Otter's Window," which "keeps to the natural setting" of Amherst's landscape (Charles Anderson 136–37), refers to the fragile hiding place of a once-common creature that was almost driven to extinction. With this poem about a sunset's play upon the landscape, Dickinson takes up another favorite subject of descriptive nature essays, but again without their learned scientific and moral interpretations. Instead, its shift from "leaping" to "stooping" and lying "low" implies a different position, especially if one considers the personification of the sun as a woman who after a quick display of her cosmic powers retreats to the sphere of "Otter," "Barn," and "Meadow." A similar restraint informs the position of the speaker, who quickly stages this exquisite show of colors, turns to more mundane references, and leaves the scene. Via this movement and gesture, which amplify the self-effacing stance inherent in the mode of description, Dickinson's local snapshot manages to combine a high moment of artistic achievement with an environmentally oriented position of humility.

Such relative de-emphasis of the speaker's authority even informs poems that are emphatically about landscapes of the mind. In "It will be Summer – eventually" (Fr374), Dickinson both recalls and predicts the "bright" details of summer in the face of a "pallid" winter scene, an imaginative move in which the land takes center stage:

> It will be Summer – eventually.
> Ladies – with parasols –
> Sauntering Gentlemen – with Canes –
> And little Girls – with Dolls –

Will tint the pallid landscape –
As 'twere a bright Bouquet –
Thro' drifted deep, in Parian –
The Village lies – today –

The Lilacs – bending many a year –
Will sway with purple load –
The Bees – will not despise the tune –
Their Forefathers – have hummed –

The Wild Rose – redden in the Bog –
The Aster – on the Hill
Her everlasting fashion – set –
And Covenant Gentians – frill –

Till Summer folds her miracle –
As Women – do – their Gown –
Of Priests – adjust the Symbols –
When Sacrament – is done –

The "pallid landscape" of winter is evoked through a quick reference to pale snowdrifts, the fields of summer by way of leisurely walkers and, especially, four native wildflowers in their distinct environments (the lilac, a swamp rose, an "everlasting" aster, and the fragile fringed gentian).[4] Dickinson conjoins these scenes without diminishing the specificity of either one, addressing the expected turn of the seasons not only as a sign of eternal grace but also as a geographic phenomenon. While the poem may suggest a Renoir landscape painting (Charles Anderson 145) or a watercolor still life that anticipates Seurat (Farr 69–70), it also has a precedent in Thoreau's "A Winter Walk," the nodal essay published in *The Dial* in 1843 that marked his turn from writing about sweeping pastoral scenes to nature essays embedded in the specifics of a delimited landscape (see Sattelmeyer xviii). The text's guiding idea is the memory of summer in the face of a winterscape:

> We skate near to where the blackbird, the pewee, and the kingbird hung their nests over the water and the hornets builded [*sic*] from the maple in the swamp. How many gay warblers, following the sun, have radiated from this nest of silver birch and thistle-down! On the swamp's outer edge was hung the supermarine village, where no foot penetrated. In this hollow tree the wood duck reared her brood, and slid away each day to forage in yonder fen. (37–38)

Dickinson also conjoins winter and summer sensations in ways that mark the details of a familiar place, yet the differences in how the texts express this idea are equally instructive, beyond the difference between Thoreau's nostalgic memory and her own more forward-oriented hope, and also beyond generic distinctions. Where Thoreau's text is densely descriptive, Dickinson's bare words point the other way. And where Thoreau emerges as a model of environmental perceptivity, and his edifying account is geared toward moral instruction ("Go to [the pickerel-fisher], and you will learn that he too is a worshipper of the unseen. Hear with what sincere deference [. . .] he speaks of the lake pickerel"; 39), Dickinson's speaker fades into the background and quietly withdraws in the end, as if "folding" up her own gown together with her poem and the image it "miraculously" evoked. Again Dickinson responds to the time's passion for local nature descriptions by combining her formal and stylistic choices with Victorian ideals of religious and "female" modesty in ways that come together as an environmentally resonant gesture.

The poem whose unassuming attention to a familiar landscape probably constitutes Dickinson's most complex and ecologically sensitive contemplation of local nature is "Four Trees – opon a solitary Acre" (Fr778).

> Four Trees – opon a solitary Acre –
> Without Design
> Or Order, or Apparent Action –
> Maintain –
>
> The Sun – opon a Morning meets them –
> The Wind –
> No nearer Neighbor – have they –
> But God –
>
> The Acre gives them – Place –
> They – Him – Attention of Passer by –
> Of Shadow, or of Squirrel, haply –
> Or Boy –
>
> What Deed is Their's unto the General Nature –
> What Plan
> They severally – retard – or further –
> Unknown –

This poem's presentation of a few, seemingly unrelated elements without a clear "Plan" has long led critics to read it as an expression of Dickinson's sense of isolation caused by the perceived absence of nature's divine order, or as an example of linguistic fragmentation that displays the poet's inner chaos.[5] Rachel Stein has given an important environmental twist to these interpretations by stressing that "the lack of 'apparent' meaning is more of a dilemma for the male nature reader" than for the female poet who replaces limiting ideas about "the nature of gender" with more haphazard relations and thus wrests "nature and women from patriarchal orders" (34). Taking a different perspective, Christopher Benfey has linked the poem's formal placement of periods, colons, and dashes to the question of giving place to the trees "in the general nature," and to "the place of human beings with regards to them" (*Dickinson and the Problem of Others* 115); he also seems to be the only critic who has stressed the "nearness" between the speaker and her world (117). I would add that this poem's slippery engagement with place also constitutes a fine-tuned response to the era's growing awareness of autonomous natural systems and people's possible relationships with them, a response whose power has much to do with its poetic revision of the conventions of nineteenth-century landscape description in ways that broaden their eco-ethical possibilities.

The poem's very interest in local geography is noteworthy, precisely because of its simultaneous concern with transcendence. This passion for place, no less intense for its contested quality, has been obscured by the long critical fascination with Dickinson's landscapes of the mind; characteristically, Douglas Anderson, who claimed that Dickinson was committed "to the mutable world" (207) only as a sphere where transcendence could be experienced, argued that in "Four Trees" "her subject seems, *merely*, place" but actually is "a nearness to tremendousness" (222; emphasis added). Yet while Dickinson certainly negotiates between the two, place probably has more weight in this poem than has been acknowledged. The trees on the acre "maintain" the speaker's "Attention" through all four stanzas, and her imagination never moves fully beyond or out of the scene's immediacy. Even as the speaker ponders the neighborly presence of God and "General Nature," she emphatically does not move through place as a lesser aspect of poetic concern. Such place orientedness echoes the era's essayists' tireless fascination with the varieties of local landscapes; Flagg's "Trees in Assemblages," for instance, has much to say about "the most lovely appearances in landscape [. . .] caused by the spontaneous growth of miscellaneous trees, some in dense assemblages and some in scattered groups, with here and there a few single trees standing in open space" (135). Dickinson's quick evocation of four trees on a solitary, windy acre in the morning sun, occasionally visited by a squirrel or a boy, registers the stark beauty and multilayered materiality of a similar stretch of land, paralleling and fostering her culture's interest in local natural places whose aesthetic qualities inspire not only a turn toward transcendence but also attention to geography.

It is equally noteworthy how the few elements that constitute this place relate to each other in multiple, environmentally significant ways, not in spite but because of the reduced use of descriptive means. Critics have mostly claimed that the world of this seemingly disrupted poem is completely devoid of connection, arguing even that "no thread of commonality holds the contents of this work together—nothing but happenstance seems to justify their inclusion in the same piece of verse" (Wolff 459–60). Only Christopher Benfey and Cristanne Miller have addressed the reciprocity, interdependence, and agency involved in its ambiguous subject-object relations (Benfey, *Dickinson and the Problem of Others* 117; Miller, *A Poet's Grammar* 255–56), without, however, exploring their environmental implications. But the poem is attentive precisely to relationships that are ecologically meaningful: the trees not only create a shifting "Shadow" on the landscape as the "Sun" travels across the sky, they also provide shelter and presumably nourishment for "Squirrel" "Or Boy"; as they break up the monotony of the "solitary Acre," they transform a cultivated piece of land into a more diverse biotope; the "Sun" provides light and energy, the "Wind" brings humidity and a different kind of movement, while "the Acre gives" all of them "Place." These links among plants, soil, climate, animal, and human being are not so much indeterminate as they are multiple, since each is connected with more than one other unit. Especially if one reads Dickinson's signature dashes not as disruptive but as connective, the poem evokes a dynamic web of relationships, which undermines the initial claim that there is no "design," "order," or "action." If one turns to Flagg's essays again, including "Among the Trees," published in the *Atlantic Monthly* in 1860, the poem resonates as a remarkably fine-tuned cultural commentary both on the ecological structures of local landscapes and on ways of communicating them. Flagg's piece describes the significance of trees as habitat and "sustenance" for other creatures, details their connectedness to climatic factors, and urges his contemporaries to turn their attention from trees' sublime beauty toward their role in the "economy of life" (257), including the flow of energy and nutrients. Dickinson's "Four Trees," too, describes dynamics in what would soon be called an ecosystem, evoking a network of organic and inorganic components in which energy flows in multiple directions, but it does so by way of a uniquely sparse poetic description, in a hypercondensed format that is open and suggestive rather than definitive and restrictive.

Indeed, Dickinson's refusal to let the speaker's perceiving consciousness control the scene or formulate definite insights is most crucial in terms of the poem's environmental overtones. Throughout the first three stanzas, she remains in the background, focusing on the objects she registers, and when she enters the scene as questioning subject, she emphasizes her limited insights, amplifying the humility implicit in the descriptive mode. Perhaps the emerging web of relationships is already a crucial part of what there is to know about the scene, maybe this is its "Plan" and "Deed," but the speaker refuses to claim she understands its "Design." Especially the final assertion that the acre's ultimate "Plan" remains "Unknown – " insists, for all the "nearness" this poem is about, on a respectful distance between speaker and nature. At a time when essayists eagerly discussed the ecological importance of the most mundane landscapes, Dickinson's poem questions the notion of epistemological certainty in regard to familiar lands as one of the bases of human presumption and undercuts the illusion of control so prevalent at the time, even in proto-ecological publications. It is interesting to note here that in the mid-nineteenth century a small number of trees in an otherwise cultivated area was a recurrent image, and not an environmentally innocent one. Susan Fenimore Cooper's *Rural Hours*, for instance, describes several pines surrounded by cornfields and orchards, whose "nearer brethren have all been swept away," calling them "a monument of the past" (116), and a single elm, whose trunk, branches, and bark she also describes at length, becomes a "Sagamore," according to *Webster's* both an Algonquian war chief and "someone who prevails": "There is an elm of great size now standing entirely alone in a pretty field of the valley, its girth, its age, and whole appearance declaring it a chieftain of the ancient race—the 'Sagamore elm,' as it is called—and in spite of complete exposure to the winds from all quarters of the heavens, it maintains its place firmly" (132). Cooper takes her culture's nostalgic conflation of ancient trees with Native Americans as a starting point to turn the charge of "savagery" against her countrymen: "In these times, the hewers of wood are an unsparing race" (132), indifferent, wasteful, and not "civilized," as they fell hundreds of trees and leave them to rot (135). Read against such concerned sympathy, which apparently was part of the period's view of isolated trees, Dickinson's evocation of four trees who "maintain" their place in a modified landscape but might "retard – or further" echoes this sensibility. But it resists the move from description to prescription, thus extending the subversive reach of the humility this poem performs all the way to include her contemporaries' most well-meaning environmental positions.

Familiarization and Defamiliarization

The environmental import of Dickinson's poetry further crystallizes in the way she views natural landscapes as familiar systems in which humans are embedded, while emphasizing that even well-known lands must ultimately remain alien to human observers. This dual move of familiarization and defamiliarization repeats on the local level a dynamic that also characterizes her small-scale poetry, where the speaker's identification with small creatures often goes hand-in-hand with a recognition of their otherness. Dickinson's renditions of local naturescapes as communities of interdependent life-forms that can, however, turn into sites of chaotic change add depth to her local green imagination because they engage a foundational conflict in environmental ethics and philosophy that took shape during her time.

In the second half of the nineteenth century, the reassuring message of Humboldt's diverse, dynamic, but orderly cosmos—in itself a key concept of holistic ecology—was challenged by Darwin's emphasis on turbulence rather than harmony and belonging, which placed humans in the midst of rather than above the struggling forces of nature. On the one hand, the older idea of nature as the familiar web of life has been at the core of environmental ethics since its emergence and remains central to what Aldo Leopold called the "land ethic": if the land is a community, "[a] thing is right when it tends to preserve the integrity, stability, and beauty of the biotic community. It is wrong when it tends otherwise" (224–25). On the other hand, the recognition of nature as unpredictable, as even a cruel Other, has served as an important countermove to this extension of moral principles, since such an extension implies an act of imaginary domestication, no matter how sympathetic. As Val Plumwood explains, "the broadening of the scope of moral concern and the according of rights to the natural world have been seen by influential environmental philosophers [Leopold, Nash, Fox] as the final step in the process of increasing moral abstraction and generalization, part of the move away from the merely particular, *my* self, *my* family, *my* tribe" (170), but the idea of "overcoming dualism does not imply dissolving difference" (189). That Dickinson gives a voice to both perspectives and their dialectical relationship is part of the environmental richness of her sparse descriptions, as well as a basis for comparison with Whitman's equally double-edged presentation of the nature nearest to him. Reading Dickinson's and Whitman's local poetry against this backdrop also contributes to the ongoing debate about in which ways the landscape concept is always already imperial or open for revision.

Dickinson's tendency to render local landscapes as deeply familiar is particularly prominent in a group of sentimental poems that conceptualize nature by way of family and household imagery. Feminist critics have revalued some of these poems by emphasizing that Dickinson "challenges the order of housekeeping in her depiction of nature and the spiritual, emotional, and creative lives of women," especially through irony (Baker 87); Rachel Stein has shown that "Dickinson wields the standard generic identification of women and nature in order to rewrite the exclusion of women from positions of public power and their relegation to the subsidiary domestic realm" (26). It is equally noteworthy, though, that such transpositions of family and domestic principles also engage ecological insights:

> Haeckel derived the new label [oecology] from the same root found in the older word "economy": the Greek *oikos*, referring originally to the family household and its daily operations and maintenance. [. . .] [I]n *Oecologie*, Haeckel suggested that the living organisms of the earth constitute a single economic unit resembling a household or family dwelling intimately together, in conflict as well as in mutual aid. (Worster, *Nature's Economy* 192)

At the same time, natural history essays used family metaphors to communicate nature's processes and new scientific ideas in a Victorian framework. Dickinson's short poems about local nature as a forest-mother who cares for her children, or as a forceful housewife who sweeps the land, participate in this exchange of new ideas, casting nature's systems as worthy of moral consideration, while also destabilizing the conceptual control that these sentimental tropes seek to assert.

The best-known Dickinson poem of this kind was probably written in 1863, and published in 1891 under the title "Mother Nature":

> Nature – the Gentlest Mother is,
> Impatient of no Child –
> The feeblest – or the Waywardest –
> Her Admonition mild –

In Forest – and the Hill –
By Traveller – be heard –
Restraining Rampant Squirrel –
Or too impetuous Bird –

How fair Her Conversation –
A Summer Afternoon –
Her Household – Her Assembly –
And when the Sun go down –

Her Voice among the Aisles
Incite the timid prayer
Of the minutest Cricket –
The most unworthy Flower –

When all the Children sleep –
She turns as long away
As will suffice to light Her lamps –
Then bending from the Sky –

With infinite Affection –
And infiniter Care –
Her Golden finger on Her lip –
Wills Silence – Everywhere – (Fr741)

Typical for her local imagination, Dickinson mentions only a few elements—"Rampant Squirrel," a "too impetuous Bird," "the minutest Cricket," and "The most unworthy Flower" "in Forest and the hill"—that are, however, precise enough to evoke a familiar landscape. The deceptively naïve celebration of "mother nature," however, is more than an abstract meditation on nature's powers, or, as Stein argues, a "response to the Puritan conception of a cold, unyielding, unknowable god" that "deifies female domesticity even as it defies the limits of the Victorian domestic sphere" (38). It is also not only opposed to Darwinian notions—Stein stresses that "the poem vindicates domesticity, inscribing maternal care as the principle of nature that insures survival of all creatures, the point that nineteenth-century sciences, such as Darwinism, denied, to the detriment of female status within those systems" (39–40)—but also in dialogue with perspectives popularized in natural history prose, including, again, Flagg's essays:

> Man now learns to regard trees in other relations beside their capacity to supply his physical and mechanical wants. He looks upon them as the prin-

> cipal ornaments of the face of creation, and as forming the conservatories of Nature, in which she rears those minute wonders of her skill, the flowers and smaller plants that will flourish only under their protection, and those insect hosts that charm the student with their beauty and excite his wonder by their mysterious instincts. ("Among the Trees" 258)

Flagg quickly moves beyond notions of trees as merely ornamental and compares local forests to traditional human families in order to express a sense of their "mysterious" web of life. Dickinson's poem alludes to the same pattern, but is actually more specific in terms of a forest's flora and fauna, and in her attention to the ways in which the "feeblest" creatures are linked to local and larger natural rhythms. Also, it is similarly nuanced in ethical terms, while complicating the nonutilitarian ethics that focuses on "Man's" growing understanding of trees' ecological significance. Dickinson's reference to nature's "infinite Affection – / And infiniter Care" suggests, by association, a human care for nature's systems, resembling Flagg's interest in the trees' apparent care for smaller creatures that also implies the ideal of human noninstrumentalism. Such a traditionally feminine ethics of care can, in Plumwood's words, "be socially progressive or regressive," but it develops an important "subversive and oppositional potential" in social and political contexts, also and especially in environmental contexts (188). At the same time, however, Dickinson's idea that "Cricket" and "Flower" address nature in a "timid prayer" brings another traditionally feminine stance into play here, that of modest reverence, which also resonates in terms of a human position toward nature, but undermines the power relationship implicit in the notion of human care for fragile natural systems. Instead of Flagg's overt interest in teaching "students" of nature, Dickinson enters the ethical paradox of understanding local nature as a domestic economy that humans should approach both with affectionate care and with a humble recognition of their own insignificance.

Other Dickinson poems express a similar awareness of nature's interacting subjects by way of family metaphors that both imply an ethics of care and grant natural systems considerable ontological autonomy. "A Lady red – amid the Hill" (Fr137), for instance, evokes a "Landscape" in which the Spring "Breezes" "Sweep vale – and hill – and tree" as if they were "pretty Housewives," to the effect that nature (rather than the outside observer) pulls together field, hedge, woods, "Orchard, and Buttercup, and Bird" as a self-sufficient household. When the speaker attempts a religious interpretation of the scene, the land resists dissolution as an image of "Resurrection" (it is only "as if") and remains present as a "very strange" earthly community. Similarly, "She sweeps with many-colored Brooms – " (Fr318) portrays the wind as a careless "Housewife in the Evening West" who drops colorful "shreds" all over the place, with a last line ("And then I come away – ") that dissolves the speaker's mock indignation, perhaps even her subjectivity. In a later version, the ending "And still the scene prevails / Till Dusk obstructs the Diligence – / Or Contemplation fails" puts even more emphasis on the resilience of nature's local economy in the face of imaginative domestication. Dickinson's sentimental poems about nature as mother or housewife, then, are not only noteworthy for their revisionist views on women's social position, but also for their "careful" descriptions of natural processes that manage to be both adept and unassuming. As such, they participate in her culture's understanding of "nature's economy" while revealing the epistemological limits of such an inevitably anthropocentric system of thought.

Yet for all her investment in grasping local nature as a familiar matriarchal household, Dickinson often undermines this association or withholds it altogether, especially when she depicts dramatic changes in seemingly pristine rural areas. As such, her poems "on transitional points in natural cycles," which Jane Eberwein and others have read as speculations on "Time and Eternity," death and immortality ("Nature" 205–6), also respond to the problem of how to talk about landscapes that turn out to be much more puzzling than family and household metaphors would admit. At a time when Darwin's theories required the recognition of nature's difference, which was especially challenging with regard to places that were sometimes perceived as extensions of human households, Dickinson's poems about forceful rains or storms enter this debate by re-imagining a nature whose apparent order is suddenly disrupted as one that forever reorganizes itself out of chaos.

Such poems that question notions of local nature as a harmonious family household include "Nature – sometimes sears a Sapling – / Sometimes – scalps a Tree" (Fr457), which, apart from its significance as eulogy, subverts the sentimental trope of a benevolent forest-mother and makes death a numbing yet vital presence among nature's "people." Other poems let go of the family association altogether. "The Wind did'nt come from the Orchard – today – " (Fr494) sketches a nearby world of "Hay," "Clovers," and "Mowers," until a "hoarse" storm upsets this sense of knowing nature in place and controlling its forces ("And that is His business – not Ours – ");

"The Trees like Tassels – hit – and swung – " (Fr523) shows how a storm turns orchard, lane, and fence into an ungodly scene where "Bright Flowers slit a Calyx," offering a vague, "mean" revelation. More dramatically still, "The wind drew off" (Fr1703) confronts nature's violence by showing how "The trees held up / Their mangled limbs / Like animals in pain," and in "The Frost was never seen – " (Fr1202), the sly killing of a garden leaves the speaker apprehensive that "Unproved is much we know – / Unknown the worst we fear – / Of Strangers is the Earth the Inn / Of Secrets is the Air – ."

In such poems, nearby fields and gardens turn from a quasi-domestic "household" into the "Inn" of "Strangers" (Fr1202), in an era when few nature essays concerned themselves with such radically alienating changes. One important exception is Thoreau's *Cape Cod*, which opens with an account of a violent storm that layered the beach with corpses and keeps coming back to the subject of death in apparently calm, stable landscapes. Dickinson's defamiliarization of neighborly fields and lanes similarly tests the idea of natural systems as turbulent and chaotic. At a time when the Humboldtian notion of nature as a harmonious system of mutually dependent communities was slowly being translated into an environmental ethic that emphasized the supposed stability of these systems, while Darwin's theories had already begun to complicate some of these notions, Dickinson's poems are noteworthy for their rendition of disturbances as part of nature's communities, deeming moments of apparent stability as transitory, and for facing local nature's unfathomable otherness without superimposing religious or moral interpretations onto its violent spectacles.

Overall, Dickinson's poems about local landscapes indirectly respond to a growing interest in describing local natural systems in ways whose environmentally significance hinges upon the unique sparseness of her verse. The lack of "definitorial detail" in her descriptions does not necessarily mean that these poems are mainly about the human psyche, as Eberwein suggests when she writes that "in her presentations of natural scenery [. . .] Dickinson eliminated most of the descriptive elements that would have recorded her precise observations and concentrated instead on her own perceiving consciousness" (*Strategies of Limitation* 142). Rather, her reduction of descriptive means also serves as an inverted contribution to the search for possible means of communicating a new sense of local nature's complex systems. In particular, she echoes and also challenges popular prose publications by taking the epistemological promise of description, as an approach that largely refrains from interpretation and analysis, to its critical edge. Tracing a limited number of the land's characteristic features in ways that forestall the idea of complete imaginative control, her poems offer fresh glimpses of local nature as autonomous systems. The insistence with which Dickinson's speakers claim that the meaning of a scene evades them even though they have just sketched it with supreme force goes far beyond a coy display of a female poet's limited powers. This commitment to uncertainty also transcends her well-known skepticism, which was particularly pronounced in terms of human access to nature, and recharges the Victorian dictate of female modesty as a position of eco-ethical interrogation. Such a position requires a momentary de-emphasizing of the human self as central agent, without, however, generally threatening the precarious speaking position of the female poet.

4

“With angry moans the fierce old mother incessantly moaning”

Whitman’s Narrative Description

When Whitman published *Specimen Days* in 1882, this unconventional autobiography included a remarkable number of sketches of his Long Island childhood, his time on a New Jersey farm, and his journeys to Canada and the American West. Most of these local notes “dwell awhile on the locality itself” (*CPCP* 695), as in the following example:

> *June 10th.*—AS I write, 5 ½ P. M., here by the creek, nothing can exceed the quiet splendor and freshness around me. We had a heavy shower, with brief thunder and lightning, in the middle of the day; and since, overhead, one of those not uncommon yet indescribable skies (in quality, not details or forms) of limpid blue, with rolling silver-fringed clouds, and a pure-dazzling sun. For underlay, trees in fulness of tender foliage—liquid, ready, long-drawn notes of birds—based by the fretful mewing of a querulous cat-bird, and the pleasant chippering-shriek of two kingfishers. I have been watching the latter the last half hour, on their regular evening frolic over and in the stream; evidently a spree of the liveliest kind. They pursue each other, whirling and wheeling around, with many a jocund downward dip, splashing the spray in jets of diamonds—and then off they swoop, with slanting wings and graceful flight, sometimes so near me I can plainly see their dark-gray feather-bodies and milk-white necks. (*CPCP* 786–87)

Similar to Dickinson’s letter in which she refers to hills and a sunset as her companions, Whitman does more here than link his life to the land. He expresses an interest in specific landscapes in ways that respond to the conventions of local nature descriptions, which popular natural history essays relied so heavily upon. Much like these essays, his sketches recount the interactions among natural phenomena in place and usually culminate in certain insights regarding the speaker’s surroundings.[1] Yet Whitman’s nature notes are also much shorter, more fragmentary, and decidedly less learned; they let the narrative of human experiences more fully slide over into accounts of nature's dynamics, and his "lessons" more often include doubts regarding the ability to speak adequately about common natural scenes—the skies are "indescribable," and a brook "is saying something, of course, (If one could only translate it)" (781). For Whitman, ultimately "there is a humiliating lesson one learns, in serene hours, of a fine day or night. Nature seems to look on all fixed-up poetry and art as something almost impertinent" (924). If this autobiography seems "quaintly modest," as Martin Murray has put it, this is not only because Whitman mentions his literary achievements merely in passing (Murray 554), but also because in the middle sections he uses the mode of nature description in ways that emphasize its humbling implications, a technique that his local poetry develops to its full potential.

Critics are currently taking a second look at local nature descriptions in Whitman's poetry, without, however, discussing their environmental implications in relation to the nature descriptions that were so prominent in the nineteenth century. Most characteristic of this absence in scholarship is Angus Fletcher's *A New Theory for American Poetry*, which argues that America's best poetry is "descriptive" and "environmental," and which has a lot to say about Whitman. But since Fletcher defines environmental poetry as one that is not "about" natural or social environments but "environs" the reader, and is interested in how "description without place [. . .] is able to express the life of an environing space, a self-organizing chorography" (12), he pulls away from description as a mode that imaginatively connects poetry to natural places. Coming from a different direction, M. Jimmie Killingsworth's *Walt Whitman and the Earth* is interested in Whitman's environmental sensibilities, claiming that Whitman "is at his best as a local poet, a loyal son of the New York islands" (74). But his argument that Whitman's island poetics is based on synecdoche and myth and revolves around the shore as a sacred place (105–6) largely brackets the role of description and the contexts of nineteenth-century environmentalism in Whitman's local imagination.

I argue here that the environmental significance of some of Whitman's most celebrated poems has much to do with his poetic involvement with the seemingly simple mode of local landscape description. By reading his work against the nature descriptions that were so prominent in geography and other proto-ecological sciences, in early preservationist arguments, and especially in the natural history essays of the time, I hope to show that much like Dickinson, he embraces some of these descriptive conventions as he evokes geographically distinct places, communicates the complex interactions among their players, and assumes speaking positions that are legible as gestures of environmental humility. Where Dickinson talks back to these discourses through sparse descriptions whose combination of radical formal reduction and an unassuming female speaker de-emphasizes the possibility of imaginative control and grants the land a maximum degree of dignified autonomy, Whitman achieves a related effect by what I call here narrative descriptions. His local poems, which tend to constitute larger narratives of the evolving human self, often rest on descriptive passages in which the speaker-poet steps back behind the natural scene he encounters and transfers the narrative momentum to the land itself, foregrounding its self-sufficient agency.

Narrative Description

The phrase "narrative description" may appear to be an oxymoron, particularly from the perspective of traditional narrative analysis, which considers descriptive and narrative passages as distinct if not mutually exclusive. However, both modes are closely related and show considerable overlap, and in the sciences, geographers and ecologists often use a "narrative-descriptive" approach to talk about the complexities of places, so that the question of how places are made "is implied or informally woven into the presentation, but not explicitly formulated or developed" (Tuan, "Language and the Making of Place" 684). I argue here that subtle shifts between narration (with a central human speaker who controls the action) and description (in which the speaker withdraws his presence and interpretive agency farthest from the scene) are a key element of Whitman's environmental poetics on the local scale. As such, they can be understood as another specific incarnation of Whitman's credo in the 1855 preface, that true poetry expresses both the self's "measureless pride which consists in never acknowledging any lessons but its own" and its equally measureless "sympathy" for the other.

Whitman's signature poem "Out of the Cradle Endlessly Rocking" distills this strategy. The poem has received substantial attention, but little has been said about the setting, although the memorable evocation of a Long Island beach is part of its achievements. Lawrence Buell briefly mentions that "Out of the Cradle" is "concerned with the composition of a specific place, and Whitman's symbolic bird is endowed with a habitat, a history, a story of its own" (*The Environmental Imagination* 7), and Killingsworth shows that the poem struggles against the limits of language in conjunction with the limits of land and the limits of life, and that the poet learns how, in order to master the world through language, he must be open to the details of nature's otherness (*Whitman and the Earth* 106, 109). My own reading of the poem with respect to Dickinson's local poetry emphasizes how Whitman's subtle revisions of the time's proto-ecological nature descriptions not only add depth to this poem's dynamic sense of place but also minimize and destabilize (rather than increase) the notion of linguistic mastery.

In the extended opening sentence, the poet who revisits a shore he knew as a child offers a moving account of the site in its geographical distinctness—not only by referencing its topographical details, but also by skipping for a moment his own movement in place and time, investing the shoreline instead with narrativity:

> Out of the cradle endlessly rocking,
> Out of the mocking-bird's throat, the musical shuttle,
> Out of the Ninth-month midnight,
> Over the sterile sands and the fields beyond, where the child leaving his bed
> wander'd alone, bareheaded, barefoot,
> Down from the shower'd halo,
> Up from the mystic play of shadows twining and twisting as if they were
> alive,
> Out from the patches of briers and blackberries,
> From the memories of the bird that chanted to me [. . .]. (*LG* 206–7)

The dramatic emphasis on "Out of," "Down," and "Up from," underscored by Whitman's characteristic use of parallelisms, creates a place that implicitly enables a narrative where not only the poet but also nature's features can move into the center as agents. And indeed, before the poet briefly moves into the foreground to sing his reminiscence, this beach becomes palpable as a place of interlocking, interacting natural elements rather than a flat stage for human action: the ocean moves on the shore, the bird sings, and shadows twist "as if they were alive." In the next section, in which the speaker imaginatively merges the present experience and the memory of his formative childhood encounter with the Long Island beach, this narrative description is even more pronounced:

> Once Paumanok,
> When the lilac-scent was in the air and Fifth-month grass was growing,
> Up this seashore in some briers,

Two feather'd guests from Alabama, two together,
And their nest, and four light-green eggs spotted with brown,
And every day the he-bird to and fro near at hand,
And every day the she-bird crouch'd on her nest, silent, with bright eyes,
And every day I, a curious boy, never too close, never disturbing them,
Cautiously peering, absorbing, translating. (*LG* 207)

Here the temporal conjunctions "Once" and "When" emphasize the connection between descriptive elements and the narrative aspects of this passage, while Whitman's parallelisms increase the lines' narrative drive. Again, the beach is not only made tangible through references to characteristic plants and animals (lilacs, grass, briars, two migrating birds with their nest and eggs), it also emerges as autonomous place by way of the emphasis on these natural elements as primary narrative agents. The birds' presence and action—the fragile eggs, the female bird who "crouches" on the nest, and the nervous movement of the male bird—give the place meaning, more than the boy's passive witnessing; and even though the boy's presence channels the specifics of this place to the reminiscing adult voice, so that the scene appears doubly enfolded in human consciousness, the description of this place as a vividly alive bird-place brackets the centrality of the poet's perception and grants the land significance in its own right.

Whitman's poem here modifies a perspective that began to develop in the environmentally oriented discussions of the time. Around midcentury, geographers explored topographical boundaries in conjunction with distribution patterns of local flora and fauna, and Philip Lutley Sclater's 1858 ornithological study marked the emergence of descriptive biogeography as a proto-ecological field (see Ball 408); natural history essays popularized these scientific approaches by mixing them with personal recollections. Characteristically, Celia Thaxter writes in *Among the Isles of Shoals*, printed in the *Atlantic Monthly* between 1869 and 1870:

> Early in March the first flocks of crows arrive, and they soar finely above the coves, and perch on the flukes of stranded anchors or the tops of kellock-sticks that lie about the water's edge. They are most welcome, for they are never seen in winter; and pleasant it is to watch them beating their black, ragged pinions in the blue, while the gulls swim on beyond them serenely, shining still whiter for their sable color. No other birds come till about the 27th of March, and then all at once the islands are alive with song sparrows, and these sing from morning till night so beautifully that dull and weary

> indeed must be the mortal who can resist the charm of their fresh music. There is a matchless sweetness and good cheer in this bravo bird. The nightingale singing with its breast against a thorn may be divine; yet would I turn away from its tender melody to listen to the fresh, cheerful, healthy song of this dauntless and happy little creature. They come in flocks to be fed every morning the whole summer long, tame and charming, with their warm brown and gray feathers, striped and freaked with wood-color, and little brown knots at each pretty throat. (582)

Thaxter's prose is typical insofar as it offers a close look at a specific place, its climate and larger ecological significance, and tells stories about its active natural players, while almost everything in her description of the song-sparrows refers back to human sensibilities—the birds are welcome, cheerful, tame and charming, pleasant to watch, their music hard to resist. By comparison, Whitman's hints give his imaginative seashore just as much geographical specificity, while also, amplified by the suggestive rhythms of his rolling lines, granting its elements a more autonomous kind of agency, as unrestricted by the "cautious" speaker's interpretations as perhaps is possible in language. This is not to downplay the poem's central moment of epiphany as the boy comes to look at the world as a poet, but to show that this epiphany is enabled by a carefully gauged attention to the self-directed dynamics of a specific physical environment. Contrary to John D. Kerkering's claim that Whitman merely "poses" as a topologist here, since "Out of the Cradle" is "more global than local," and "location [. . .] matters less as a particular place than as an alternative to the sea and death" (239), I suggest that the material geography of the shore holds a central position in the world of this poem, and that Whitman achieves this effect not only through the rendition of precise natural detail but also through a narrative-descriptive emphasis on nature's agency. This also makes for an unexpected link between Whitman's extensive "Out of the Cradle" and Dickinson's four-line sketch "An Everywhere of Silver," since her poignant portrait, too, evokes a shoreline as an interactive natural place and principal agent.

This dynamic is linked to another aspect of the poem's green resonances, namely, its gestures of environmental humility. From the beginning there is a unique gentleness to the boy-poet's "[b]areheaded, barefoot" approach to the land and birds, whom he tries to disturb as little as possible, "cautiously" keeping his distance to the point of being no more than a "shadow"; additionally, he owes his poetic inspiration to his attentiveness to a scene that can itself be called humble—a "dusky bird" on a "gray beach"—rather than to being overwhelmed by one of nature's more dazzling shows; and his way of "throwing" himself "on the sand, confronting the waves," his desperate calls for an answer, and the promise to keep in mind the lesson he learned are all rather overt gestures of humility that enact that "freedom from pride or arrogance" which would define such a stance (Webster, *Dictionary* [1847]). Moreover, there is overall a de-emphasis of interpretive control that also implies environmental humility, especially in Robert Gibson's terms of accepting our limited grasp of nature's processes, our prevailing uncertainty and indeed ignorance (158). This may seem paradoxical because the speaker reads the place in search of a "key," claims that he "will conquer it," and translates both the bird's song and the sea's answer; Kerkering, in the only comment I have found to address this issue, writes that "despite the humility of the phrase 'never more shall I cease perpetuating you,' the speaker approaches this song in a manner that, ultimately, is more instrumental than deferential" (239). I would stress here the intricate dynamics between the two positions, in which a profoundly felt humility envelops, counteracts, and forever changes the speaker's bouts of poetic pride. After the speaker claims that he of "all men" will grasp the scene's meaning, he glides down the beach and blends into it; his idea of singing "clearer and louder" is followed by the promise to never "cease perpetuating" the bird; and his proclamation "(for I will conquer it,)" is literally bracketed and accompanied by questions ("what is it?"; "Is that from your liquid rims and wet sands?"). So in the end, he arrives at a position of confidence that is forever altered by, and includes, a humbling empathy for the fragility of the most mundane natural places. Finally, and perhaps most significantly, his search for an answer culminates not in a closure that gives meaning to the bird's story of love and loss, but in the incessantly repeated "Death, death, death, death, death," which absorbs all meaning and cancels it:

> The word final, superior to all,
> Subtle, sent up – what is it? – I listen;
> Are you whispering it, and have been all the time, you sea-waves?
> Whereto answering, the sea,
> Delaying not, hurrying not,
> Whisper'd me through the night, and very plainly before daybreak,
> Lisp'd to me the low and delicious word death,
> And again death, death, death, death,

> Hissing melodious, neither like the bird nor like my arous'd child's heart,
> But edging near as privately for me rustling at my feet,
> Creeping thence steadily up to my ears and laving me softly all over,
> Death, death, death, death, death. (*LG* 211)

Death is the culmination of how this local place resists comprehension, an answer that dissolves all stories—the bird's story as well as the poet's "translation" of it—so that all that is left is an active, incomprehensible place. The poet may boast that "already a thousand singers, a thousand songs, clearer, louder and more sorrowful than yours, / A thousand warbling echoes have started to life within me, never to die" (*LG* 211), but the sea's answer "death" voids precisely this claim. Even as the poet's imagination tries to "leap quickly beyond" place, the seashore's presence here outlasts any boy or poet, also because it remains unfathomable. Here, too, the poem indirectly corresponds to Dickinson's "An Everywhere of Silver," which also pulls away from human signification, facing the elusiveness of a shore's meaning. Yet while her unassuming speaker, who throughout the poem is hardly perceptible as an interpreting agent, does no more than hint at the slipperiness of human signification, Whitman's more expressive speaker vacillates between confident gestures of masculine self-assertion and the admission of his limited insights with significantly more verbal force, showing humility and pride to be more actively in conflict with each other.

In the framework of contemporaneous discourses, Whitman's reluctance to pin down the meaning of a nearby place marks another subtle revision of the way in which nature essays approached local landscapes. In most of these essays, detailed descriptions are interspersed with scientific, practical, and moral comments, so that the land's material properties and the speaker's interpretations of it compete for semantic dominance over the text, with the speaker ultimately installing himself at the center. The following passage from Thoreau's *Cape Cod* is in many ways characteristic:

> The trees [. . .] were either narrow and high, with flat tops, having lost their side branches, like huge plum-bushes growing in exposed situations, or else dwarfed and branching immediately at the ground, like quince-bushes. They suggested that, under like circumstances, all trees would at last acquire like habits of growth. [. . .] In another place, I saw some not much larger than currant-bushes; yet the owner told me that they had borne a barrel and a half of apples that fall. If they had been placed close together, I could have cleared them all at a jump. [. . .] This habit of growth should, no

doubt, be encouraged; and they should not be trimmed up, as some travelling practitioners have advised. (37–38)

Compared to this knowledgeable, nature-sensitive wanderer who is the supreme measure of the land and always ready to give advice, the speaker in "Out of the Cradle" gives prominence to the land's autonomy by acknowledging the presence of a human observer eager but unable to find meaning there that would not destabilize his own position. The mind-set Whitman's poem explores with related yet different means is the devout desperation of a crying boy-poet whose tortured yearning to grasp and adequately express the meaning of a familiar natural scene takes him to the edge of questioning the power of language and the centrality of his self, toward "death"—the edge he imaginatively crosses in "As I Ebb'd with the Ocean of Life."

"As I Ebb'd," the poem that immediately follows "Out of the Cradle" in the 1892 *Leaves of Grass*, is in many ways its dialectical companion piece. Critics have long recognized this relationship, stressing that while "'Out of the Cradle' is about mothers, oceans, poetry, love, and commitment, 'As I Ebb'd' is about fathers, the shore, the failure of poetry, personal inadequacy, and profound uncertainty" (Gutman 31), and that both "present the poet as fallen transcendentalist overwhelmed [. . .] by the particulars of life, human suffering, and individual death" (Loving, *The Song of Himself* 248). From an environmental perspective they share another commonality, since both evoke the seashore as a dynamic place while momentarily de-emphasizing the speaker's physical and linguistic agency, in ways that I call narrative descriptions here and that embrace and also revise the conventions of local nature descriptions. Yet it is in "As I Ebb'd" that Whitman's almost complete transferral of control to a triumphantly sovereign nature, to the point of imagining his own death, turns this common mode into a platform for expressing some of his most radical environmental sensibilities.[2]

In the moving opening scene, the shore serves as a corollary and sounding board for the speaker's meditation on his own, low mood, and yet it comes progressively into view as a place that also acts:

As I ebbed with the ocean of life,
As I wended the shores I know,
As I walk'd where the ripples continually wash you Paumanok,
Where they rustle up hoarse and sibilant,
Where the fierce old mother endlessly cries for her castaways,

> I musing late in the autumn day, gazing off southward,
> Held by this electric self out of the pride of which I utter poems,
> Was seiz'd by the spirit that trails in the lines underfoot,
> The rim, the sediment that stands for all the water and all the land of the
>   globe.
> Fascinated, my eyes reverting from the south, dropt, to follow those slender
>   windrows,
> Chaff, straw, splinters of wood, weeds, and the sea-gluten,
> Scum, scales from shining rocks, leaves of salt-lettuce, left by the tide,
> Miles walking, the sound of breaking waves the other side of me,
> Paumanok there and then as I thought the old thought of likenesses,
> These you presented to me you fish-shaped island,
> As I wended the shores I know,
> As I walk'd with that electric self seeking types. (*LG* 212–13)

The repeated "As I" of the first three lines emphasizes the initial focus on the self-absorbed speaker, whose mystifying notion of ebbing "with the ocean of life" evokes sea and shore as external images of his own thoughts; the passage ends with two more "I"s and culminates in the speaker's "electric self." But the narrative keeps sliding into descriptive accounts of the seashore as a living system "where the ripples continually wash" the shore, "Where they rustle up hoarse and sibilant." "[S]eized" by the ocean, the poet's musings begin to resonate as a story of Paumanok's coast in autumn: as the poet's self-absorption is punctuated by the place, by a force that "trails in the lines underfoot," he begins "to follow those slender windrows" and notices the details of the shore's rough materiality; and the sea becomes a central driving force, which "ebbs" and "rustle[s]," whose tides "continually wash" the land and "present" a wealth of organic and inorganic particles, while the speaker does little more than react. Critics usually move from a brief mention of the poem's scene to its figurative import, following what seems like Whitman's own lead in a poem he originally titled "Bardic Symbols." Challenging this emphasis, Killingsworth has offered a stimulating interpretation of how the poem suggests openness and "willingness to engage," yet he too emphasizes that the drifted matter ultimately "becomes the 'types' that he seeks in the poem, the symbols for the bard with depressed spirit" (124); Paul Outka sees the speaker's struggle with "the gap [. . .] between the textual and the nontextual natural" as the poem's central idea (51). I would argue that the life of a local landscape is in itself a central insight that "seizes" the poet.

Such insights also figured prominently in nineteenth-century publications about marine geographies. The *Atlantic Monthly* alone, where "As I Ebb'd" first appeared in 1860, published reviews of titles such as *Physical Geography of the Sea* (1855), *The Aquarium: An Unveiling of the Wonders of the Deep Sea* (1856), and *The Common Objects of the Seashore* (1857), essays such as David William Cheever's "The Aquarium" (1861) on marine species' adaptation to their environments, and excerpts from Thoreau's *Cape Cod* (1864) and Celia Thaxter's *Among the Isles of Shoals* (1869–70).[3] *Cape Cod*, for example, first published in *Putnam's Monthly* in 1855, describes the shore's many forms of aquatic and terrestrial life and its wealth of decaying matter, as well as the dunes' movement as "a tide of sand impelled by waves and wind, slowly flowing from the sea toward the town" (161), explaining, with reference to renowned geologist Edward Hitchcock, "that the ocean has, in course of time, eaten out Boston Harbor and other bays in the mainland, and [. . .] the minute fragments have been deposited by the currents at a distance from the shore, and formed this sand-bank" (16). Whitman's "As I Ebb'd" engages this new awareness of marine landscapes as intricate, extraordinarily active systems; his "friable shore, with trails of debris" may be a realm of religious, personal, and political inspiration, but it is also a richly diverse beach that moves and acts, much like and at times more so than the wandering speaker.

As a poem, however, "As I Ebb'd" also dramatizes the era's broader interest in local nature's agency through the personification of the sea as "fierce old mother" and of the beach as "father."[4] The speaker's conflict with his overpowering nature-parents suggests the struggles involved in recognizing not only nature's autonomy but also its possible dominance. On the one hand, the exuberant poet who is rebuked by nature because he "was assuming so much" admits that he has "not once had the least idea" about himself or "the least thing" around him. On the other hand, the familial constellation implies the "child's" resistance, his urge to overcome the parental constraints; even as the speaker shows remorse at his futile attempts to speak about nature he also feels "oppressed," and in spite of his self-doubts he urges the sea, "deny not me, / Rustle not up so hoarse and angry against my feet as I touch you or gather from you," and calls out to the island, "I hold you so firm till you answer me something." At a time when botanists, geologists, and marine scientists were discovering new aspects of local nature's complexities, but also had to readjust the scope of their claims and realize, as Cheever's 1861 essay put it, that "all that we drag from the bottom [. . .] are but a few disconnected species of that infinite whole which makes up their home" (336), the tensions expressed in Whitman's personal poem crystallize the contradictory impulses that came with the new awareness of the indisputable authority of nature's self-sustaining systems. By providing nature not only with agency but also with authority, a subjecthood that resists control, Whitman imaginatively turns the sea and shore into subjects who strain against being conceptually grasped and thus contained.

Moreover, Whitman's account of a poet who is pushed by the parental sea and shore to recognize their supreme power, so that all he can do is try to reassert his own muted confidence, also gestures toward the possibilities and limitations of a nature-centered ethics. When the speaker begins to read the seemingly well-known environment on its own terms, this goes hand-in-hand with an overwhelming sense of his relative insignificance:

> As the ocean so mysterious rolls toward me closer and closer,
> I too but signify at the utmost a little wash'd-up drift,
> A few sands and dead leaves to gather,
> Gather, and merge myself as part of the sands and drift. (*LG* 213)

Throughout the poem, gestures of moving closer to the drifts on the shore (he "drops" and "bends" to the earth) indicate that the speaker's humbled sense of self is indeed a humility before the earth, an increasing earth-orientedness that culminates in his gentle pledge "I mean tenderly by you" (*LG* 214). In her reading of the poem as "the loss of democratic ensemble" (163), Betsy Erkkila has stressed that the isolated bard feels like a castaway for whom the self and "the world he perceives have disintegrated" (*Political Poet* 164, 165), and Killingsworth has emphasized that the poet at this point seems "unable to find a place [. . .] to attach" and is "without a connection" (*Whitman and the Earth* 124–25). Yet while it is true that old structures lose their hold for the speaker, a new system of identification offers itself. After all, he now sees himself as "part of the sands and drift to gather," an identification with the small that does not necessarily suggest a loss of self. A few years earlier, Thoreau had been ecstatic about the revelations regarding human-nature relations that can spring from immersion in a well-known place, exclaiming in *Walden*, "Am I not partly leaves and vegetable mould myself?," and, toward the end of the book, "What is man but a mass of thawing clay?" (93, 205); in *Cape Cod* he wrote that, observing the waves "[c]reeping along the endless beach amid the sun-squawl and the foam, it occurs to us that we, too, are the product of sea-slime" (147). Whitman's speaker, in his desperate acceptance of identity with "a trail of drift and debris," formulates a similar insight. At a time of growing alarm over the modification of marine environments and the "extirpation of aquatic animals" (see Marsh, *Man and Nature* 105–8), such a transferral of the principles of human interaction to sea, shore, and "Tufts of straw, sands, fragments" renounces physical and conceptual domination, suggesting instead an ethics of affection and potentially care based on utter humility.

However, "As I Ebb'd" also indicates the limits of such an urge toward a non-anthropocentric stance, boldly facing death as its logical consequence. Killingsworth and Outka offer diverging interpretations of the poem's ending. Emphasizing the speaker's survival, Killingsworth finds that the poet is able to overcome the loss of self that culminated in his near death; the "identification with the father and his own frailties" let him emerge from the crisis "chastened but realigned" and "reconnected" to himself and the world around him (127). Outka argues that it is how the poet imagines his own death and decomposition that allows him to suture the split between language and the material world; aligning himself "with the ecosystem, he speaks, 'at last,' for a moment the earth's poetry" (53). My sense here is that while both of these interpretations address key aspects of the paradox that this poem confronts, the poem privileges neither the survival nor the death of the speaker but precisely resists the narrative linearity that such a decision would assume. The moving gesture of physically speaking in death—"(See! from my dead lips the ooze exuding at last! / See – the prismatic colors, glistening and rolling!)"—cannot really provide a solution to the dilemma that in *speaking* about nature, we must already dominate it, nor can the survival of the chastened poet provide such a solution. Rather, Whitman succeeds in both imagining the impossible, namely, our becoming one with the world even as this implies a loss of self, and capturing the very impossibility of such a move as a viable speaking position. Instead of suggesting death as the inevitable end of human life which materially reconnects the body with the natural environment as it decomposes with the leaves around it, he points to death as a present—poetic rather than narrative—possibility of being in nature. When the poet continues to speak after conjuring up his own decomposition, he does not leave it behind but carries its presence into the continuation of the poem and of *Leaves of Grass* as a whole. Death here is not a state at the end of a linear life narrative, but a presence that connects the poet's body to the natural environment even as he seals his irrevocable distance from it in speaking the words that constitute his poem. So in summoning death here, the poem does not create a complex memento mori, nor does it merely point to the fact that decomposition turns the human body over to other organisms. While doubtless these are significant aspects of the poem, it forcefully testifies to the aporia of human existence in nature. At the cultural moment when modern environmentalism emerged, Whitman's figure of the dead poet articulating living speech embodies the necessity for an utterly humble, self-effacing speaking position—as well as the ultimate inaccessibility of such a position that would not dominate nature. As such, the poem also addresses the paradox inherent in the conventions of landscape descriptions, a mode that minimizes but cannot undo the conceptual control involved in speaking about nature. Rather than attempting to resolve this conflict, "As I Ebb'd" uses the imaginative space afforded by the genre of poetry to enact the conundrum of the epistemological modesty that is part of the promise of description but is impossible to realize.

Apart from these two major seashore poems, Whitman's very different "When Lilacs Last in the Dooryard Bloom'd" performs similar environmentally suggestive moves from speaker-centered to nature-centered accounts, so that a range of American landscapes, including a proverbially elusive swamp, emerge as natural systems that cannot be fully subjugated to human visions of cultivation or linguistic control. As an elegy that was first included in the 1865 "Sequel" to *Drum-Taps* and later headed a group of poems called "President Lincoln's Burial Hymn," "Lilacs" offers an important variation on what I here call narrative description. While the codified use of nature in this formulaic genre of mourning strengthens the symbolic significance of lilacs (as love of exuberant nature), star (as Lincoln and the Civil War dead), and thrush (as the poet's voice) rather than their resonance as living elements of actual local landscapes, these codified links between death and nature also underscore the central role death plays in Whitman's sensitive evocations of people's humbled interaction with local environments, which the two shore poems have already suggested. That the wandering poet in "Lilacs" speaks from the experience of death right from the poem's beginning makes all the difference. He does not have to recall the unassuming position of a child who seeks to understand a bird's death, or be rebuked by nature because he tried to "speak" it and respond by imaginatively facing his own death, in order to realize the need to approach nature without assumptions of mastery and control, however impossible such a stance may be. In "Lilacs," the deaths of President Lincoln and thousands of Civil War soldiers are always already with him, so that he carries on the dynamic from the end of "As I

Ebb'd"—death not as end point (not even for Lincoln's body) but as continuing presence, whose realization engenders a humble relationship with familiar nature without undoing one's own language and humanity. Like the shore poems "Out of the Cradle" and "As I Ebb'd," the swamp poem "Lilacs" expresses a sense of place by mediating a human-centered narrative and repeated loco-descriptive elements in ways that charge the environment itself with narrativity. But unlike the other two poems, "Lilacs" intertwines at least two narrative strands—that of the mourning poet who moves from the lilac-covered dooryard into the bird's swamp, and that of Lincoln's dead body being carried through the landscapes of post–Civil War America—both of which are frequently displaced by portraits of the land that emphasize nature's agency. The accuracy of the nature descriptions, which many critics have discussed,[5] plays a role in this dynamic, but it is the ubiquity of death that gives its narrative-descriptive rendition a new eco-ethical quality.

In this multilocal poem, the narrative arc strings together a range of natural places before culminating in a swamp, places whose elements have a considerable impact on the humbled speaker who seems to merely drift from one location to the next. In the opening scene, he calls out to star and night, but "the black murk that hides the star" and the "surrounding cloud" keep him down; later, the lilac bush is "tall-growing" and "rising," and the bird "warbles" in the swamp, "avoiding" the settlements, while the deferential speaker enters the scene only toward the end; and when he quietly takes a "delicate" lilac sprig, he brackets his interpretation, toning down the somewhat pompous claim that he knows the bird's condition: "(for well dear brother I know, / If thou wast not granted to sing thou would'st surely die.)" (*LG* 277). The poem maintains this perspective on active local geographies, linked to a deferential speaking position, when the mourning poet talks about the journey of Lincoln's coffin:

> Over the breast of the spring, the land, amid cities,
> Amid lanes and through old woods, where lately the violets peep'd from the ground, spotting the gray debris,
> Amid the grass in the fields each side of the lanes, passing the endless grass,
> Passing the yellow-spear'd wheat, every grain from its shroud in the dark-brown fields uprisen,
> Passing the apple-tree blows of white and pink in the orchards,
> Carrying a corpse to where it shall rest in the grave,
> Night and day journeys a coffin.

The land itself seems to be carrying the coffin here, and the journey "over" the land becomes one "amid" lanes and woods, so that the coffin is embraced by the earth's ample growths long before it will be buried in the ground. Whitman's parallel constructions, each opening with a preposition or verb that emphasizes movement, amplify this sense of a "natural" dynamic, while the sensitive speaker has receded into the background. Throughout the next few sections, the speaker similarly negotiates his poetic agency in relation to nature's processes and frequently defers to them: the thrush calls until he promises to "come presently"; the "Sea-winds" blow until he imagines himself merging "with these the breath of [his] chant"; and when he wonders about decorating the burial-house with "pictures" of nature, they are not fully framed or controlled but keep "growing," "flowing," and "expanding." In the face of overwhelming human death, the disquieted poet yields control to nature's particulars without falling silent.

When the speaker finally enters the swamp, it is again the "knowledge of death" and "thought of death" that make him recognize nature's agency in ways that do not threaten his own being:

> Then with the knowledge of death as walking one side of me,
> And the thought of death close-walking the other side of me,
> And I in the middle as with companions, and as holding the hands of
> companions,
> I fled forth to the hiding receiving night that talks not,
> Down to the shores of the water, the path by the swamp in the dimness,
> To the solemn shadowy cedars and ghostly pines so still.
> And the singer so shy to the rest receiv'd me,
> The gray-brown bird I know receiv'd us comrades three,
> And he sang the carol of death, and a verse for him I love.
> From deep secluded recesses,
> From the fragrant cedars and the ghostly pines so still,
> Came the carol of the bird.
> And the charm of the carol rapt me,
> As I held as if by their hands my comrades in the night,
> And the voice of my spirit tallied the song of the bird. (*LG* 281)

Accepting death as his companion, the poet repeats the downward movement that characterized his encounter with the seashore in "As I Ebb'd." This time, however, he is received without words, just as he himself is without words, as if the state of mourning has precluded excessive and "arrogant" human language. But silence or death is not the solution, as they never can be in "As I Ebb'd." The thrush that sings "the carol of death" also "receives" the poet, and poetry remains part of this human-nature interaction inflected by death. The gesture of "receiving" the grieving poet perfectly captures the idea of an active nature whose authority does not cancel out that of the poet, all the more so since "receiving" also has the connotation of "paying attention," suggesting a mutuality that is further reinforced when the charm of the bird's carol "raps" the poet, affecting him deeply without overpowering him.

In the second part of section 14, after "the voice of [the poet's] spirit tallied the song of the bird" (*LG* 281), the bird fully takes over, and sings, rather than being translated and understood by the speaker in "Out of the Cradle."[6] That the hermit thrush does not sing to his mate but glorifies death turns him from a muse for the speaker into a poet himself; the bird's song is not superseded by that of the human speaker but is a self-contained poetic unit. In the 1871 version, the bird's song even had a separate subtitle, "Death Carol," suggesting how much this section serves as a poem within a poem, controlled only minimally by the human speaker. The bird interprets "the sight of the open landscape and the high-spread sky" and "life in the fields" as "fitting" to death. Even though his lyrical agency ultimately falls back to the human poet, who implicitly "translates" his melody into speech that comments upon death, Whitman suggests a natural scene here that both interprets itself and reads death as an experience that blurs the difference between humans and nature.

A comparison with the nature writing of the time, such as Higginson's descriptions in "The Life of Birds" (1862), shows to what extent attempts to "translate" birdsong were among the time's proto-ecological interests, and how Whitman's elegy uses the means of poetry to circumvent some of its pitfalls in ways that are suggestive in terms not only of finding a language for a mourning culture but also of representing nature's elements as self-directed subjects. Here is how Higginson describes his encounter with a wood thrush:

> [T]he clear, calm, interrupted chant of the Wood-Thrush fell like solemn water-drops from some source above. I am acquainted with no sound in Nature so sweet, so elevated, so serene. Flutes and flageolets are Art's poor efforts to recall that softer sound. It is simple, and seems all prelude; but the music to which it is the overture must belong to other spheres. It might be the *Angelus* of some lost convent. It might be the meditation of some

> maiden-hermit, saying over to herself in solitude, with recurrent tuneful pauses, the only song she knows. (373)

This speaker, too, is "rapt" by the birdsong; one could even say he is so humbled by it as to wonder if it is not more excellent than human music. Yet the experiences of the refined speaker are the measure here (he is acquainted with no comparable sound), and through sentimental allusions he genders the encounter in ways that emphasize his interpretive power and transform the bird into a metaphor for female modesty. While this is certainly due to the mix of science and sentiment, description and narration, that marks natural history essays as a genre, it also highlights how Whitman's poetic description of a similar scene is environmentally suggestive not only because of ornithologically relevant descriptions of the bird but also because of a human speaker for whom, through the experience of death, conventional knowledge, sentimental allusions, and a patronizing attitude no longer work, and who instead willingly lets himself be guided without losing his self. A brief look at another Higginson passage that tries to grasp the song of a robin through a mix of narration, description, and transcription further highlights the related yet different positions taken by both speaker and bird in this unequal dialogue:

(Before noticing me,)	*chirrup, cheerup ;*
(pausing in alarm, at my approach,)	*che, che, che ;*
(broken presently by a thoughtful strain,)	*caw, caw ;*
(then softer and more confiding,)	*see, see, see ;*
(then the original note, in a whisper,)	*chirrup, cheerup ;*
(often broken by a soft note,)	*see, wee ;*
(and an odder one,)	*squeal ;*
(and a mellow note,)	*tweedle.* (372)

This table tells the story of a wanderer who tries to minimize his disturbing presence as well as his interpretive agency (he tucks his descriptions away in parentheses), and who is somewhat redeemed when the bird continues its song. But Whitman's poem grants the bird the power and autonomy to address the universe, and on the most unfathomable, humbling of topics, so that not only all cuteness (and the threat of banality) are absent, but issues of superiority or control, even new knowledge, are no longer germane. The speaker may come away with a profound insight, but he keeps it to himself.

From an eco-ethical perspective, then, "Lilacs" shows how compassion for the dead is, for all its political and spiritual significance, also a principal force behind Whitman's recurrent expressions of deference toward the land. The multiple, terribly concrete experience of death makes the mature poet engage with the land around him in ways that neither subject them to systems of rational understanding or physical control, nor threaten his own poetic voice: his mourning paves the way for his attention to nature's dynamics, leads him to temporarily question his ability to sing, and prepares him to be "received" by swamp and bird on equal terms. With a speaker this sensitive to the fragility of all life, poetic vision and nature's self-sufficiency reach a wonderful balance, one "tallying" the other, and environmental humility reaches a new dimension.

In all three poems discussed here, Whitman's approach to local natural landscapes also indirectly intersects with Dickinson's. Her reduced descriptions that give prominence to the land's interactive presence by minimizing the speaker's interpretive agency structurally parallel Whitman's way of telling stories about human encounters with familiar landscapes that slide into narrative descriptions of the self-sufficient land, doubting, bracketing, or undoing the speaker's interpretations. In Dickinson, however, the self-effacing speaker tends to remain just present enough to depict the land with minimal means, often quietly withdrawing in the end; the paradoxical sense of authority these poems imply is one of creating such evocative portraits of the world without letting this ability turn into visions of total mastery. Whitman's male speakers tend to come to such a position via a detour—primarily through the acknowledgment of death, in the face of which all language threatens to collapse—yet it is no less radical for its more contested quality.

Familiarization and Defamiliarization

In their descriptive portraits of local environments, Whitman and Dickinson not only convey a deep sense of familiarity with the details of the land, they also disrupt such familiarity. This double movement is an important element of their local ecopoetics: the idea that natural and human systems are linked, as well as resemble each other, is a vital basis for eco-ethical thought and action, while the recognition of nature's autonomy and difference is a necessary countermove, since even the most well-meaning dissolution of difference constitutes an act of imaginary appropriation and can give way to exploitative practices. While Dickinson sounds out this tension through metaphors of family, Whitman speaks to these concerns through his engagement of organicism, which was, apart from its literary currency, a concept naturalists were developing, and which holds, much like the metaphor of family, an important position in the history of ecology and environmentalism. Whitman's way of familiarizing local landscapes as organic wholes, and of defamiliarizing them by showing the limits of such organic models, contributes to the complexity of his local ecopoetry.

Organicism is well known to be a foundational principle of *Leaves of Grass*, which is modeled after nature's processes on various levels. Organicism as an environmental concept, however, has not been examined in detail in relation to Whitman's poetry. Nineteenth-century organicism developed in response to older ideas of mechanism and vitalism, and its claim that living processes can be understood best by considering the autonomous organization of systems rather than their individual parts also deeply informed Darwin's theories. Robert J. Richards explains that "the nature that Darwin experienced with the aid of Humboldt [. . .] was a cosmos, in which organic patterns of land, climate, vegetation, animals, and humans were woven into a vast web pulsating with life" (525); later, Frederick Clements's notion that organic matter in a particular area forms a kind of "superorganism" that eventually reaches its stable climax state, which dominated ecological studies from the turn of the twentieth century until the 1930s (Worster, *Wealth of Nature* 175), "grew" out of organicism. However, ecology as a serious science also depended on abandoning the inherent mysticism of organicism. Laura Walls stresses that Thoreau, as a Humboldtian proto-ecologist, had already "helped to advance an alternative tradition of romantic science and literature that looked toward ecological approaches to nature and that was suppressed, then forgotten, by later organicist interpretations" (*Seeing New Worlds* 4). When Whitman's poetry embraces the organic interwovenness of natural and human systems, yet at the same time pushes beyond organicism's supposed eternal harmonies to express a sense of nature's difference, it engages his culture's struggles with a concept that both fostered and hindered the move toward modern ecology, and participates in carving out a language for new, ecosensitive ways of relating to familiar natural environments that were just in the making.

"Crossing Brooklyn Ferry" is perhaps not an obvious choice for discussing how Whitman understands local landscapes as organic wholes. But this poem, whose pivotal idea of "crossing" place and time pushes against its paradoxical "groundedness" in a liquid locale at a specific time, unfolds, as Lawrence Buell has put it, "a lovely description of the speaker's meditation as he relishes landscape, river, and sky during a leisurely seeming homeward commute" (*Writing for an Endangered World* 95). But it also keeps transmuting the story of the perceiving poet into descriptive accounts of the dynamics of the place, portraying it as an organic system in which humans are embedded and that therefore seems wonderfully familiar. The passage early in the poem when the speaker on the ferry remembers everything he watched and saw during earlier crossings is a good example:

> I too many and many a time cross'd the river of old,
> Watched the Twelfth-month sea-gulls, saw them high in the air floating with motionless wings, oscillating their bodies,
> Saw how the glistening yellow lit up parts of their bodies and left the rest in strong shadow,
> Saw the slow-wheeling circles and the gradual edging toward the south,
> Saw the reflection of the summer sky in the water,
> Had my eyes dazzled by the shimmering track of beams,
> Look'd at the fine centrifugal spokes of light round the shape of my head in the sunlit water,
> Look'd on the haze on the hills southward and south-westward,
> Look'd on the vapor as it flew in fleeces tinged with violet,
> Look'd toward the lower bay to notice the vessels arriving,
> Saw their approach, saw aboard those that were near me,
> Saw the white sails of schooners and sloops, saw the ships at anchor,
> The sailors at work in the rigging or out astride the spars,
> The round masts, the swinging motion of the hulls, the slender serpentine pennants,
> The large and small steamers in motion, the pilots in their pilot-houses,
> The white wake left by the passage, the quick tremulous whirl of the wheels,
> The flags of all nations, the falling of them at sunset,
> The scallop-edged waves in the twilight, the ladled cups, the frolicsome crests and glistening [. . .] (*LG* 136–37)

Even though the speaker emphasizes his past act of looking, the rhythmic repetitions make his perception part of the dynamic scene, which may appear to be mechanically ordered from above but is also miraculously self-organized, even as it ultimately depends on the poet's vision. The gulls are carried by their wings, floating on air and water, while the hills, water, and ships are loosely linked by rising vapor; the poet's "dazzled eyes" become one with the "reflection of the summer sky in the water," while his head seems to be swimming in the river; ships and sailors blend into the place, while the "scallop-edged waves," with their echo of clams and mussels from the deep, and the "the frolicsome crests" enfold the "ladled cups" of the ferry's wheel—nature and culture are complexly intertwined herein, a self-sustaining, harmonious system that is clearly more than the sum of its parts. Instead of Dickinson's emphasis on family resemblances, Whitman expresses such interwovenness through an organic holism whose spiritual and aesthetic qualities were part of Humboldt's natural history (see Dettelbach) and of Darwin's proto-ecological perspectives. As Richards underscores: "organic patterns [. . .] woven into a vast web pulsating with life" were a key "aestheticized experience" that delivered to Darwin a crucial vision which then informed his theory of nature (525).

While it is true that such an organicism renders the most overwhelmingly diverse local scene not only deeply familiar but also knowable and potentially useful, Whitman's speaker celebrates this organic whole not primarily because it sustains him (the idea of "[t]he impalpable sustenance of me from all things at all hours of the day" is followed by the notion of his being "disintegrated" in the next line) and counters the idea of comprehension. As in the other local poems discussed here, a moment of profound doubt is part of this account as well. In the middle of his optimistic vision, the speaker perceives "dark patches" falling upon him and confesses that "[t]he best I had done seem'd to me blank and suspicious, / My great thoughts as I supposed them, were they not in reality meagre?" (*LG* 138). Often taken as an indication of a psychological crisis and as a moment of increased empathy between poet and reader through the admission of human failings (see Nelson 157–58), the speaker also doubts the reach of his vision and grants nature its incomprehensible otherness.

Considering midcentury environmental discussions, Whitman's concluding call "Flow on, river! flow with the flood-tide, and ebb with the ebb-tide!," followed by twenty lines that urge the elements of this landscape to continue to frolic, stand up, throb, live, play, fly, receive, hold, and diverge, might even imply a nudge against the time's rampant utilitarianism. Just then, New York Harbor was turning into a hazardous wasteland, a place whose fishing grounds were under such great pressure that "the well-joined scheme" was on the verge of breaking down (see Waldman 38–42, 84). Indeed, midcentury New York City suffered from severe "waste management problems" and "struggle[d] to keep disease and pollution from overtaking the city," as Maria Farland has stressed in her reading of "This Compost" in the context of the time's sanitary and health crisis ("Decomposing City" 803); interestingly, Whitman's early prose sketches, including "A Plea For Water" and "Wholesome Water," show him worried about urban environments "crammed with filth, excrement, and waste products" ("Decomposing City" 805). If "Crossing Brooklyn Ferry" is an urban poem in which "refreshing nature imagery" cleanses the city (Reynolds, *Walt Whitman's America* 109), this notion of a clean and cleansing nature was already under threat. Whitman is certainly not expressing any direct environmental concern here; Killingsworth even finds that from an ecocritical viewpoint the poem falters when the speaker stretches his soul all the way to include urban realities in his evocation of "sacred space and sacred time" (*Whitman and the Earth* 131). But the poem's celebration of an organic wholeness in which humans are integrated, together with the yearning for its continuation, anticipates a change that may refer to more than the end of ferries. The final address to the dynamics of this natural-cultural place, culminating in the line "Keep your places, objects than which none else is more lasting," also bestows upon it what Aldo Leopold in his land ethic would call "the right to continued existence."

Written the same year as "Crossing Brooklyn Ferry," "This Compost" is a poem in which a local natural site in its organic interconnectedness becomes deeply unfamiliar. It was originally entitled "Poem of Wonder at the Resurrection of Wheat," but the poem expresses more than a sense of wonder at nature's processes. It also offers a narrative description that probes the limits of an organicist approach, fully confronting nature's otherness. This move is condensed in the memorable opening line, "Something startles me where I thought I was safest" (*LG* 309). Revisiting a place he used to know as familiar, the speaker feels compelled to withdraw from this reassuring perspective. Several lines amplify his sense of dissociation:

> I withdraw from the still woods I loved,
> I will not go now on the pastures to walk,
> I will not strip the clothes from my body to meet my lover the sea,
> I will not touch my flesh to the earth as to other flesh to renew me. (*LG* 309)

The speaker's trust in one larger life force that holds natural systems together and his ability to conceive of himself as part of this dynamic interconnectedness both disintegrate, leading him to formulate a list of clear-eyed questions about nature's most unfathomable quality—the ability to create life out of the "foul liquid and meat" of death. After this intense moment of doubt, he does for a moment reengage the familiarizing mode and reconnect with woods, forests, and swamps as wonderfully interrelated systems, eleven parallel lines that rhythmically describe all kinds of "appearing" and "rising" natural particulars; the section culminates, however, in the surprising exclamation "What chemistry!" (*LG* 310).

If the poet has come across something that the comforting organicist notion of nature's well-joined scheme cannot fully account for, the rational sciences seem to offer alternative models of talking about those aspects of nature that leave you "terrified at the Earth" (*LG* 311). Liebig's organic chemistry, which Whitman had embraced enthusiastically in an 1847 review, may have regarded the decomposition of matter into new life as a kind of resurrection (see Matteson 392), paralleling Higginson's attempts to reconcile religious interpretations of spring with scientific insights. But it was also a science directed against older theories that saw humus as some vague "organic force" (Merchant, *Ecological Revolutions* 207). Yet while Whitman's "This Compost" does resound as an homage to Liebig, it also pushes against the limits of organicism's inherent mysticism. Much later, this move was necessary to pave the way for ecology as a fully fledged science, and in the 1930s the ecosystem model was formulated explicitly against organicist ideas (Worster, *Nature's Economy* 302). Whitman's local poetry subtly engages both the mystical notion of natural scenes as wonderfully interwoven wholes and a more rational one of intricate living systems. Remarkably, gestures of humility inform both perspectives: when he imagines local naturescapes as organic wholes, as in "Crossing Brooklyn Ferry," his sense of wonder keeps him from formulating visions of linguistic mastery, and when he withdraws from the idea of nature as mystical entity, as in "This Compost," he still brackets science's claim of total knowability.

Reading Whitman's local poetry back against Dickinson's highlights once more the environmental implications of their shared but differently inflected descriptive approach. At a time when natural history essays, with their numerous descriptions of the interactions between animal and plant life, climate and soil, water and landforms in natural systems, were a driving force in America's increasing environmental awareness, Whitman's and Dickinson's poems, in spite of their intense symbolic implications, also insisted on the physical magnitude of geographical places and conveyed a sense of local naturescapes as living systems. Moreover, when nature essayists embraced landscape description as a mode that promises a relative de-centering of the speaker, moving toward a new environmental ethics of reciprocity that they often also explicitly endorsed, Dickinson's descriptive minimalism and Whitman's narrative descriptions formulated similar yet more richly ambivalent positions of environmental humility. The humility of their landscape poems derives not only from description as a stance that promises to refrain from valuation, analysis, and definition, but also from the ways in which their speakers question the very possibility of doing so, of de-emphasizing or even canceling human intervention and domination. In their descriptive passages, the speaker only seemingly disappears to make room for nature's autonomous agency; the observer remains present, and it is the observer's attitude that makes all the difference. Rather than being humble in essence, Dickinson's and Whitman's poems perform humility in the act of speaking: as they enact a continuing fascination with familiar lands, yet express an awareness that even the most ordinary landscape can never be fully described, they suggest a self-aware yet humble stance that sustains an inherent conflict of ecology while sidestepping a lapse into silence. Ultimately, their ongoing attempts to imaginatively grasp the character of the land but refrain from asserting symbolic power over it give voice to the paradoxical situation that the very act of speaking already appropriates that about which we speak—in other words, that we cannot live without appropriating, even when we "merely" describe.

III · Narrating the Regions

Regional perspectives form an integral part of Dickinson's and Whitman's poetry about nature and human-nature relations. Dickinson, who famously claimed to "see – New Englandly" (Fr256), occasionally portrays the Northeast as a pastoral middle ground where people "grow" as if they were parts of the biotic community, and talked about "Men that made the Hay" (Fr610) and other old-fashioned farming routines at a time when change was imminent. Whitman, her fellow northeasterner who had, however, also traveled through parts of the South and West, embraces a broader range of regions in his work, both in poems such as "A Paumanok Picture," "Pioneers! O Pioneers!," and "O Magnet-South" and in his all-American catalogues. Characteristically, "Our Old Feuillage" alludes to people's interactions with the land in the Northeast ("On interior rivers by night in the glare of pine knots, steamboats wooding up, / In farmers' barns oxen in the stable, their harvest labor done, they rest standing, they are too tired"), the West ("The scout riding on horseback over the plains west of the Mississippi, he ascends a knoll and sweeps his eyes around"), and the South ("Southern fishermen fishing, the sounds and inlets of North Carolina's coast, the shad-fishery and the herring-fishery, the large sweep-seines, the windlasses on shore work'd by horses, the clearing, curing, and packing-houses"). Even though Dickinson's interest in America's regions is by no means as prominent or as diverse as Whitman's, both poets talk about nature in regional terms. Comparison of their work on this scale offers a new perspective on the green resonances of their poetry because regions are "the site of economic production [. . .] closely bound up with the larger rhythms of the national and global economy, and regional identity is constructed disproportionately around the kinds of work performed there" (Smith 108). When Dickinson and Whitman write about nature and human-nature relationships in America's three core regions, they write about farming, fishing and logging, agrarianism and expansionism, touching upon some of the larger economic, social, and political implications of their culture's views of the land. In the following two chapters I argue that Dickinson and Whitman portray regional environments as dynamic platial configurations by way of equally dynamic modes of poetic expression that include specific narrative elements—elements that reconsider some of America's most prominent cultural narratives about how to use the land economically. Both poets imagine regions as storied places at a time when conservationists and preservationists also used a range of narratives to reevaluate America's formative ideas about the land as an economic resource. But while these proponents of more environmentally attuned practices tell stories that emphasize nature's inherent value, warn against its indiscriminate exploitation, and promote a shift toward wise management and environmental protection, Dickinson's and Whitman's poems unfold scenarios that shift the ethical focus from narrative closure and a usually simple morality toward activating, and humbly acknowledging, the impossibility of solving the basic ethical dilemma of human existence in nature.

Dickinson and Whitman wrote about New England farms, western prairies, and the rich southern soil when deep changes in the economic setup of America's regions went hand-in-hand with the development of regionally inflected ideas about conservation and preservation. In America's three main regions, the massive redistribution of "natural wealth" through new technologies (Steinberg, *Down to Earth* 55) sparked specific environmental ideas. For the increasingly industrialized Northeast, Judd has argued that communitarian principles, including "a faith in common stewardship, an aggressive anthropocentrism, and the concept of an ordained landscape" (*Common Lands, Common People* 8), made common farmers and fishers trailblazers of nature conservation. This interpretation challenges older notions that conservation ideas emerged among elite easterners (see Merchant, *Ecological Revolutions* 227). For the South, Albert Cowdrey has shown that in reaction to diminishing wildlife in a region that heavily relied on hunting (94; see also Anthony Wilson 112), pre–Civil War nature protection was linked to "aristocratic pleasure, sovereign right, bureaucratic regulation, or scientific thought" (94). In the postwar South, environmental concern increased as a result of the large-scale logging and mechanized agriculture that arrived in "neofrontier" areas (Dorman 107). In the West, environmental advocacy began after the Civil War with the advent of large-scale logging and grew considerably through the activism of John Muir, especially after he moved to

Yosemite Valley State Park in 1868. His texts about nature as an economic and spiritual resource were eagerly embraced by the American middle class, generally troubled by modernization (Dorman 105–7), which shows the national resonance of these discussions.

Some historians trace precursors of the conservation movement back to the early nineteenth century, when John James Audubon, George Catlin, Francis Parkman, James Fenimore Cooper, and William Cullen Bryant expressed concern about nature's massive destruction (see Nash, *Wilderness and the American Mind* 96–102); according to Daniel G. Payne, Catlin proposed national parks as early as 1832 (48). These developments paved the way for conservation and, later, preservation to become broader cultural movements in the second half of the century, finding their most dramatic expressions in the protection of the Yosemite Valley (1864) and the establishment of Yellowstone (1872), the Adirondack Forest Preserve (1885), and Yosemite National Park (1890). Although conservationists saw nature as a limited but renewable resource that required wise management in the interest of "sustainable economic growth," while preservationists sought to protect pristine nature from intensive economic exploitation and preserve it "for a more symbiotic purpose, recreation," the difference was one of degree, since both utilitarian conservationists (such as Marsh) and moral-aesthetic preservationists (such as Thoreau and Muir) were interested in using nature economically (Dorman xiii). What is more significant for a contextual analysis of Dickinson's and Whitman's poetic strategies is that such speeches, editorials, and books not only called attention to natural phenomena and described their characteristics but also worked with key narrative patterns, harking back to a set of interrelated cultural narratives that have shaped America's contradictory relationship to the land. In particular, conservationists told stories about northeasterners, westerners, or southerners in their economic relationship to the natural environment that revisited narratives of America as nature's nation, manifest destiny, and the frontier. In the first of these narratives, the settlers' arrival in the New World, viewed as a new Eden, marks the starting point of an idyllic life in pastoral harmony, an agrarian middle ground characterized by hard work on small farms and the appreciation of nature's sublime aspects in certain undomesticated areas. In the narrative of America's manifest destiny, the New World is destined to be settled by an expanding, progressive, Anglo-Saxon nation. In the frontier narrative, the New World is a wilderness to be mastered and "civilized," in a process that guarantees the regeneration and democratization of individuals and institutions. As Marsh, Thoreau, Muir, and others engaged these narrative patterns, they tended to emphasize causal links between negative developments, pointed to conflicting interests, and suggested remedies, forming an important "narrative" context for Dickinson's and Whitman's regional poetry.

In particular, George Perkins Marsh, the "Prophet of Conservation" (Lowenthal), used narrative elements to communicate his conviction that people should use nature for economic purposes but reconsider its indiscriminate exploitation, as shown by the following 1849 letter to botanist Asa Gray:

> I spent my early life almost literally in the woods; a large portion of the territory of Vermont was, within my recollection, covered with natural forests; and having been personally engaged to a considerable extent in clearing lands, and manufacturing, and dealing in lumber, I have had occasion both to observe and to feel the effects resulting from an injudicious system of managing woodlands and the products of the forest. (qtd. in Lowenthal, "Introduction" xviii)

This autobiographical sequence about believing in people's supreme right to use nature indirectly refers to the frontier narrative of people "clearing" undomesticated wilderness areas in the interest of America's economic growth and territorial expansion. When the woodsman comes to realize that he has inadvertently participated in the forest's destruction and that the solution might lie in improved management, his short moral tale also alludes to the related narrative of "nature's nation," of America as a place wherein to re-create heaven on earth. The passage here reaches back to two biblical ideas of human-nature relationships, expressed, for instance, in Genesis 1:28, where God blesses man and woman and tells them: "Be fruitful, and multiply, and replenish the earth, and subdue it: and have dominion over the fish of the sea, and over the fowl of the air, and over every living thing that moveth upon the earth" (King James Version). While these lines urge humans to subdue nature and use it in their own interest—which has been taken as a blueprint for an unabashedly exploitative attitude—they also ask humans to "replenish the earth," which conservationists such as Marsh have read in terms of more complex notions of good stewardship. How prominently a reinterpretation of biblical narratives figured in Marsh's utilitarian conservationism can be seen in this famous passage from *Man and Nature*:

> Man has too long forgotten that the earth was given to him for usufruct alone, not for consumption, still less for profligate waste. Nature has provided against the absolute destruction of any of her elementary matter [. . .]. But she has left it within the power of man irreparably to derange the combinations of inorganic matter and of organic life, which through the night of aeons she had been proportioning and balancing, to prepare the earth for his habitation. (36)

According to Marsh, the story of humans as God's special creation needs to be reinterpreted, because people have turned out to be less than perfect stewards whose abuses of their powers constitute a betrayal of nature's trust and generosity—a conflict that can be resolved by refraining from excess and adhering to the principle of "usufruct," which leaves people's superiority intact and even reinscribes it on a more perfect level. Marsh's text accesses a whole network of stories about people's conflicted economic relationships with nature, shedding light on Dickinson's and Whitman's regional poems insofar as they, too, negotiate their time's shifting utilitarian perspectives by way of narrative elements that have complex, often religiously charged eco-ethical overtones.

Henry David Thoreau shared with Marsh the belief in a middle landscape that would accommodate certain degrees of modernization as well as undomesticated natural places, yet he questioned people's utilitarianism on a more fundamental level, also urging awareness of nature's unparalleled aesthetic qualities. His unfinished "Huckleberries" includes the following allegory:

> But ah we have fallen on evil days! I hear of pickers ordered out of the huckleberry fields, and I see stakes set up with written notices forbidding any to pick them. I do not mean to blame any, but all—to bewail our fates generally. We are not grateful enough that we have lived a part of our lives before these things occurred. What becomes of the true value of country life—what, if you must go to market for it? It has come to this, that the butcher now brings round our huckleberries in his cart. Why, it is as if the hangman were to perform the marriage ceremony. (492)

Thoreau's lament about the decline of a subsistence economy in idyllic pastoral places is based on a story of individual fruit pickers still familiar with the "true value of country life" being displaced by landowners who seek control for the sake of large-scale crops and profits, a micronarrative whose contrast between biblical innocence and modern guilt and whose rhetoric of evil forces, fate, and blame allude to notions of America as a new garden being desecrated in ways that surely lead to doom. However, Thoreau ends the essay with an activist call to establish public domains that would be exempt from such degradation and useful in more general moral and aesthetic terms: "I think that each town should have a park, or rather a primitive forest, of five hundred or a thousand acres, either in one body or several—where a stick should never be cut for fuel—nor for the navy, nor to make wagons, but stand and decay for higher uses—a common possession forever, for instruction and recreation" (500). Again, for assessing the green resonances of Dickinson's and Whitman's poetry—especially their occasional nostalgia for old-fashioned modes of farming and for timeless places that seem unaffected by economic activities—it is instructive to consider the "stories" included in such explicitly eco-ethical publications of their time.

Finally, John Muir, who went furthest in urging the aesthetic and especially the spiritual appreciation of wild nature, also uses narrative elements to convey his message, as the opening of his essay "Wild Wool," published in the *Overland Monthly* in 1875, indicates:

> Moral improvers have calls to preach. I have a friend who has a call to plow, and woe to the daisy sod or azalea thicket that falls under the savage redemption of his keen steel shares. Not content with the so-called subjugation of every terrestrial bog, rock, and moor-land, he would fain discover some method of reclamation applicable to the ocean and the sky, that in due calendar time they might be made to bud and blossom as the rose. Our efforts are of no avail when we seek to turn his attention to wild roses, or to the fact that both ocean and sky are already about as rosy as possible [. . .]. Wildness charms not my friend, charm it never so wisely; and whatsoever may be the character of his heaven, his earth seems only a chaos of agricultural possibilities calling for grubbinghoes and manures. [. . .] [T]he barbarous notion is almost universally entertained by civilized men, that there is in all the manufactures of nature something essentially coarse which can and must be eradicated by human culture. I was, therefore, delighted in finding that the wild wool growing upon mountain sheep in the neighborhood of Mount Shasta was much finer than the average grades of cultivated wool. (Muir, *Nature Writings* 598)

The conflict between a farmer who feels "called" to tame even oceans and skies and a narrator who emphasizes untamed nature's inherent value again plays upon several cultural narratives regarding America's relationship with the earth. The ironic depiction of the farmer turns the common dichotomy between "civilization" and "savagery" on its head, thus destabilizing the notion of manifest destiny as a story of progress. At the same time, references to redemption, heaven, and earth recast earthly nature as a spiritual entity, revisiting the Judeo-Christian notion of man's dominion and shifting the idea of stewardship further toward a more biocentric ethics. As such, Dickinson's and Whitman's poems about what "Is often seen – but seldom felt" on New England's farms, or about woodcutters who are unable to perceive the pristine beauty of the forests they are destroying, were framed by a broader narrative exchange regarding nature's aesthetic and spiritual values, and the moral dilemma of using its resources solely for economic purposes.

In such a context Dickinson's and Whitman's poems about farming, fishing, and logging become legible as nuanced contributions to controversial arguments about how to live comfortably with and from the land in an increasingly industrial economy without irreversibly destroying nature. I argue here that their regional poems engage the foundational conflicts between dominion and stewardship, civilization and wilderness, abundance and scarcity, and ultimately, life and death, by performing a move that is structurally similar to one that the conservationists of the time were performing—that is, by telling *stories* that are linked to America's core cultural narratives about life in and with nature while challenging some of their basic assumptions. Dickinson's and Whitman's regional poems may not always have identifiable agents, conflicts, or even a clear beginning and end; Dickinson's lyric poems, especially, tend to have a relatively weak narrativity compared to Whitman's more epic works, which often have small but identifiable narrative clusters.[1] Still, elements of plot, setting, and personification give a narrative edge to their regional poems that enables a reading against certain stories of the land that conservationists and preservationists were telling. More specifically, the following two chapters explore how Dickinson's and Whitman's poems engage narrative elements that evoke America's historically different regions with their characteristic modes of production and the conflicts that emerge from them. Yet while these identifiable ministories resemble those included in the conservationist and preservationist arguments of the time insofar as they tend to have moral implications and point to larger conflicts that transcend regional boundaries, they do not try to suggest a new master narrative that subsumes or reconciles all others, nor do they imply the possibility of alternative, nondominating stories of human life on earth.

Rather, their poems about an agrarian nostalgia that ultimately leads to death, or about the troublesome joys of controlling nature, present readers with a language that boldly sounds out the quandary of an industrialized "nature's nation," replacing the demands of narrative closure with baffling expressions of an ethical dilemma.

Environmental geographer Joan Iverson Nassauer has recently sketched a scenario that provides a suitable metaphor for such a narrative poetics. She argues with Edward Relph that in our economic relationships with nature, we first of all need to acknowledge "the limitations of what we know and even what we *can* know when we change the environment" (76), and condenses this notion as follows:

> A picture of environmental humility might look like a prairie in a garden in a prairie—all writ large on the landscape. At the broadest scale, environmental humility would require that tended places fit into a larger ecological scheme—avoiding the wet prairie or the driest prairie where a garden would not thrive. At a middle scale, the well-placed garden would look recognizably neat, an inviting place where we might expect to find the gardener landscape. At a smaller scale, we might find a small patch of prairie in the garden, alongside the pumpkin patch and the rows of carrots. More than any other part of the picture, this little prairie symbolizes our environmental humility. It says that even where we think we know, we suspect we have more to learn about what the garden can produce. (77)

Neither Dickinson nor Whitman writes literally about "a prairie in a garden in a prairie." But they both envision economic relationships to nature that correspond to the land's characteristic features, and people who listen to what the land has to say or at least consider this imperative. As such, their regional poems acknowledge how difficult it is to know how to live ethically with the land, and even if we think we know, how difficult it is to live accordingly.

5

"A Field of Stubble, lying sere"

Dickinson's Reluctant New England Narratives

Emily Dickinson lived in the middle of an agricultural enclave in an increasingly industrialized region. In the mid-1850s, Amherst was a rural farming community, but industrial North Amherst was already referred to as a "city" (Habegger 669n70), and by the 1880s, the town's hat factories had expanded right in front of the Dickinson homestead (Erkkila, "Dickinson and Class" 18). Dickinson's letters occasionally talk about Amherst's ways of working the land in these times of change—she reported that "Old Amos weeds and hoes and has an oversight of all thoughtless vegetables" (L49) and that she "hayed a little for the horse" (L215); she expressed concern that the rye field she and her mother had planted might be mortgaged (L16); she wondered if "[t]he trees are getting over the effect of Canker worm" (L131). Some of her reflections on New England's agricultural practices are particularly rich in cultural implications, such as this mock indignation about "gentlemen" who debase themselves by "plucking" trees and fields and eagerly storing the produce:

> Gentlemen here have a way of plucking the tops of trees, and putting the fields in their cellars annually, which in point of taste is execrable, and would they please omit, I should have fine vegetation & foliage all the year round, and never a winter month. Insanity to the sane seems so unnecessary—but I am only one, and they are "four and forty," which little affair of numbers leaves me impotent. (L209)

For all its playfulness, this leisurely lady's complaint about economic practices that ruin the land aesthetically contains a narrative that echoes broader sentiments of nature's appreciation espoused by moral-aesthetic preservationists, as well as more specific upper-class interests that fed into New England's intensifying environmental concern.[1] At the same time these lines, especially in their irony, imply a couched critique of nature's "insane" commodification in which New England's utilitarian conservationists, paradoxically, themselves participated. Even the earthly paradise she envisions, which refers to the cultural narrative of America as the new Garden of Eden, can be linked to conservationist notions of restoring nature's divine harmonies and preservationist ideals of undomesticated nature as a spiritual realm. Ultimately, however, Dickinson's suggestion that one might simply live off the land without destroying it, and that there would be no "winter"—neither hunger nor a loss of innocence—because nature would miraculously feed people, seems just as fantastic as the "insane" work of the gentlemen she criticizes. In other words, to try to draw a viable conclusion from her text would be missing its point; rather, it admits, in a roundabout way, to our "impotence" in terms of effectively countering certain economic developments. Letters such as this one offer a glimpse of the workshop of a poet who occasionally engages her region's shifting agrarian setup by way of narratives that address some of the "insane" conflicts in people's economic relationships with the land, in a cultural climate where conservationists and preservationists were performing similar moves. Yet instead of feeding the illusion that there are alternative stories that might resolve these conflicts, she focuses on eloquently sounding out some of their irresolvable contradictions.

So far, Dickinson's views of New England as a geographic entity have received comparatively little sustained attention, even though she wrote poems about New England farming that matter apart from their religious and broader cultural implications.[2] Approaching these poems from an environmental perspective, it is helpful to consider the conservationist and preservationist arguments that developed in the wake of the region's changing agricultural practices. After all, it was in New England, and Massachusetts specifically, that a new industrialized agriculture, based on rather grand notions about managerial control of nature, became dominant, while noteworthy conservation practices, equally shaped by utilitarian reform ideas, pointed in a different direction. For instance, ordinary New England farmers and fishers replaced patterns of ruthless exploitation with techniques developed to ensure nature's resources for future generations (see Judd, *Common Lands, Common People*). At the same time, George B. Emerson's influential *Report on the Trees and Shrubs Growing Naturally in the Forests of Massachusetts* (1846) derided the relentless cutting of New England's forests, urging more careful management and the propagation of native trees (see Merchant, *Ecological Revolutions* 228). And Thoreau, who used George Emerson's *Report* for his own naturalist explorations of the region's diminished forests (Worster, *Nature's Economy*

68), formulated arguments in defense of a pastoral middle landscape that combined utilitarian conservation with a preservationist appreciation of undomesticated wilderness (see Nash, *Wilderness and the American Mind* 94–95). Moreover, many of the conservation and preservation arguments of the time relied as much on facts and figures as on certain story patterns of past mistakes and late insights. In such a framework, Dickinson's occasional use of narrative elements that question the farmers' obsession with "toils" and "triumphs," or praise the "congenial time" of haying from the unsettling perspective of the dead, as well as her keen eye for the tensions between different economic, philosophical, and ethical positions that may be impossible to resolve, become legible as indirect commentaries that are noteworthy for their multifaceted expressions of the dilemma of viewing nature both as a means of production and as a realm that may be in need of protection.

Reluctant Farm Narratives

The poems in which Dickinson looks most specifically at the working lives of New England farmers tend to be poems of harvest. In an agrarian economy, the time of harvest condenses people's dependency on the natural environment, ritually expressed in the Thanksgiving celebration. More generally speaking, it is also the time when people's economic engagement with the land yields its most immediate results, making their attitudes toward nature intensely visible. Dickinson accesses these aspects of harvest through certain narrative elements that highlight her era's conflicting notions about types of economic interaction with nature, while also reaching back to more general American ideas about how to relate to the land. Reading these "stories" of harvest against those that conservationists of her time were telling helps to address some of her regional poetry's specific green implications, rather than subsuming them under autobiographical or psychological concerns.

A compelling example here is a poem Dickinson called "Portrait of the Parish" when sending it to her nephew in 1877:

A – Field of Stubble, lying sere
Beneath the second Sun –
It's Toils to Brindled People thrust –
It's Triumphs – to the Bin –
Accosted by a timid Bird

Irresolute of Alms –
Is often seen – but seldom felt,
On our New England Farms – (Fr1419)

The poem can be read, as Adam Sweeting has suggested, as being concerned with neighbors who do not recognize the season's "psychological complexities," including "the isolated moments in time, the sharp angularity of the seasonal divide, the portents of death" (129). Yet it also contains a multilayered story of harvest whose sequence of events crystallizes a conflict between different approaches to living with the land that cannot be resolved by way of the poem's seemingly simple moral. On a quasi-realistic level, the poem tells a story of New England farmers as "Brindled People," whose bodies were tanned by the sun as they moved the crops "to the Bin." While the poem offers an almost Whitmanian look at the workers' bodies here, appreciating their physical presence and strength, the focus on their direct contact with the land, their dependency on it for sustenance, and their "Toils," implies that such an obsession with labor aligns them with work oxen or horses. The idea of "Triumphs" also suggests that they view harvesting as a struggle against a potentially resistant "field of stubble" that they now have mastered. On the same level, there is the contrasting story of a bird who also depends on the land's fruit but is "timid" rather than dominant, simply feeds on "alms" instead of working, and pays a friendly "visit" instead of struggling against a foe. The second narrative serves as an ironic, critical commentary on the first, suggesting that a less "toilsome" approach might feed the farmers just as well, while the causal connection expressed through the notion of "alms" problematizes the bird's dependency not only on what the field willingly offers, but also on what the farmers leave behind. On another, allegorical level, the poem also invokes two biblical stories. The farmers' "toils" echo Genesis 3:17, in which God articulates the terms of Adam's punishment: "cursed is the ground for thy sake; in sorrow shalt thou eat of it all the days of thy life." The bird's visit alludes to Matthew 6:26: "Behold the fowls of the air: for they sow not, neither do they reap, nor gather into barns; yet your heavenly Father feedeth them. Are ye not much better than they?" The implicit criticism of the farmers' approach is thus redoubled, but it is also inverted, since giving "alms," a biblical virtue and duty, shifts here from God to the farmers who provide for other creatures in need. Finally, these two stories are framed by yet another narrative, in which the aesthetic and religious sensibilities of the observing speaker contrast with her contemporaries' insensitivity, and which contains a subtle admonition to not only "see" but also "feel" what such scenes have to teach.

The context of mid-nineteenth-century environmental discourses highlights the rich, green resonances of these narrative strands. Thoreau's "Wild Apples," for instance, published in the *Atlantic* in 1862, challenges New England's farming practices on related religious, aesthetic, and moral grounds:

> There is thus about all natural products a certain volatile and ethereal quality which represents their highest value, and which cannot be vulgarized, or bought and sold. No mortal has ever enjoyed the perfect flavor of any fruit, and only the godlike among men begin to taste its ambrosial qualities. For nectar and ambrosia are only those fine flavors of every earthly fruit which our coarse palates fail to perceive,—just as we occupy the heaven of the gods without knowing it. When I see a particularly mean man carrying a load of fair and fragrant early apples to market, I seem to see a contest going on between him and his horse, on the one side, and the apples on the other, and, to my mind, the apples always gain it. [. . .] Though he gets out from time to time, and feels of them, and thinks they are all there, I see the stream of their evanescent and celestial qualities going to heaven from his cart, while the pulp and skin and core only are going to market. (447)

Thoreau, too, tells a story of farmers who are overly concerned with their harvest's economic value, and whose obsession with overcoming nature turns them into "meaner" creatures, on a level with workhorses. And he, too, suggests that letting their lives be dominated by hard labor keeps these New Englanders from perceiving the ephemeral beauty of nature's products and from simply enjoying the fruits of "the heaven of the gods" they "occupy," a line of thought that further echoes and perpetuates notions of an earthly paradise that are at the core of the idea of America as nature's nation. For all of his seemingly inconsistent claims and tendency to speak tongue in cheek, Thoreau's moral tale serves as a warning against exaggerated agrarian diligence, combining aesthetic and religious sensibilities to argue for a limited and, if you will, sympathetic economic approach. Many contemporaries were similarly concerned, even if they proposed different solutions. George Perkins Marsh, who was appalled at "man's" destructive impact yet considered the mastery of nature a Christian mission, sought to develop a more sustainable agriculture; a few years later, the radical preservationist John Muir considered farming itself to be a key obstacle because it put people in an adversarial relationship with the earth; and although he turned his back on traditional Christianity, he argued for appreciating nature's beauty as that of God's temples (see Oelschlaeger 184).

This context shows how Dickinson's "portrait" of a "parish" embraces narrative elements whose aesthetic and religious implications subtly respond to conservationist and preservationist arguments, but it also highlights that she withholds precisely the solution the narrative dynamic would invite, offering here what I call a "reluctant" farm narrative. The entire poem, with the various stories to which it alludes, moves toward two concluding couplets that seem to spell out a moral imperative, but its implications remain slippery. Juxtaposing "often" and "seldom," and concerned with perception and emotions, it stays vague about what exactly people "often see" but "seldom feel." This reluctance also has to do with the central position of the bird's being "irresolute," a position the speaker herself echoes. One critic has argued that the speaker identifies with the visiting bird, whose hunger "and the bleakness of its prospects of finding any food are seldom felt by the self-satisfied citizenry of New England farms" (Goudie 32). But why is the bird "irresolute of alms"? Perhaps because the farmers left too little, or because any harvest deprives birds of their natural food source and reduces those who are entitled to the fruits of the fields in ecological as well as biblical terms to the position of taking alms. Both readings seem especially plausible at a time when nature essayists stressed that "birds long retain their tradition of old places, and strive to keep their hold upon them; but we are building them out year by year" (Cabot 216) and argued that farmers should harvest less thoroughly because "the negligence of the tiller of the soil is [. . .] a great gain to the small birds" (Flagg, "The Winter-Birds" 321). But perhaps the bird is irresolute because farmers, rather than God, are now feeding it; considering the conservationists' interest in restoring a God-given harmony between humans and nature, such irresoluteness would imply a more radical critique of man's overconfidence. Finally, the bird's irresoluteness also complicates the biblical allusion to people's being fed without working. It is part of the poem's achievement that it invokes conflicting stories of how to relate to the land economically without providing narrative closure. Yet while the sensitive speaker may be as hesitant to formulate a moral as the bird is irresolute of alms, the poem urges concern for the place of our nonhuman co-inhabitants in an agrarian economy, perhaps even for what birds "feel" at harvest, in ways that point toward environmental sympathy, sidestepping the anthropocentrism implicit in the idea of stewardship. Humans may have lost their environmental innocence for good, but trying to regain it, even though an unattainable goal, can still be a viable motor for change.

In other harvest poems, Dickinson links stories about farming to those about death and mortality in ways that also yield green subtexts when read in context. Read in isolation, these poems' New England resonances may seem to amount to little more than a tinge of the domestic (Phillips 6) or local color (Mulder 552), especially since linking harvest to death was a conventional literary move in a culture as obsessed with death and dying as mid-nineteenth-century New England. But these poems' narratives of old-fashioned farming practices are also in themselves "deadly," in ways that point beyond an allegory for the human cycle of life and death. At a time when many conservationists referred to the ostensibly ideal features of an agrarian middle ground, Dickinson's poems intertwine nostalgic narratives about the routines of old-fashioned subsistence farming with narratives of death, in ways that subtly undercut such idealizing views of traditional farming practices.

A key poem here is "'Twas just this time, last year, I died" (Fr344), whose figure of the speaking corpse is usually read as a curious example of the sentimental consolation lyric that Dickinson wrote throughout her life (Janet Buell 329; Fuss 9). From an ecocritical perspective, it is noteworthy that the poem takes human death as the occasion for a review of New England's traditional agriculture:

'Twas just this time, last year, I died.
I know I heard the Corn,
When I was carried by the Farms –
It had the Tassels on –

I thought how yellow it would look –
When Richard went to mill –
And then, I wanted to get out,
But something held my will.

I thought just how Red – Apples wedged
The Stubble's joints between –
And the Carts went stooping round the fields
To take the Pumpkins in –

I wondered which would miss me, least,
And when Thanksgiving, came,

If Father'd multiply the plates –
To make an even Sum –

And would it blur the Christmas glee
My stocking hang too high
For any Santa Claus to reach
The altitude of me –

But this sort, grieved myself,
And so, I thought the other way,
How just this time, some perfect year –
Themself, should come to me –

In one of the few critical comments on the poem's *Lebenswelt*, Eberwein finds that steeped in sentimental obsession with death, it "pay[s] roundabout homage to the ideal of domestic bliss by citing the commonplace comforts the dead miss out on: harvests, Thanksgiving celebrations, Christmas stockings, and the ordinary comforts of farm and family" (*Strategies of Limitation* 116). Part of what makes this scene ideal and common at the same time are its stories of agricultural balance and harmony: the wagon with the speaker's body passes rustling corn; a man or boy takes the corn to the mill while ripe apples are "wedging" the field's stubbles; while the equally personified carts move about the fields to collect pumpkins. Even the deceased speaker's concern about who would miss her "least" fits into this overall scheme of agrarian harmony. The query has been taken to refer to the speaker's family (Eberwein, *Strategies of Limitation* 116; Fuss 9), and Vivian Pollack even finds that this is "one of her most obviously hostile autobiographical poems" that hints at Dickinson's difficult relationship to her father (*The Anxiety of Gender* 55). But the comment refers as much to the fields, apple trees, and corn as to her family (or *as* her family), as well as implying a degree of interdependence.

Yet this seemingly stable, interconnected agrarian idyll is enveloped in a double story of loss and death. Not only does the poem have a speaker who died about a year earlier, but the awareness of the death of all earthly existence during harvest, which unifies the poem, also creates a sense of another, impending loss, made explicit when the speaker responds to the tension between life and death by thinking "the other way": since she cannot rejoin the idyll (which only exists in her memory to begin with), she consoles herself by imagining "How just this time, some perfect year – / Themself, should come to me – ." If one takes "Themself" to include both her relatives and the "familiar" fields and produce, she anticipates nothing less than the entire farming scene joining her in the "altitudes" of heaven. In the contexts of the time, what seems like a comforting thought and even solution in terms of traditional Christianity is also legible as a muted expression of a sense of death immanent in New England's agrarian traditions, but in such a paradoxical setup that the very idea of a viable solution seems misguided.

About a year later, in 1863, Dickinson wrote another poem that uses the conventional combination of harvest and death in environmentally suggestive ways. In "I'm sorry for the Dead – Today – " (Fr582), the childlike speaker is fully immersed in the joys of making hay, this time expressing sympathy for the dead who cannot participate:

> I'm sorry for the Dead – Today –
> It's such congenial times
> Old neighbors have at fences –
> It's time o' year for Hay,
>
> And Broad – Sunburned Acquaintance
> Discourse between the Toil –
> And laugh, a homely species
> That makes the Fences smile –
>
> It seems so straight to lie away
> From all of the noise of Fields –
> The Busy Carts – the fragrant Cocks –
> The Mower's metre – Steals –
>
> A Trouble lest they're homesick –
> Those Farmers – and their Wives –
> Set separate from the Farming –
> And all the Neighbor's lives –
>
> A Wonder if the Sepulchre
> Dont feel a lonesome way –
> When Men – and Boys – and Carts – and June,
> Go down the Fields to "Hay" –

Whether this is a mourning poem related to the Civil War (Coleman Hutchison 18) or a description of a country graveyard (Mulder 553), it also evokes stories of harvest as "Congenial times" of "Old neighbors" leaning over fences, of "discourse" and laughter during everyday work, of an easy familiarity between farmers and place (so much so that the "Broad – Sunburned Acquaintance" refers to the farmers' bodies as much as the wide sunny space of the field, and the "homely species" implicitly designates the workers as a familiar part of the land). The poem idealizes New England farming as a busy yet relaxed activity in which unassuming people follow nature's rhythms as they always have and maintain an eye for the land's beauty. Yet again, the thematic presence of death impacts upon the scene. The speaker's proclamation that she is "sorry for the Dead – Today" pushes against her seemingly innocent joy, since death is already a subliminal part of "all the noise of Fields." While this is generally implied in the time of autumn—a scene of impending death in nature that coincides with the joys of harvest—the only solution to this speaker's troubles would be, paradoxically, a collective death to make the deceased less "lonesome."

The green implications of these two eulogies become more evident against the backdrop of conservationist publications that idealized pastoral middle landscapes and small-scale subsistence farming in the form of stories of loss, regret, and mourning. The following passage from Marsh's influential "Address Delivered before the Agricultural Society of Rutland County" (1847) offers a characteristic example:

> [T]here is reason to fear that the valleys of many of our streams will soon be converted from smiling meadows into broad wastes of shingle and gravel and pebbles, deserts in summer, and seas in autumn and spring. The changes, which these causes have wrought in the physical geography of Vermont, within a single generation, are too striking to have escaped the attention of any observing person, and every middle-aged man, who revisits his birth-place after a few years of absence, looks upon another landscape than that which formed the theatre of his youthful toils and pleasures. The signs of artificial improvement are mingled with the tokens of improvident waste, and the bald and barren hills, the dry beds of the smaller streams, the ravines furrowed out by the torrents of spring, and the diminished thread of interval that skirts the widened channel of the rivers, seem sad substitutes for the pleasant groves and brooks and broad meadows of his ancient paternal domain. (*So Great a Vision* 19)

Placing great rhetorical urgency on the valleys of "smiling meadows," Marsh links a pastoral idyll to the anticipation of its demise, its transformation into "broad wastes of shingle and gravel and pebbles." In particular, the story of a representative man who finds the pleasant places of his childhood dominated by "bald and barren hills" and "dry beds of the smaller streams" evokes the bygone "brooks and broad meadows of his ancient paternal domain" to dramatize the loss. Around midcentury, in the face of New England's rapidly changing geography, an ostensibly harmonious agrarian economy was already becoming an ideal of the past, and utilitarian conservationists evoked its idyllic charms, including biblical allusions to an earthly paradise that "man" should re-create on earth, in order to urge people to increase in the region the "signs of artificial improvement" rather than those of "improvident waste."

Dickinson's poems tell related stories without utopian delusions, but also without despondency. While contemporary discussions about the possibilities and limitations of living sustainably with and in nature—or of trying to view nature as resource *and* value—were torn between grand schemes of improved management and the urge to preserve the past, her poems about New England farming in which death is subliminally present have speakers who embrace tentative positions rather than lapsing into moralism; in "'Twas just this time," the speaker remembers how she "wondered," and remain poised in a state of in-between—captured in the moment of wanting "to get out" of her coffin but being "held" back—before arriving at a paradoxical conclusion; and in "I'm sorry for the Dead," she is concerned about "seeming" and "wondering" and ends with a negative question. And yet these poems, too, implicitly question the time's excessive profit- and market-orientedness, and include a sense of the imperfection and transitoriness of a seemingly harmonious agrarian idyll. They are reluctant without being inconclusive: for all their sense of the paradoxical character of human existence in nature, Dickinson's regional poems suggest a preference for mutual human-nature relations in which people are attuned to the land they work and view nature as an autonomous realm rather than a passive entity.

Nostalgia

A peculiar feature of the reluctant farm narratives Dickinson tells in her New England poems is an element of nostalgia, a sentimental longing for a supposedly ideal past often viewed with suspicion because nostalgia seems both conservative and unsophisticated.[3] However, nostalgia is not per se reactionary. As Linda Hutcheon has written in "Irony, Nostalgia, and the Postmodern," it "can be made to 'happen' by (and to) anyone of any political persuasion" (qtd. in Scanlan 4), and Sean Scanlan emphasizes nostalgia's "various links to memory, history, affect, media, and the marketplace," and its "continuing power":

> In current criticism [. . .] nostalgia as warning, as pejorative marker of certain historical changes, has given way to nostalgia as a more ambivalent, more engaged, critical frame. Now, nostalgia may be a style or design or narrative that serves to comment on how memory works. Rather than an end reaction to yearning, it is understood as a technique for provoking a secondary reaction. (3)

As an inherently ambivalent "technique for provoking a secondary reaction," nostalgia also figures as a force in current environmental debates; according to Donald Worster, "[n]ostalgia runs all through this society—fortunately, for it may be our only hope of salvation" (*The Wealth of Nature* 3). Historically speaking, environmental nostalgia as a mode of critical commentary emerged in the nineteenth century—"the more Americans saw the devastation of forests and wildlife hitherto considered inexhaustible the more nostalgic they began to feel for what historian Donald Worster has called 'a lost pastoral haven'" (Stewart 54). It was in New England that a particular kind of traditionalism first engendered early forms of conservationist and preservationist activism:

> Northern New England, a region of farms, villages, and small cities anchored to an agrarian past by strong family ties, well earned its reputation for traditionalism in the nineteenth century. Yet people immersed in this traditional culture participated enthusiastically in early efforts to protect and sustain their natural resources. Traditionalism, in fact, encouraged this participation. (Judd, *Common Lands, Common People* 264)

A closer look at Dickinson's regional nostalgia from such a perspective helps to see how her backward-oriented accounts of New England farming do not in fact evade modernity but face it, by giving a sense of loss of the past a place in the changing present. While America's dominant narratives of expansionism and industrial development were firmly focused on on the future and environmental debates tried to reconcile a progressive reform rhetoric with the urge to protect at least some "wilderness" spaces, Dickinson's poetry recounts calm stories of the past that resonate as meditations about the transitory character of New England's agrarian setup, human existence, and their place in the natural environment—ambivalent commentaries on former times that develop an energy of their own in a changing present.

One of her very late poems, from 1881, exemplifies how the nostalgia that informs her evocations of "pastures" of the past potentially develops a critical resonance in the present:

> A faded Boy – in sallow Clothes
> Who drove a lonesome Cow
> To pastures of Oblivion –
> A statesman's Embryo –
>
> The Boys that whistled are extinct –
> The Cows that fed and thanked
> Remanded to a Ballad's Barn
> Or Clover's Retrospect – (Fr1549)

These two quatrains are a sentimental reverie for an agrarian idyll in which people allegedly related to nature in trouble-free, harmonious, one-on-one relationships. Instead of one of the more clearly utilitarian, forceful agricultural activities such as plowing or haying, the speaker remembers a boy taking care of a cow, the two mirroring each other in their oblivious and peaceful way of simply being on the land. The miniature story of "Cows that fed and thanked" further emphasizes an individualized relationship between humans and livestock and a certain mutuality, endowing nonhuman beings with a certain communicative agency. Yet even before the second stanza declares this paradisiacal world "extinct," a sense of transitoriness informs the scene, in the "fading," the loneliness, and the "sallow" clothes (a yellowish green that according to *Webster's* denotes both a pale sickliness and the color of hay), as well as in the way the boy seems to drive the cow and himself out of the picture. This is another Dickinson poem about New England's changing agrarian culture whose central stories are of the past, and whose "moral," should there be one, is not fully spelled out. While the speaker's dreamy reminiscence suggests a yearning for those bygone days, the image of a boy as "statesman's Embryo" also naturalizes the transformation as one of growing up rather than dying.

What distinguishes this piece from Dickinson's other New England poems is its more direct interest in the cultural functions of such nostalgia. The world this poem evokes may be irrevocably "extinct," but its stories have been "Remanded to a Ballad's Barn / Or Clover's Retrospect – ," rescued from the "pastures of Oblivion" and given a place in her poem. The ballad is an ancient lyric form with a prominent narrative quality, a poem or song meant to transmit a culture's historical events to future generations; it is also associated with oral traditions rather than professionalism, and with remoter regions rather than centers of power.[4] In a structurally similar manner, "Barn" and "clover" in an agrarian economy evoke the common storing of a year's harvest to sustain people throughout the coming winter and provide seeds for the new fields in spring. A "ballad" that functions like a "barn": Dickinson creates a curious, self-reflexive figure here for her New England poetry that remembers stories of the region's supposedly idyllic agrarianism for whatever they may contain for later generations. In particular, her "Ballad's Barn" serves as a poignant image for her peculiar brand of environmental nostalgia as potential poetic nourishment for a changing future.

A brief look at the presence of nostalgia in the writings of contemporary conservationists further highlights its cultural resonances in her work. Thoreau was among those who most vocally expressed the era's sense of loss, and occasionally turned to nostalgia when writing about a well-balanced economy of wild and cultivated land, hard work and joy. For instance, after celebrating the wild apple as an incarnation of that harmony, he lamented: "The era of the Wild Apple will soon be past. It is a fruit which will probably become extinct in New England. [. . .] I fear that he who walks over these fields a century hence will not know the pleasure of knocking off wild apples. Ah, poor man, there are many pleasures which he will not know!" ("Wild Apples" 466). After a biblical warning about the coming days of doom, the passage culminates in his suggestion of communal parks to protect at least a few remnants of uncultivated space. Where Lance Newman stresses that Thoreau, instead of lapsing into nostalgia, offered an organic utopia (67), I would point out that such a move beyond nostalgia remains contingent upon its recognition. Read together with Dickinson's work, Thoreau's text shows how her New England poems, too, convey a sense of loss as they take "a backward look" at an agricultural system whose human-nature relationships were characterized by a certain degree of mutuality and that was on the verge of becoming history. But they remain decidedly oblique about the broader implications of those sentimental memories, let alone their possible cultural function as a motor of change.

In several of her poems, then, Emily Dickinson points beyond occasionally coy, largely poetological statements about "The Products of [her] Farm" (Fr1036), and relates culturally specific episodes of New England's changing agricultural setup. This narrative element of her regional work can be productively read against conservationist publications of the time insofar as they, too, are interested in stories that reveal the growing conflicts in the wake of such major economic shifts and explore a range of possible responses. Yet although Dickinson's poems draw from a culture of farm-related storytelling, nowhere does she formulate the ethical imperative of any one superior narrative, not even the ambivalent concept of human stewardship. Apart from this reluctant narrativity that sidesteps the urge to resolve the dilemma of humans as both part of creation and in a position to use it, her poems about farmers' toils and triumphs, and about impending change and death, try to make sense of shifting human-nature relations by turning backward, expressing not only ambivalence but also nostalgia in regard to the region's peculiar forms of agrarianism. Such a perspective need not be reactionary; it can be "conservative" in the sense that it seeks to preserve memories of the practices and sensibilities of a rural subsistence culture within a rapidly changing economy. Joan Iverson Nassauer recently has argued:

> As we confront the limitations of our ecological knowledge, *we need to know conservatively in the landscape*, saving every possible remnant of remaining indigenous ecosystems even if we cannot anticipate all of their potential values. Similarly, we are wise to observe what we can about indigenous ecosystems and *imitate these observable properties when we construct and maintain the landscape where we live.* (77; emphasis in original)

If ecocentrism is not a viable option for a modern industrial economy, a modified utilitarianism that remains humble enough to "confront the limitations" of human knowledge and to pay attention to and preserve aspects of the land's history might be part of a possible alternative. In this sense, Dickinson's New England poems preserve the memory not so much of ideal, sustainable practices as of subject positions that unsettle the totalizing vision of human dominion over the earth. Viewed differently, even her relative reluctance to talk at all about New England farming, compared to her much more numerous poems on small and local nature, can be linked to such a "conservatism." When New England was on its way to becoming one of the country's most industrialized regions, Dickinson's prominent interest in undomesticated forests, wildflowers, and insects performed an equally "nostalgic" countermove.

6

"Clearing the ground for broad humanity"

Whitman's Affirmative Regional Narratives

Whitman's *Specimen Days*, the unconventional story of his life that is also a narrative of America as a diverse geographical place and contested economic terrain, contains a passage that responds to what his contemporaries had to say about the West as a natural place and means of production:

> Speaking generally as to the capacity and sure future destiny of that plain and prairie area (larger than any European kingdom) it is the inexhaustible land of wheat, maize, wool, flax, coal, iron, beef and pork, butter and cheese, apples and grapes—land of ten million virgin farms—to the eye at present wild and unproductive—yet experts say that upon it when irrigated may easily be grown enough wheat to feed the world. Then as to scenery (giving my own thought and feeling,) while I know the standard claim is that Yosemite, Niagara falls, the upper Yellowstone and the like, afford the greatest natural shows, I am not so sure but the Prairies and Plains, while less stunning at first sight, last longer, fill the esthetic sense fuller, precede all the rest, and make North America's characteristic landscape. (*CPCP* 864)

This seemingly casual reappraisal of the prairies as "North America's characteristic landscape" shows Whitman engaging with the discussions of his time about shifting regional identities, discussions in which economic developments were increasingly linked to environmental concerns. His lines acknowledge voices that value regions as sources of economic growth as well as those that appreciate their distinct "natural shows"; "experts" interested in improved agricultural management as well as others who emphasize the need to protect undomesticated areas; religiously infused notions about America's "destiny" as well as personal "thoughts and feelings" about nature's aesthetic qualities. This passage is noteworthy not only because it displays Whitman's awareness of such debates, but also because it presents the dominant cultural narrative of "wild and unproductive" lands of "inexhaustible" resources whose "sure future" it is to be turned into "ten million virgin farms" in ways that recognize and reproduce this narrative's power and persuasiveness regarding an alternative narrative of people who prefer a more moderate approach to cultivating the West and engage in wilderness protection. In a number of poems, Whitman similarly brings together narrative elements that echo his culture's debates about viewing nature primarily as an economic resource or primarily as an ecological entity worthy of protection, using the generic possibilities of poetry to more fully sound out the ethical implications of this conflict. Rather than simply condoning the ruthless domination of nature, his poetry affirms the shaping power of certain utilitarian narratives, as well as the difficulty of alternative stories to develop a similar force.

On a more general level, this passage from *Specimen Days* is also noteworthy as an example of Whitman's investment in America's distinct regions. While much of his work was directed against the pull of exclusive regional identifications, and his 1855 preface urged that "[t]he American bard shall [. . .] not be for the eastern states more than the western or the northern states more than the southern" (*LG* 1855, 625–26), the recognition of regional differences constitutes a prerequisite for his ideal "great aggregate Nation" ("A Backward Glance," *CPCP* 668), a counterbalance that helps to ground his continental perspective in concrete places. That Whitman's poetry affirms the diversity of America's "contemporary lands" even as it tries to transcend regional affiliations is a cornerstone of his environmental poetry. When America's regions were taking shape as *the* Northeast, *the* South, and *the* West in the national imagination, *Leaves of Grass* talks about regional forms of production and the resulting frictions without turning "northerly wilds," "prairies wide," and southern "fields of rice" into mutually exclusive enclaves whose geographic and historical conditions determine more or less environmentally sensitive human-nature relations. Rather, his regional poetry highlights different manifestations of the basic conflict between the views of nature-as-resource and nature-as-value, affirming these conflicts as part of the American story.

While Whitman's regional poems have not been discussed together, several studies of his northeastern, western, and southern poetry are crucial for my rereading of his regional work in terms of the environmental politics of the time. Regarding the Northeast, commonly understood as the place of origin for Whitman's entire oeuvre,[1] M. Jimmie Killingsworth's *Walt Whitman and the Earth* discusses Whitman as a local and regional poet whose bioregionalism informs his ecological "island poetics" and is linked synecdochically to national and global issues, while also comparing his island poems to an agrarian pastoralism. For the South, critics such as Andrew Hudgins and Deborah Kolb have focused on how Whitman's views of the region's geographies were shaped by political convictions; my own essay "Managing the Wilderness: Walt Whitman's Southern Landscapes" begins to explore the environmental implications of his southern poetry. For the West, Killingsworth's monograph discusses the representation of the land's exploitation in "Pioneers! O Pioneers!" and "Song of the Redwood-Tree," while Ed Folsom's essays on the prairies show how for Whitman the West's democratic import was linked to specific ideas about nature conservation and Gay Wilson Allen's "How Emerson, Thoreau, and Whitman Viewed the Frontier" analyzes Whitman's interest in exploiting western resources in environmentally insightful ways. Also relevant here is the Whitman chapter in Cecelia Tichi's *New World, New Earth,* which reads "Song of the Broad-Axe" and "Song of the Redwood Tree" in the context of conservationism's ideal of civilizing nature as a way to ensure social progress (155), stressing that Whitman leaves this rhetoric of controlling nature largely unchallenged—against which I would argue that overall, his regional poetry does take issue with this anthropocentric and utilitarian stance, affirming it only after testing its power against alternative stories. My aim here is not to excuse or justify Whitman's poetic choices, but to suggest their complex functions in the environmentalist contexts of the second half of the nineteenth century, also and especially in terms of their references to culturally productive narrative patterns. Rather than fully condoning or directly challenging exploitative attitudes, his poems offer rather discriminating accounts of human-nature interactions and thus respond to the eco-ethical dilemma of knowingly abusing creation in the interest of human progress.

Such a regionalism differs in scope and function from Emily Dickinson's occasional turns toward New England's agriculture. Similar to her harvest poems, however, Whitman's poems about fishing around Long Island, felling western redwoods, and the conspicuous stillness of southern swamps include clusters of narrativity that refer to some of the same conflicting stories that conservationists and preservationists were evoking in their publications as well, a connection that also invests Whitman's irritating celebrations of nature's exploitation with fresh meaning. Unlike Dickinson, Whitman recounts stories of nature's domination in ways that affirm their basic utilitarianism yet do not leave this utilitarianism undisputed. When conservationists and preservationists responded to the ruthless exploitation of nature by juxtaposing the idea of America's manifest destiny with alternative principles—from nature's management to wilderness preservation—his poems can be read as attempts to deal with the continuing hold of narratives of control on the American imagination, affirming the irresolvable tensions they created in a context in which ideas of human-nature reciprocity were beginning to gain momentum.

The Northeast

Several of Whitman's major poems about natural places focus on the Northeast; the chapter on his local landscape poetry has shown how his mediations between human agency and nature's autonomy in places on and around Long Island make for some of the most stirring expressions of environmental humility in his oeuvre. Yet his northeastern poetry also moves beyond individual encounters with local landscapes, exploring people's collective modes of making economic use of the region. His Northeast is an area of "coal and iron" ("Our Old Feuillage"), the place of "New-England's farms" ("A Twilight Song"), and, most often, the "Land of boatmen and sailors! fishermen's land!" ("Starting from Paumanok"); as such it is a significant economic site.

Whitman wrote about a Northeast of farming, hunting, and fishing when not only its agriculture but also its marine industries were changing considerably. Up until the 1840s and 1850s, fishing had been central to New England's economy, but overfishing, pollution, and a network of dams led to a sharp decline in the population of native fish. Moreover, the whaling industry began to dwindle during the Civil War, not only because new materials were replacing whale products, but also because excessive hunting had severely decimated many whale populations.[2] Such changes caused Thoreau to spend long sections of his *A Week on the Concord and Merrimack Rivers* deploring the impact of dams on the region's fish, while Marsh urged in *Man and Nature* that "[Man] has already exterminated at least one marine warm-blooded animal—Steller's sea cow—and the walrus, the sea lion, and other large amphibia, as well as the principal fishing quadrupeds, are in imminent danger of extinction" (105). Marsh also emphasized the particular fragility of aquatic environments:

> Man has hitherto hardly anywhere produced such climatic or other changes as would suffice of themselves totally to banish the wild inhabi-

> tants of the dry land [. . .]. But almost all the processes of agriculture, and of mechanical and chemical industry, are fatally destructive to aquatic animals. (107)

Set side by side with such publications, Whitman's lyrical embrace of the Northeast's flurry of economic activities becomes legible as a perplexing but nonetheless highly perceptive environmental commentary. Where Dickinson's accounts of New England farming remain skeptical toward her region's economic practices, his northeastern poems and passages contain narrative elements that face the ethical dilemma of human existence in nature by probing the irresistible attractions of controlling the world.

The 1860 poem "A Song of Joys" is usually read as a weaker reiteration of *Song of Myself* that celebrates "the vitality and variety of the American experience" as a national experience (Diedrich 653). But it is also a poem about the area between Manhattan and Chesapeake Bay, its workers, landscapes, and products, and indirectly responds to industrialism's negative impact on these lands and waters by way of narrative segments about the paradoxical pleasures of the unbridled domination of nature, pleasures that are so profound that they cannot be checked even by increasing ethical concern.

Right at the beginning, the speaker moves from a cursory regard for nature's unique characteristics ("the voices of animals") and an appreciation of its economic riches ("grain and trees") to a long celebration of the thrills of people's "resistless" power (including "the horseman's and horsewoman's" joys of force and speed; *LG* 150). While this poetic tour de force full of exclamation marks and expressive "O"s suggests that such "common" joys are legitimate because they affirm human existence, the "merry shrieks" over such "maddening" pleasures already indicate that they are on the verge of becoming excessive and uncontainable. Against this overall affirmation, the speaker also softens the joy of being "conscious of power" through the alternative "joy of that vast elemental sympathy," and "the joy of increase, growth, recuperation" through the "joy of soothing and pacifying, the joy of concord and harmony" (*LG* 150). Ultimately, however, he undermines such binaries, as "recuperation" is a part of the joys of "growth," and the "soothing and pacifying" respond to such excesses without undoing or reversing them.

Apart from this prelude, "A Song of Joys" includes two passages that evoke more detailed stories of people's "employments," the ethical frictions caused by their "joyful" mastery of nature, and the "maddening" intractability of these tensions. First, Whitman unfolds a reminiscence of youthful clam fishing:

> O to have been brought up on bays, lagoons, creeks, or along the coast,
> To continue and be employ'd there all my life,
> The briny and damp smell, the shore, the salt weeds exposed at low water,
> The work of fishermen, the work of the eel-fisher and clam-fisher;
> I come with my clam-rake and spade, I come with my eel-spear,
> Is the tide out? I join the group of clam-diggers on the flats,
> I laugh and work with them, I joke at my work like a mettlesome young man;
> In winter I take my eel-basket and eel-spear and travel out on foot on the ice
> – I have a small axe to cut holes in the ice [. . .].
>
> Another time in warm weather out in a boat, to lift the lobster-pots where they are sunk with heavy stones, (I know the buoys,)
> O the sweetness of the Fifth-month morning upon the water as I row just before sunrise toward the buoys,
> I pull the wicker pots up slantingly, the dark green lobsters are desperate with their claws as I take them out, I insert wooden pegs in the joints of their pincers,
> I go to all the places one after another, and then row back to the shore,
> There in a huge kettle of boiling water the lobsters shall be boil'd till their color becomes scarlet. (*LG* 150–51)

This section conjoins the joys of nature's beauty with those of human control, whose conflict is increased by the centrality of the lobsters' desperation. The way in which this report of boiling animals alive—one of the more violent aspects of hunting and fishing—remains overall expressive of human "joys" can be productively compared to a passage from *Walden*, where Thoreau remembers how he "caught a glimpse of a woodchuck stealing across [his] path, and felt a strange thrill of savage delight, and was strongly tempted to seize and devour him raw," reflecting upon this moment as follows:

> The wildness and adventure that are in fishing still recommended it to me. I like sometimes to take rank hold on life and spend my day more as the animals do. Perhaps I have owed to this employment and to hunting, when quite young, my closest acquaintance with Nature. They early introduce us to and detain us in scenery with which otherwise, at that age, we should have little acquaintance. Fishermen, hunters, woodchoppers, and others, spending their lives in the fields and woods, in a peculiar sense a part of

> Nature themselves, are often in a more favorable mood for observing her, in the intervals of their pursuits, than philosophers or poets even, who approach her with expectation. (141)

Thoreau's woodchuck remains as abstract as the "thrill of savage delight" to which he does not yield, and the ethical conflict of his story is first relegated to a collective, professional level and then resolved by integrating it into an overall pattern of a life close to nature that increases people's environmental sensibilities. One could also say that Thoreau attempts to reconcile here the domineering approach of manifest destiny and the paradisiacal harmony of nature's nation. The difference, it seems to me, is not that Whitman leaves people's violence against nature unchallenged, but that he faces more directly the disconcerting thought that fishing may be pleasurable because of the brutal control it involves, and that he does not sublimate or try to otherwise resolve the conflict, even though the narrative structure implies such a progression.

In a second passage, lines on the "joys" of warfare lead to a dramatic "story" of whaling, symbolically linking the two (which is itself interesting, considering Marsh's complaint in *Man and Nature* that man leads "an almost indiscriminate warfare upon all the forms of animal and vegetable existence around him" and "gradually eradicates or transforms every spontaneous product" of nature [40]):

> O the whaleman's joys! O I cruise my old cruise again!
> I feel the ship's motion under me, I feel the Atlantic breezes fanning me,
> I hear the cry again sent down from the mast-head, There – she blows!
> Again I spring up the rigging to look with the rest – we descend, wild with excitement,
> I leap in the lower'd boat, we row toward our prey where he lies,
> We approach stealthy and silent, I see the mountainous mass, lethargic, basking,
> I see the harpooneer standing up, I see the weapon dart from his vigorous arm;
> O swift again far out in the ocean the wounded whale, settling, running to windward, tows me,
> Again I see him rise to breathe, we row close again,
> I see a lance driven through his side, press'd deep, turn'd in the wound,
> Again we back off, I see him settle again, the life is leaving him fast,
> As he rises he spouts blood, I see him swim in circles narrower and narrower, swiftly cutting the water – I see him die,

> He gives one convulsive leap in the centre of the circle, and then falls flat and still in the bloody foam. (*LG* 152)

Whitman's speaker is both an experiencing "I" and a witness here, immersed in the scene while standing apart from and thus ready to comment on it. Yet as he reports on the whalers' excitement and their fearful joy in the wounded animal, while registering the death struggle and killing, there is again no resolution or moral judgment—at a cultural moment when whaling was becoming a topic of contention, but not in terms of ethical reservations in regard to the individual animal. A chapter by Marsh on the "Destruction of Fish," for instance, details how "human agency has [. . .] produced great changes in the population of the sea, the lakes, and the rivers" (99) and how the "demand for oil and whalebone [. . .] has stimulated the pursuit of the 'hugest of living creatures' to such activity that he has now almost wholly disappeared from many favorite fishing grounds" (100). Still, Marsh is mainly interested in improved management:

> There are many sterile or wornout soils in Europe so situated that they might, at no very formidable cost, be converted into permanent lakes, which would serve not only as reservoirs to retain the water of winter rains and snow, and give it out in the dry season for irrigation, but as breeding ponds for fish, and would thus, without further cost, yield a larger supply of human food. (104–5)

In the light of such attempts to alleviate anthropogenic environmental disturbances by improved human schemes, Whitman's lines can certainly be charged with repeating the violence they note. But they also emphasize what remains subliminal in Marsh's text—the "maddening" joys of the power to dominate nature, which play into both the excessive destruction of nature and conservationist attempts at environmental reform.

That Whitman's poem indeed implies such ethical concern is suggested by two gloomier passages tucked away among its largely affirmative sections. At one point, after the speaker imaginatively chases fish that "seem to fill the water for miles," he expresses awareness of some moral dilemma:

> (O something pernicious and dread!
> Something far away from a puny and pious life!
> Something unproved! something in a trance!
> Something escaped from the anchorage and driving free.) (*LG* 151–52)

This evocation of "something pernicious and dread," while directly linked to the fishing narrative yet typographically bracketed, acknowledges "some" destructive urge as part of humankind's way of being in the world and implies that ethical concern may not be able to prevent excess—which is not cynical, or a simple embrace of such excess, but a paradoxically humble gesture of affirming the irresolvable conflict of our human existence in nature. The speaker again comes close to offering a moral commentary when he expresses a double desire "To lead America – to quell America with a great tongue" (*LG* 153). Wynn Thomas has claimed that this phrase encapsulates Whitman's "obscure unease at the kind of society he saw developing all around him" after the Civil War (6), which, in my view, also includes the excess of nature's subjugation that remained largely unchecked in spite of a growing awareness of its irreversible damages. The speaker who wants to "quell America" proceeds to face the ambivalence of the human-nature interactions he has reported:

> Yet O my soul supreme!
> Know'st thou the joys of pensive thought?
> Joys of the free and lonesome heart, the tender, gloomy heart?
> Joys of the solitary walk, the spirit bow'd yet proud, the suffering and the struggle?
> The agonistic throes, the ecstasies, joys of the solemn musings day or night?
> Joys of the thought of Death, the great spheres Time and Space? (*LG* 154)

Circling back to the poem's opening, a "supreme" soul is checked here by "tenderness" and "gloom," by conflicting "ecstasies" and "joys," and, especially, by a "spirit bow'd yet proud." In other words, the humbling acknowledgment of one's failings will forever be challenged by the proud longing for omnipotence that is impossible to "quell," which is how the poem ends: "To be indeed a God!" (*LG* 155). As such, "A Song of Joys" also indirectly engages the story of creation, which conservationists were often alluding to in order to show what happens when people reject the constraint implied in God's verdict that humans shall "toil" in a land of "thorns and thistles" (Gen. 3:17 [King James Version]). Through its emphasis on the joys of controlling nature, Whitman's poem enacts the human yearning for an end to scarcity (a whale, in particular, suggests a paradisiacal wealth of usable materials) while also facing the negative consequences involved in the project of creating a New Earth, rethinking our human hubris in ways that point toward an eco-ethical problem.

Turning here to Dickinson's New England poetry further clarifies the environmental implications of such a perspective. Compared to Dickinson's often nostalgic accounts of old-fashioned farming, Whitman deals more directly with the Northeast's intensifying exploitation, and read against her sensitive accounts of some of the "insane" tensions involved in working the land, his emphasis on rather drastic aspects of nature's distress, and on people's powerful fixation on being in control, seems more audacious. Yet the juxtaposition also suggests that if there is a legitimate joy in momentarily overcoming nature for economic reasons, the farmer's "animalistic" obsession with profits and the ecstatic joys of whaling may be equivalent expressions of the same ethical friction, caused by a human urge to be in command of nature that may be impossible to "quell."

The West

Whitman's poetry is often understood to have moved from east to west, paralleling his culture's historical expansion. This orientation is largely grounded in Whitman's fascination with the West's natural features, both as symbol and as the material basis for a diverse national future. But in his celebrations of the "the dominion-heart of America" where the "main social, political, spine-character of the States" will soon be settled as a "giant growth" ("Democratic Vistas," *CPCP* 951–52), accounts of how the region is used economically are so prominent that they leave comparatively little room for a nonutilitarian recognition of its characteristics. For an environmental discussion of his western poetry, it is helpful to note that when Whitman began to work on *Leaves of Grass*, the idea that at least some of the West's unspoiled natural features should be preserved was still an exception—James Russell Lowell's article "Humanity to Trees" (1857) was far ahead of its time—and that even in the 1870s, when Whitman wrote "Song of the Redwood Tree," this discussion was just about to gain momentum. John Muir began to publish essays on the need to legally protect Yosemite in 1871, but his work developed a popular impact only in the 1880s and 1890s, together with Marsh's "urgent plea to consider the forests" (Tyrrell 19) and the 1890 census report about the West's "dwindling supplies of timber and arable land" (Gottlieb 54). In a time of such change, Whitman's poetry takes up the ideological pressures of the national narrative of manifest destiny, in the form of unsettling "stories" of a broad cultural myopia in regard to its destructive impact.

"Song of the Redwood Tree," first published in *Harper's Magazine* in 1873, has long been criticized for its "maddening" embrace of America's dominant frontier mentality (Allen, "How Emerson, Thoreau, and Whitman Viewed the Frontier" 126). Gay Wilson Allen, in particular, has juxtaposed Whitman's apparent belief in an inexhaustible nature with Emerson's urge to find a balance with nature and Thoreau's frontier skepticism, and M. Wynn Thomas has read the poem as "unintentional propaganda" and a crude "attempt to justify, even to incite, indiscriminate felling" (137–39). M. Jimmie Killingsworth's work is particularly important here because he considers this "most reprehensible poem" ("The Voluptuous Earth" 22) as an example for how abstraction and distance can allow "the nature-as-object view to drift toward the nature-as-resource ideology" (*Whitman and the Earth* 64); he develops a compelling reading of the poem's problematic implications grounded in Whitman's combination of personification, conventional poetic language, and discourses of environmental racism (69–71). However, several contextual readings have drawn further attention to the poem's unexpected nuances. Diane Kirk's Ph.D. dissertation, "Landscapes of Old Age in Walt Whitman's Later Poetry," provides a survey of shifting scientific debates, arguing that Whitman modeled his poem after Asa Gray's 1872 idea of the redwoods' "natural" disappearance rather than Muir's 1876 call for their preservation, while also claiming that it is less a California poem than a "landscape image of human aging" (10–29). James Perrin Warren's "Contexts for Reading 'Song of the Redwood-Tree'" links the poem to Whitman's old age, Gray's theory of gradual modification, Muir's spiritual positions, and *Harper's Magazine*'s socially and politically rather uncritical publishing policy (to help explain the poem's anthropocentric evolutionism). And while Steven Blakemore and Jon Noble's "Whitman and 'the Indian Problem': The Texts and Contexts of 'Song of the Redwood-Tree'" reads the poem against the precarious situation of both redwoods and Native Americans in nineteenth-century California, as an attempt to "absorb" both and thus grant them a presence in his poetry, Linda Furgerson Selzer's "Walt Whitman, Clarence Major, and Changing Thresholds of American Wonder" shows how the poem manages to link the time's fascination with technological progress with discourses of natural wonder. My point here is that Whitman also takes up his culture's diverging views about western nature in the form of narrative elements that echo certain patterns of meaning making that environmentalists were also using then, and that the poem ultimately acknowledges the ethical conflicts inherent in these stories as constitutive of American culture.

In "Song of the Redwood Tree," in which the speaker professes to hear a tree's death song while the woodsmen remain oblivious, the tree's life story forms the poem's most perplexing narrative strand. In being felled, one representative redwood offers something akin to a narrative life review, and reports, in two long, italicized passages, that for him and his brothers "time has ended" and "term has come," that they now "leave the field" for a "superber race," and dedicate to them "these areas entire, lands of the Western shore," with "Nature's calm content" and even "with tacit huge delight" (LG 174–75; italics removed). Critics have expressed incredulity at this rhetorical move to have the "mighty dying tree" gladly acquiesce in his own demise so as to make room for an invading white human race. Thomas has stressed that Whitman turns one of his most touching poetic strategies, letting nature speak on its own behalf, into a "propaganda trick" (139) for manifest destiny; Killingsworth has juxtaposed this use of personification with that of "Out of the Cradle" and "Lilacs," suggesting that the poet assumes too much identity with the trees here, turning himself into their "privileged spokesperson" (*Whitman and the Earth* 66).[3] But the tree's life story also contains a counternarrative that belies the dominant "story" that he and his brother trees abdicate willingly. As the speaking tree reviews the redwoods' long history of living in place (close to the "neighboring waters" and "these skies and airs, these mountain peaks, Shasta, Nevadas, / These huge precipitous cliffs, this amplitude, these valleys, far Yosemite"; *LG* 175), he characterizes his own species as "perennial" and "hardy"—botanical terms that according to the midcentury *Webster's* also mean "perpetual; unceasing; never failing" and "bold; brave; stout; daring; resolute; intrepid," as well as "stubborn to excess," which makes their embrace of a sudden death unconvincing. Moreover, he goes over the trees' lives as having been full of "venerable and innocent joys" and "great patient rugged joys" and explicitly invests his own kind with subjectivity—"(For know I bear the soul befitting me, I too have consciousness, identity, / And all the rocks and mountains have, and all the earth,)"—which is especially interesting if one considers that he uses a negative construction ("Nor yield we mournfully majestic brothers"; *LG* 174), as if the trees do not concur with the master narrative of their willing abdication. Killingsworth finds that Whitman allows "the spirit of the redwood to speak in human language only long enough to bless the people who destroy the very life of the forest" (*Whitman and the Earth* 71), but I would stress that the tree's "story" alludes to the cultural scheme of America's manifest destiny in slightly more ambivalent ways, including elements that strain against such cooptation.

It has been variously pointed out that in the years before and after the poem's publication, there were two opposing views about how the expanding nation should relate to these ancient trees. In 1872, the authoritative botanist Asa Gray developed the misleading theory of "natural erosion," which was so influential that even John Muir admitted to having shared it initially (see Kirk 20–21). Passages in Gray's speech, however, indicate that he was aware that the trees were not disappearing "naturally" but as the result of wasteful lumbering methods (Kirk 22), and Muir had already started publishing pleas to save the redwoods in 1871, presenting alternative data in 1876 (Kirk 20). In 1874, when Whitman published his poem, George Perkins Marsh added several lines to his *Man and Nature* that highlight this confusion and show how difficult it was even for prominent conservationist and preservationist thinkers to confront the devastating environmental consequences of the large-scale cutting of the redwoods, or try to change these practices:

> California fortunately still preserves her magnificent sequoias, which rise to the height of three hundred feet, and sometimes, as we are assured, even to three hundred and sixty and four hundred feet, and she has also pines and cedars of scarcely inferior dimensions. The public being now convinced of the importance of preserving these colossal trees, it is very probable that the fear of their total destruction may prove groundless, and we may still hope that some of them may survive even till that distant future when the skill of the forester shall have raised from their seeds a progeny as lofty and as majestic as those which now exist. (333–34)

Marsh tells a story here about certain misconceptions that led to fearful results, were corrected when it was almost too late, and are slowly making room for new convictions that may give reason for fresh hope in the future. Whether Marsh refers to ruthless logging practices or to the spurious biological theories that seemed to justify them, his report indirectly questions the idea of the rightful exploitation of nature while leaving an overall utilitarian perspective intact. Instead of charging Whitman with environmental chauvinism, or exempting him from such charges, I am referring to this context here to suggest that his decision to have the redwoods use their voice to willingly renounce their lives, while also allowing them to recall their own history so that this renunciation becomes unconvincing, does not, as it is sometimes argued (see Thomas 140), have to signify a failure of poetic imagination. Rather, taking place before the controversy over Gray's theory was resolved, Whitman's rhetorical move can also be read as a response to the ideological pressures to make the trees' demise fit snugly into a nationalist, utilitarian framework. That his trees themselves almost, but not fully, give in to this pressure is perhaps not so much detestable as painful, as it faces the ethical dimension of a debate that was firmly grounded in an anthropocentric fascination with scientific explanations and improved economic schemes.

The second narrative strand that plays into this poem is that of American settlers moving westward and becoming a superior human race in the process, a "story" told here by the speaker in his own voice and in his paraphrase of the redwood's song. These new men are mainly represented by a vanguard of "choppers," "quick-ear'd teamsters and chain and jackscrew men" with "strong arms," whose felling of the trees clears the space for "many a thrifty farm, with machinery, / And wool and wheat and the grape, and diggings of yellow gold." But again, the poem does not simply justify or idealize the process, since the narrative of the woodsmen also pulls in a different direction. The forest workers are dwarfed by the trees' towering physicality; they do not hear the redwood's song (although they are "quick-ear'd" when it comes to work calls); and, unlike the trees, they remain largely silent. And while they supposedly prepare the way for others who "come from Nature's long and harmless throes, peacefully builded thence," their felling of the trees "[w]ith crackling blows of axes [. . .] / Riven deep by the sharp tongues" is a brutal rather than "harmless" or "peaceful" process, especially compared to the trees own "innocent joys." These men may be only harbingers of "the new culminating man [. . .] promis'd long" (*LG* 175), whose supremacy is merely stated, but the fact that they are such shadowy creatures, unable or unwilling to register the trees' majestic history reinforces the ethical dilemma on which America's future rests.[4]

In the late-nineteenth-century context, such a "story" of oblivious woodsmen recalls a sobering passage in Thoreau's *The Maine Woods* that follows the slaughter of a moose: "This afternoon's experience suggested to me how base or coarse are the motives which commonly carry men into the wilderness. The explorers and lumberers generally are all hirelings, paid so much a day for their labor, and as such they have no more love for wild nature than wood-sawyers have for forests" (683–84). Thoreau here revises his earlier idea that "[f]ishermen, hunters, woodchoppers" are "in a more favorable mood for observing" nature (*Walden* 141), mourning the loss of their and his own innocence and blaming the woodsmen for their lowly motives. Whitman, by contrast, not only provides a more direct presence for the killing, but also skips Thoreau's direct criticism of such "hirelings." That "Song of the Redwood-Tree" stays away from overt moral judgment does not have to mean that the older Whitman was lagging behind Thoreau in terms of environmental sensibilities, as Thomas and Allen have argued. It may well indicate that he acknowledges the economic pressures of America's manifest destiny by enacting its numbing effects, on the poet himself as well. Turning to the frontier West, Whitman confronts the environmental myopia on which the national story of manifest destiny must be based and which it also engenders.

Finally, these two narrative strands are represented by a poet who himself plays an ambivalent role. He is the one who turns the tree's song into a dedication to an expanding nation, but he is also a sensitive witness who registers the redwoods' ecological presence (their "myriad leaves," "lofty top rising two hundred feet high," "stalwart trunk and limbs," and "foot-thick bark"), who "plainly" hears what the woodsmen do not (including the dying tree's "murmuring, fateful giant voice" and "the crash, the muffled shriek, the groan"), and who, in noting the scene's violence, appears to be yearning to be absolved from guilt. Killingsworth links the "undercurrent of guilt and grieving" to a "return of the repressed," mainly in terms of the fate of Native Americans, and finds that the "unquiet" the speaker feels regarding nature's otherness is not very profound or arresting (*Whitman and the Earth* 66, 71). But as a poet interested in the West as an economic region, he has to stay in control, much like the woodsmen, or, in fact, anybody intending to live off the land. The eco-ethical problem Whitman turns to here is that in using nature as a resource, the ideological pressures of this perspective must momentarily override the sensibility of nature's being an autonomous realm and an object of aesthetic or spiritual value. Instead of trying to resolve this impossible tension in the present, the speaker relegates it to the future, envisioning a more nature-oriented West "to come":

> But more in you than these, lands of the Western shore,
> (These but the means, the implements, the standing-ground,)
> I see in you, certain to come, the promise of thousands of years, till now
> deferr'd,
> Promis'd to be fulfill'd, our common kind, the race.
> The new society at last, proportionate to Nature

In man of you, more than your mountain peaks or stalwart trees imperial,
In woman more, far more, than all your gold or vines, or even vital air.
(*LG* 176–77)

With such laudable hopes placed in a generation of people who will relate to nature more reciprocally, Whitman still privileges, as Warren has shown, "the human 'promise' more than any natural one," while also "broaden[ing] the terms of his vision, [. . .] which joins the lands and the swarming race" ("Contexts" 175–76). Furthermore, in the later nineteenth century, utilitarian conservationists equally turned toward the future as they envisioned alternatives to the prevailing frontier mentality. Marsh, for example, in his chapter "Restoration of Disturbed Harmonies," characterizes a new generation of American pioneers as follows: "In reclaiming and reoccupying lands laid waste by human improvidence or malice, [. . .] the task of the pioneer settler is of a very different character. He is to become a co-worker with nature in the reconstruction of the damaged fabric which the negligence or the wantonness of former lodgers has rendered untenable" (*Man and Nature* 35). Yet where Marsh embraces responsibility and accountability in ways that point toward a resolution, Whitman's poem acknowledges more fully the dilemma that the destruction of nature in the name of economic progress could only be justified if the emerging society were indeed perfect, but also that even the most "natural" society could never retroactively justify such destruction. The difficulty, if not impossibility, of going beyond an anthropocentric perspective in an overall economic framework may be precisely the point of this poem.

In her discussion of "Song of the Redwood-Tree," Tichi finds that "the demise of the redwood is not treated poignantly or with pity. No aura of regret, ambiguity, or even sadness settles from Whitman's tone" (248); and Allen interprets Whitman's embrace of the exploitation of nature to improve people's standard of living as a sign that he "saw no conflict between man and nature" ("How Emerson, Thoreau, and Whitman Viewed the Frontier" 122). It seems, however, that the opposite might equally be true. The poem faces the conflict of a confident capitalist nation whose ideal is to be "proportionate to Nature," as the speaker claims twice, but whose notion of progress depends on and engenders problematic botanical theories, deaf and dumb workers who subjugate ancient forests, and poets who try to justify a destruction they perceive to be unjustifiable—in short, a whole culture willfully silencing its sympathy. Whitman here engages with the paradox that if the West is the designated heartland of America's progress and a place of magnificent natural beauty, the near-term prospects for its natural environment are bleak. It is the poem's investigation of America's overconfidence in an economic approach to nature that also acknowledges the fallibility of the reigning ideology.

The South

Whitman is not usually considered to be a poet of the American South. Yet from his earliest poetic sketches to his last publications, he kept turning southward and included references to the region in many of his best-known poems. The vital role that the region's natural particulars play in Whitman's poetry complicates widespread notions that the South mattered to him primarily as a site of romantic passion and political conflict.[5] Similar to the the Northeast and the West, the South figures in *Leaves of Grass* as a distinct locale, and more specifically, as a place where people relate to place through their modes of production—as "land of cotton, sugar, rice" ("Starting from Paumanok"), of "mules, cattle, horses," and of "Southern fishermen fishing" ("Our Old Feuillage"). But Whitman's views of the South also complicate his overall representation of American regions as places that are significantly shaped by people's economic activities. The South in *Leaves of Grass* may be the region of "the shad-fishery and the herring-fishery, the large sweep-seines, the windlasses on shore work'd by horses, the clearing, curing, and packing-houses / Deep in the forest in piney woods turpentine dropping from the incisions in the trees, there are the turpentine works" ("Our Old Feuillage"), but the *details* of people's economic engagement with these lands remain largely untold. This omission is as noteworthy in terms of the defining role of slavery for the pre–Civil War southern economy as it is in environmental terms. Read in conjunction with his northeastern and western poems, this absence constitutes another manifestation of the irreconcilable tension between using nature as a resource and being mindful of its inherent value that plays such a significant part in Whitman's regional poetry. Whitman's South is a region where it may be possible to give in to the longing for a relationship with the land that is not dominated by utilitarian interests, but only at the price of momentarily disregarding people's specific modes of production, together with their ethical implications.

In terms of environmental history, the pre– and post–Civil War South that forms the backdrop for Whitman's poetry was a region where neither the exploitation of the land nor the environmental concern that followed in its wake reached the intensity of that in the Northeast and West. In the 1850s, 87 percent of the South was still considered uncultivated (Cowdrey 94), but in the settled areas it was a mixed farming region (Doughty 343), where livestock breeding and monocultures—kept profitable only through the continued, massive exploitation of slaves—led to substantial soil exhaustion and erosion, and where large amounts of fertilizer were used to increase production despite a dramatically declining soil quality. Yet on the whole the environmental onslaught in the South was not as intense as in the Northeast, and not as ideologically charged as in the West. Prior to the Civil War, the South's population numbers and level of industrialization kept the exploitation of nature at a moderate level (Smallwood 333), its forests spared owing to massive cutting in the Northeast (Melosi 318). When in the 1870s and 1880s industrial logging did destroy the region's virgin forests, the situation was in between that of the Northeast, already turned into a wasteland, and the West, which still promised material abundance. In terms of environmental concern, as well, the region lagged behind both the Northeast, the place of origin of American conservationism, and the West, the locus of its most successful activism, because even though erratic efforts at soil conservation in the South dated back to prerevolutionary times, they were difficult to implement, since the majority of white southerners perceived such efforts as infringing on their individual freedom (Smallwood 332–33). Even after the Civil War, as the South contributed "some leaders" who pushed for forest reserves, "the impetus for conservation, like much of the force for exploitation, came from outside the South" (Smallwood 333). At a time of such impending environmental pressures, Whitman's southern poetry does not—as does his poetry on the other regions—access narratives of planting or fishing but stays on the level of calm descriptions of a place whose nature seems to have remained unspoiled by large-scale exploitation. As such, it expresses the yearning to live with nature without irrevocably destroying it—indeed, the need of the imagination for such a place of difference—while the cultural myopia this requires also reveals the impracticability of such a strategy.

"O Magnet-South," written in 1860 and originally titled "Longings for Home," is a poem whose speaker is so overcome by a backward-oriented yearning for his imaginary birthplace that an engagement with the immediate prewar South, politically and geographically, is pushed to the margins. His escapist, dreamlike journey has been read as an exaggerated expression of Whitman's passion for the South, as well as a possible indication of a romantic involvement in New Orleans in 1848; Luke Mancuso has emphasized how the poem's "cultural work of nostalgia for the antebellum heritage" based on slavery served to pacify the South on the verge of war (38). Interestingly, the poem intertwines this impossible longing for a South unmarked by political strife and slavery with a longing for a region equally unmarred by the land's large-scale economic exploitation. If the poem's dominant theme is, as Edward Huffstetler claims, the "irresistible, even mystical, allure the American South has for those who live there, as well as the infamous Southern love of place" ("'O Magnet-South'" 475), this is contingent on turning a blind eye to the political and economic/environmental realities of the region on the eve of the Civil War.

The poem evokes a lush, paradisiacal back country in ways that make the South's economic practices almost invisible. "The grains" merely hints at crops; the exclamation "O the cotton plant! the growing fields of rice, sugar, hemp!" lists the region's characteristic produce without expanding on the modes of production (neither in terms of the slave economy nor in terms of agricultural practices); and the line "A Kentucky corn-field, the tall, graceful, long-leav'd corn, slender, flapping, bright green, with tassels, with beautiful ears each well-sheath'd in its husk" turns to the plants' beauty rather than their economic value. That the poem mentions these crops at all makes a difference, though (such references are often absent in his more locally oriented poetry), because apart from their metaphorical implications—they move from cotton to plants less associated with slavery and signify a border state rather than the Deep South—they also make the absence of more detailed explorations of southern agriculture conspicuous. The same is true for the workers who would be planting or harvesting these crops. The only two people mentioned in the poem are not (any longer) engaged in economic relationships to the land: "(here in these dense swamps the freebooter carries his gun, and the fugitive has his conceal'd hut;)" (*LG* 396). The presence of an adventurer who sustains himself by plundering, and a former slave who has escaped from enforced labor—a fugitive from the systematic exploitation of humans for the systematic exploitation of the land—make the poem's lack of attention to the region's economic system, especially its slave-based farming, more pronounced. In a decade when the South's situation became increasingly difficult politically and, less dramatically, ecologically, the speaker emphasizes "sluggish rivers" and "transparent lakes," a "hummock-land" with "pleasant openings" and "dense forests"—an anachronistic dream of a region that is agrarian in its basic outlook but, miraculously, remains almost completely unmarked by economic perspectives.

In this imaginary region of the past, nature is not just uncontrolled but also largely uncontrollable, especially in the poem's central, extended swamp scene. Narrativity comes into play here mainly as that of the land itself (comparable to the local dynamics in "Out of the Cradle" and "As I Ebb'd" discussed earlier) rather than in terms of people's engagement with it. Whitman's "Magnet-South" is populated by belligerent plants and animals who make any attempt from the outside to enter or control the region impossible:

> The cactus guarded with thorns, the laurel-tree with large white flowers,
> The range afar, the richness and barrenness, the old woods charged with
> mistletoe and trailing moss,
> The piney odor and the gloom, the awful natural stillness,
> (here in these dense swamps the freebooter carries his gun, and the fugitive
> has his conceal'd hut;)
> O the strange fascination of these half-known half-impassable swamps,
> infested by reptiles, resounding with the bellow of the alligator, the sad
> noises of the night-owl and the wild-cat, and the whirr of the rattlesnake,
> [. . .] (*LG* 396)

This place is "rich" yet "barren," not an area of tobacco, rice, and cotton but a "half-known half-impassable" realm whose natural particulars potentially act as aggressively as the armed freebooter. Considering that in the second half of the century, southern logging and mechanized farming began to intensify but were held at bay by the sheer inaccessibility of potentially valuable areas,[6] this naturally fortified place develops a resonance in terms of a South that resists not only political integration but also economic exploitation.

A look at the role that swamps, and southern swamps in particular, played as environmentally potent images around that time further clarifies the poem's environmental implications. Thoreau, for example, frequently turned to swamps when he discussed alternatives to a purely economic outlook:

> Hope and the future for me are not in lawns and cultivated fields, not in towns and cities, but in the impervious and quaking swamps. When, formerly, I have analyzed my partiality for some farm which I had contemplated purchasing, I have frequently found that I was attracted solely by a few square rods of impermeable and unfathomable bog—a natural sink in one corner of it. That was the jewel which dazzled me. I derive more of my

> subsistence from the swamps which surround my native town than from the cultivated gardens in the village. There are no richer parterres to my eyes than the dense beds of dwarf andromeda (*Cassandra calyculata*) which cover these tender places on the earth's surface. [. . .]
>
> Yes, though you may think me perverse, if it were proposed to me to dwell in the neighborhood of the most beautiful garden that ever human art contrived, or else of a Dismal Swamp, I should certainly decide for the swamp. How vain, then, have been all your labors, citizens, for me! ("Walking" 666)

Thoreau's ideal bog is diverse and sensually appealing, but also "impermeable" and "unfathomable," much like the wetland in Whitman's poem. Moreover, with their reference to his neighbors' "lawns and cultivated fields," Thoreau's lines highlight to what extent such a vision of a place uninhibited by economic structures remains framed by precisely such structures. His swamp as a place of difference is dialectically related to the managed fields and forests that engender the yearning for an alternative in the first place, but also make the existence of such protected areas possible because they sustain a growing population in an increasingly industrialized, urbanized society. The same is true for "O Magnet-South," whose speaker returns there from elsewhere, and where a number of briefly mentioned fields guarantee the economic survival of the region. Finally, Thoreau's text also shows how much the idealization of a peculiar area as an isolated outpost of wildness amounts to a specific way of mastering what cannot be otherwise controlled, since he imagines turning a swamp into his backyard and stresses the alternative kind of sustenance he derives from it, thus taming it both conceptually and practically; Whitman's poem delimits and idealizes the South in structurally similar ways.

Yet where Thoreau integrates a sensuous swamp scene into a larger vision of reform, seeing "hope and the future" in a well-balanced middle landscape of cultivated and wild spaces, Whitman's poem focuses on the yearning for such a wild place without attempting to resolve the conflict between using nature as a resource for human consumption and approaching it ethically, as a realm with a right to exist on its own terms. "O Magnet-South" imaginatively "preserves" a clearly demarcated, ecologically diverse area in ways that also show the limitations of such a move. Through its interest in tropical flora and fauna ("the parrots in the woods" and "the papaw-tree and the blossoming titi"), in Native American place names ("the Roanoke, the Savannah, the Altamahaw, the Pedee, the Tombigbee, the Santee, the Coosa and the Sabine"), and in species that would soon be endangered or become extinct (such as American alligators, found exclusively in the South and hunted heavily since frontier times, and parakeets, who were shot as pests and caught as pets, facing extinction toward the end of the nineteenth century; see Melosi 319), together with its atmosphere of "awful stillness," the poem creates a geographical and temporal bubble that ultimately signifies stagnation and death. In an era when the designation of wilderness areas and parks was already being discussed, albeit not yet for the South or for wetlands, Whitman's poem implies that exempting certain areas from necessarily destructive economic development may fulfill our nostalgic desires but is unsuited as a practical implement.[7] As such, the poem turns the South into a site where the expanding industrial nation can project environmental fears and "longings irrepressible" without risking a challenge to its dominant utilitarian outlook. And yet it faces the impossibility of such a move, not so much because agriculture still looms at the margins, but because in spite of nature's vitality and life force in this "Magnet-South," its flora, fauna, and geological features are kept in a "gloomy" state that suggests changelessness, even decay. In the interplay with a heavily exploited Northeast, and the promise of a seemingly boundless West, Whitman's imaginary South becomes something like Joan Iverson Nassauer's "prairie in a garden in a prairie," a relatively undeveloped place within a wider economic unit through which people humbly acknowledge that their schemes can never match nature's complex features. Whitman's southern "wilderness" points both ways: a nostalgic reverie that provides a place for the memory of nature's earlier incarnations, and an unsettling suggestion that such patches of the past offer no solution.

Environmentally speaking, then, Whitman's regional poems incorporate two opposing forces. They affirm people's paradoxical joy in dominion over nature, which overrides their sympathy and is difficult to "quell," since the ideological pressures of manifest destiny are so powerful that a reciprocal relationship to nature has to be postponed. Yet they also celebrate an immediate nonutilitarian appreciation of natural systems that depends upon the relative absence of modern economic development. What Whitman's poetry shares with Dickinson's regional imagination, apart from several crossovers between his northeastern notions and her views of New England farming, are certain poetic references to America's conflicting cultural narratives about economically oriented relationships with the natural world. Like Dickinson, Whitman, too, alludes to the tensions between foundational stories of nature's subjugation, which inform the paradigm of America's manifest destiny, and those about an original or re-created paradisiacal state of harmony, which feed into the notion of America as nature's nation. However, Whitman tends toward a more unflinching look at the pain and devastation inflicted upon the nonhuman world and thus confronts more directly the ethical conflicts resulting from "man's" being both of and outside of nature.

That the questions their poems touch upon are often those that conservationists and preservationists circulated at the time does more than show their regional imagination to be somewhat attuned to these debates. It also highlights how, as poets, they incorporate narrative elements that shaped the time's environmental arguments while resisting the narrative urge to move from conflict to resolution, embracing more ambivalent positions instead. In this framework, their discursive strategies—Dickinson's well-known tendency to face paradoxical constellations and remain reluctant to draw nonambivalent conclusions, and Whitman's characteristic way of embracing and indirectly affirming his culture's conflicting practices—acknowledge the impossibility of resolving the dilemma of nature's economic appropriation. In different but related ways, Dickinson's reluctance to express a clear preference for reciprocal modes of living off the land that would be viable in the here and now, and Whitman's disconcerting affirmation of the brute domination that plays a part in people's economically defined interactions with nature, suggest that a return to a paradisiacal state of innocence is impossible, and that the eco-ethical dilemma of forcibly exploiting the world for the sake of material progress forms an integral part of the story of America as nature's nation.

IV · Envisioning the Earth

In their shared fascination with the natural world, Dickinson and Whitman reached far beyond the more immediate levels of small, local, and regional phenomena. Both poets tried to bring all of "this earth" into their work, with an urgency that, for all their baffling differences of form, voice, and perspective, merits a critical comparison. In particular, when they wrote about earthly matters on the largest scale, they did more than turn to faraway countries and continents and thus imaginatively crisscross the globe. While Dickinson's "Vision[s] of the World Cashmere," of "Brazilian Pampas," of Teneriffe's "Retreating Mountain!" testify to lasting transnational yearnings, and Whitman's catalogues seek to democratically embrace the world's diverse places even as they threaten to tip over into colonializing fantasies, they also share a global perspective in a more literal sense, insofar as both imagine the globe as one interconnected physical entity. In this chapter I discuss how Dickinson and Whitman imagine the whole earth, both as the largest possible place that forms the basis of a global, interrelated web of nonhuman and human life, and as an autonomous cosmic entity, a celestial body moving in space as its own peculiar realm of existence. Specifically, I hope to show that the global is the realm where they "envision" the earth, engaging imaginative perspectives that allow them to grant nature and human-nature interactions a quasi-physical presence, even though they cannot possibly be grasped or encompassed by the senses or experienced in their totality. Their mode of global envisioning, in the double sense of "visualizing" the earth as a material entity and of "picturing" or projecting the earth as a cosmic phenomenon, corresponds in crucial ways to formative proto-ecological ideas of the time that addressed global matters in new ways. This global vision is grounded, on the one hand, in tangible empirical perspectives on smaller scales, and, on the other hand, in speculative acts of creative imagination. Yet unlike the scientifically oriented proto-ecological publications of their time, Dickinson's and Whitman's poems, while deeply informed by the sciences, also imagine quasi-personal relationships with the entire earth, which both strengthens the experiential aspect that is so difficult to sustain on a global scale, and calls attention to the eco-ethical implications of such global poetic endeavors. Moreover, this relational quality also potentially counteracts grandiose and self-important gestures of imagining the world.

In ecocriticism, the global scale has been considered a challenge because environmental consciousness and ethics are traditionally understood as evolving from more immediate realms of human living. People's sense of place, in particular, seems to depend upon direct contact with and attachment to phenomena close to their home, so much so that geographer Yi-Fu Tuan famously warned that "[t]opophilia rings false when it is claimed for a large territory. A compact size scaled down to man's biological needs and sense-bound capacities seems necessary" (*Topophilia* 101). More recently, Lawrence Buell still finds that "as environmental criticism moves to a global level of analysis, it understandably gets more multivocal, contentious, and fraught," and that "[a]s scale and mobility expand, placeness tends to thin out" (*The Future of Environmental Criticism* 90, 91). And yet, as Buell himself, Greg Garrard, and others have noted, much is to be gained from a more focused critical attention to changing ideas about the globe—both regarding the social, economic, and political forces of globalization, including postcolonial and transnational movements, and in terms of seeing the earth as a living entity, or even a kind of Gaia superorganism, that is essentially stable and self-sustaining (see Garrard 161–75).[1]

For an ecocritical analysis of Dickinson's and Whitman's earth poetry, it is constructive to consider to what extent a global outlook, especially one that is environmentally oriented, was already part of their cultural moment. A new, proto-ecological interest in the earth's dynamic interconnectedness, and in life on earth as one great whole, can be traced back at least to the early nineteenth century, when the older, holistic endeavors of natural theology and natural history were reframed by more decidedly empirical natural sciences, and when geography, long committed to describing the earth, came of age as a scientific discipline. It is especially productive to consider Dickinson's and Whitman's poetry in relation to the ways in which scientific publications on global processes, too, engaged the imagination. More than a century before the first photograph from space made the earth visible as a single entity, proto-ecological discourses depended as much on empirical insights as on a vision that pushed beyond what was immediately physically attainable. Against this backdrop, Dickinson's and Whitman's global poetry becomes legible as an environmentally sensitive engagement with emerging notions of the whole earth as a living, vulnerable natural phenomenon—owing to both their empirically grounded interest in "this earth" and their related commitment to visualizing and imagining nature on a scale at which it is difficult to be grasped rationally.

In particular, Alexander von Humboldt's *Cosmos*, published between 1845 and 1862, marked a major moment in the development of an empirically based and imaginatively inspired global awareness that was also distinctly proto-ecological. Humboldt was the most important global natural scientist before Darwin, and his international reception and influence can hardly be overestimated. As Laura Walls puts it, "in the United States, [Humboldt] succeeded in bringing into being a discourse, a way of speaking, about nature that we now call environmental: namely, a planetary interactive causal network operating across multiple scale levels. Darwin, one of Humboldt's closest readers, would envision an interactive network of chance and inheritance working across time and space" (*The Passage to Cosmos* 11). Whitman knew Humboldt's ambitious study rather well (see Reynolds, *Walt Whitman's America* 244–45; Walls, *The Passage to Cosmos* 280), and it is unlikely that the significance of this publication, which was discussed enthusiastically throughout the United States when it began to appear in translation in 1850, would have escaped Dickinson. In his magnum opus and culmination of a long history of "the idea of the Cosmos as a natural whole" (Walls, *Seeing New Worlds* 83), Humboldt introduced a new science of nature's connections he called "physical geography" or "earth physics" (Sachs 128), now seen as a direct precursor of ecology:

> Observation of individual parts of trees or grass is by no means to be considered plant geography; rather, plant geography traces the connections and relations by which all plants are bound together among themselves, designates in what lands they are found, in what atmospheric conditions they live, and tell us of the destruction of rocks and stones by what primitive forms of the most powerful algae, by what roots of trees, and describes the surface of the earth in which humus is prepared. (Humboldt, qtd. in Walls, *Seeing New Worlds* 79)

Humboldt combined the old holistic approach with a new synthetic one that emphasized the study of relations over the study of individual phenomena and, as Anne Godlewska stresses, was groundbreaking in the significance it granted to scale and "the 'way of life' of plants, animals and humans" (236–38). Moreover, as Walls explains, unlike the older "rational holism," in which notions of nature's unity were "based on a central organizing law defined as Logos, the Word of God," Humboldt's new "empirical holism" was based on both material evidence and, quite centrally, the creative imagination (*Seeing New Worlds* 76). When Humboldt wrote about the earth as an interwoven entity and celestial body, he linked the empirical to a more imaginative way of seeing; his central idea that by studying nature's parts one can develop an understanding of the whole was "guided by intuition" and in turn "forward[ed] intuition" (*Seeing New Worlds* 78–81). That he called on his readers to use "the power of fancy" (*Cosmos* 149) and challenged the separation between the empirical sciences and literature insofar as both are, to a degree, "rooted in the depth of feeling and interwoven with the creative force of imagination" (*Cosmos* 11) makes his work particularly relevant for discussing the ecological implications of Dickinson's and Whitman's ways of envisioning the earth.

Another text relevant here, and one with which Dickinson, in particular, was certainly familiar (see Sewall 345), is Edward Hitchcock's *Religion of Geology and Its Connected Sciences* (1851). On one level, Hitchcock's *Religion of Geology* could not have been more different from Humboldt's *Cosmos*, because where Humboldt provided a survey of a universally ordered, harmonious system without explicitly referring to God's supreme design (see Rupke xxiii–xxiv), Hitchcock was committed to reconciling the latest scientific insights with spiritual dogma. Yet Hitchcock too was an important transitional figure, who helped pave the way for understanding nature's global processes through a holistic approach. His *Religion of Geology* proposed theories of the earth's geological changes over large periods of time that anticipated modern ecological concerns, even as he integrated these theories into an overall scheme of God's infinite benevolence (Judd, "Natural History and the Beginning of Forest Conservation in America" 17). Similarly, his studies on fossil tracks in the Connecticut River valley, publicly displayed in Amherst, and his theories of modern astronomy brought new dimensions to discussions of natural relationships in large time frames. Overall, his publications, which urged readers to imagine themselves on other continents or in the era of dinosaurs, engaged people's creative, imaginative faculties as intensely as Humboldt's, even as he emphasized the need for sound scientific methods:

> Every schoolboy now knows that this globe, enormous though it be compared with what the eye can take in from the loftiest eminence, is but a mere speck in creation, and, with the exception of the moon, appearing from other worlds only as one of the smallest stars in their heavens; so small that its extinction would not be noticed. To the ignorant mind, distances and magnitudes exceeding a hundred miles are conceived of only with great difficulty. But the astronomer, when he conceives of magnitudes, must make a thousand miles his shortest unit, and a million of miles when he conceives of distances in the solar system. And when he attempts to go beyond the sun and the planets, the shortest division on his measuring line must be the diameter of the earth's orbit; and even then he will be borne onward so far, not on the wings of imagination, but of mathematics, that this enormous distance has vanished to a point. Even then he has only reached the nearest fixed star, and, of course, has only just entered upon the outer limit of creation. He must prepare himself for a still loftier flight. He must give up the diameter of the earth's orbit as the unit of his measurements, because too short, and take as his standard the passage of light, at the rate of two hundred thousand miles per second. (*Religion of Geology* 453)

Hitchcock's struggles to reconcile religious and scientific thought form a particularly interesting reference point for Dickinson's and Whitman's earth poems, which are infused with religious paradigms while also pointing beyond them.

Only a few years after Hitchcock, George Perkins Marsh's *Man and Nature* suggested that it is imperative to develop an integrative vision of the earth, calling on people's willingness to fathom what "we can hardly imagine" (463) on yet another level. His study combines descriptions of local natural systems with dramatic accounts of their anthropogenic demise in vastly different places and times, creating a global picture of negative "changes produced by human action in the physical conditions of the globe" (3). For instance, he summarizes the transformation of the exceptionally fertile "Territory of the Roman Empire" into an area of "Physical Decay" as follows:

> It appears, then, that the fairest and fruitfulest provinces of the Roman Empire, precisely that portion of terrestrial surface, in short, which, about the commencement of the Christian era, was endowed with the greatest su-

> periority of soil, climate, and position, which had been carried to the highest pitch of physical improvement, and which thus combined the natural and artificial conditions best fitting it for the habitation and enjoyment of a dense and highly refined and cultivated population, are now completely exhausted of their fertility, or so diminished in productiveness, as, with the exception of a few favored oases that have escaped the general ruin, to be no longer capable of affording sustenance to civilized man. (10)

Throughout his study, he turns to similar instances to make his contemporaries see what they found difficult to imagine—that because nature "knows no trifles, and her laws are as inflexible in dealing with an atom as with a continent or planet" (464), minor changes in nature can have unfathomable detrimental consequences, to the point even that "the earth is fast becoming an unfit home for its noblest inhabitant" (45). Marsh thus develops a vision of a global environmental crisis, urging his readers to reconsider their actions and exert "caution in all operations which, on a large scale, interfere with the spontaneous arrangements of the organic or the inorganic world" (3). In such a context, neither poetic visions of the earth's fragility nor poetic schemes of global control seem ethically neutral; both appear embedded in a network of growing environmental concern on the largest feasible scale.

Together, these studies also draw attention to a fundamental dilemma that may well be inherent in attempting to grasp the earth in its entirety. For Humboldt, Hitchcock, and Marsh, imagining nature and human-nature relationships on such a level, as well as devising theoretical and practical paradigms, was both an elevating and a deeply humbling endeavor. Humboldt's vision of providing a descriptive history of the world, from botanical details to cosmic constellations, seems grounded in unparalleled hubris, yet he kept questioning the reach of the very intuition he so celebrated; as Walls puts it, Humboldt can sound "heroically ambitious" and "plodding and modest" at the same time (*Seeing New Worlds* 78). In the case of Marsh, the tension is just as pronounced. As a representative figure of environmental reform, his progress-driven enthusiasm for technological remedies (from draining lakes to fertilizing deserts) that might undo past environmental changes occasionally overrides his key idea that extreme foresight should be used in all modifications of nature. Yet he also expresses a kind of pragmatic humility: "These achievements are more glorious than the proudest triumphs of war, but, thus far, they give but faint hope that we shall yet make full atonement for our spendthrift waste of the bounties of nature" (*Man and Nature* 44). In such a context, the audacity of Dickinson's "I take no less than skies" (Fr358), and of Whitman's declaration that "The whole earth, this cold, impassive, voiceless earth, shall be completely justified, / Trinitas divine shall be gloriously accomplish'd and compacted by the true son of God, the poet" ("Passage to India"), echo the boldness of Humboldt's, Hitchcock's, and Marsh's differently inflected global ideas. Yet at the same time, and perhaps more importantly, Dickinson's doubt whether it is indeed "for us" "to dwell in such a place" (Fr1435) and Whitman's sense that the earth might be indifferent "to our affections" ("Passage to India") also engage the sense of environmental humility some of their contemporaries would express, turning it into a critical aspect of their global environmental imagination.

When Dickinson, then, crafted the image of the earth as "a Pit – / With Heaven over it, [. . .] with fathoms under it – / Its Circuit just the same" (Fr508), and Whitman proclaimed that "[i]t is no small matter, this round and delicious globe moving so exactly in its orbit for ever and ever, without one jolt or the untruth of a single second" ("Who Learns My Lesson Complete"), this global fascination was part of broader cultural shift. As on smaller scales, their poetic engagement with these discussions not only hinges upon specific thematic resemblances but also emerges from certain epistemological and ethical perspectives. Their global poems were certainly shaped by the transcendentalist interest in the mind that would be inspired to comprehend and indeed create nature's whole, but they also acknowledge the significance of specific natural phenomena in the process, and question the reach of the imagination even as they rely on it to fathom the earth.

7

"The Earth and I and One"

Dickinson's Vision of Global Dwelling

If Dickinson's imaginative engagement with nature is most intense and diverse on the level of small creatures in their micro-environments, it seems most elusive on the global scale. This has less to do with quantity than with the religious overtones of almost all her thinking about "this earth." In particular, Dickinson's global meditations often negotiate the glory of this world against orthodox Calvinism's idea that the denial of life on earth will be rewarded in heaven. Yet when she addresses the tensions between concepts of an exclusive heaven and the more life-affirming notion of grace, between faith and skepticism, and between conventional Christianity and transcendentalism, she also tends to imagine the world as a physical entity and place, as an early letter to Susan Gilbert suggests:

> I write from the Land of Violets, and from the Land of Spring, and it would ill become me to carry you nought but sorrows. I remember you, Susie, *always* – I keep you ever here, and when *you* are gone, then I'm gone – and we're 'neath one willow tree. I can only thank "the Father" for giving me such as you, I can only pray unceasingly, that he will bless my Loved One, and bring her back to me, to "go no more out forever." "Herein is Love." But *that* was Heaven – *this* is but *Earth*, yet Earth so *like* to heaven, that I would hesitate, should the true one call away. (L85)

For all her use of conventional tropes and the sentimental language of flowers, Dickinson's familiarity with common local plants furnishes the basis here for suggesting a familiarity with nature in larger realms ("the land of") and everywhere on this planet (an "Earth so like to heaven"). In this way, her sense of being locally at home resonates in terms of being at home globally, or as a global sense of place, which includes life and death not only as spiritual but also as biological dynamics. The wordplay that turns the conventional juxtaposition of earth and heaven into a celebration of this world *as* heaven contributes to this crossover of the local and global, religion and geography, in ways that evoke a tangible globe. Perhaps most fascinatingly, Dickinson talks about her relationship to Susan in terms of her ties to local and global nature. The way in which she links her love of Sue to her love of flowers, and also links her refusal to let Sue go metaphorically and metonymically to her refusal to let this earth go, emphasizes nature's local and global interrelatedness, and, more importantly, the speaker's intensely personal relationship to flowers and even the entire earth—a relationship that is emotionally charged, potentially egalitarian, and ethically meaningful. Similar examples of envisioning a material earth to which one can imaginatively relate can be found in other Dickinson letters as well. Whether she exclaims in a later note to Sue, "Oh Matchless Earth – We underrate the chance to dwell in Thee" (L347), or writes to Elizabeth Holland, "Mother does not yet stand alone and fears she never shall walk, but I tell her we all shall fly so soon, not to let it grieve her, and what indeed is Earth but a Nest, from whose rim we are falling?," while finding that "Earth would not seem homelike without your little sunny Acts" (L619), the idea of one interconnected place and living body informs her views of "this world" in ways that also matter environmentally.

Dickinson wrote letters and poems in which she pictured "This Bashful Globe of Ours" (Fr677) at a moment of transition in her culture's understanding of the world, when religious modes of envisioning creation in its entirety were challenged by a wealth of empirical data. While the influence of this transition on Dickinson has been traced by several scholars, its ecological relevance has remained largely unexplored. For instance, Jane Eberwein discusses how Amherst's orthodox Congregationalism inspired Dickinson to both seek and doubt links between science and creation ("Dickinson's Local, Global, and Cosmic Perspectives" 34), but emphasizes how she struggled with the threats Darwin's theories posed for traditional religion, and that her main global or cosmic concern was immortality (42). Likewise, Richard E. Brantley's *Experience and Faith: The Late-Romantic Imagination of Emily Dickinson* shows that her poetry is informed by theological questions and scientific rationalism, and that it often expresses a "religion of nature" shaped by "poetic faith" and "naturalized imagination" (80); yet while his fine readings often have environmental implications, Brantley is mainly interested in Dickinson's shift from empiricism back toward a primary concern with religious faith. Robin Peel's *Emily Dickinson and the Hill of Science*, too, addresses numerous links between religion and specific scientific disciplines in Dickinson's poetry, while Paul Giles's recent article "'The Earth reversed her Hemispheres'" sees her global work embedded in religious and geographical discourses, and characterized by a perplexing simultaneity of near and far, interior and exterior, past and future. What I am concerned with here is how Dickinson's characteristic mediations between religiously inspired modes of viewing creation and an empirically informed this-worldliness participate in her culture's move toward formulating environmentally suggestive global visions. In particular, the ambitious scientific publications of her time often extrapolated from experiential insights on nature's smaller scales to discuss global phenomena as equally dynamic and interdependent, in ways that also play into Dickinson's poetry. Yet while such studies remained directly or indirectly invested in mastering creation and were often linked to imperial dynamics, Dickinson engages the conventions of poetry to envision a wonderful global interrelatedness in ways that, paradoxically, de-center her speakers' controlling agency.

A discussion of Dickinson's global environmental imagination might well begin with her valentines from 1850 and 1852. "Awake ye muses nine, sing me a strain divine" (Fr1), which proclaims that "All things do go a courting, in earth, or sea, or air, / God hath made nothing single but thee in His world so fair!," mockingly surveys how everything on earth comes together in pairs, in order to convince the addressee of the "naturalness" of going "a courting." In this rather conventional piece, the nature metaphors are as predictable as the references to God's divine plan (see Pollack, "Emily Dickinson's Valentines" 63), yet in an era characterized by a newly empirical and ecologically oriented interest in global natural dynamics, its evocation of a worldwide system of insects, flowers, earth, heaven, moon, and sun also develops subtextual green resonances:

> The bee doth court the flower, the flower his suit receives,
> And they make merry wedding, whose guests are hundred leaves;
> The wind doth woo the branches, the branches they are won,
> And the father fond demandeth the maiden for his son.
> The storm doth walk the seashore humming a mournful tune,
> The wave with eye so pensive, looketh to see the moon, [. . .]
> The *worm* doth woo the *mortal*, death claims a living bride,
> Night unto day is married, morn unto eventide;
> *Earth* is a merry damsel, and *Heaven* a knight so true,
> And Earth is quite coquettish, and he seemeth in vain to sue.

For all its playfulness, the emerging global "unity" absorbs and transcends the duality the speaker seems mainly interested in, as well as her pubescent swooning. The first lines here reach progressively outward in ways that make the interactions among small and large "things" graspable as both locally situated and world spanning; and since the list of loving pairs includes cosmic constellations, the earth also comes into view as an autonomous entity, living in space as its characteristic environment. On a different level, the speaker's focus on supposed marital alliances—including the conventional personification of the earth as a "merry damsel" met by a heaven-knight, and the "worm" wooing the "mortal"—invests the links between all these phenomena with quasi-relational qualities, which, at least indirectly, makes room for equally relational and potentially ethically informed relationships between humans and global nature.

Reading this poem against such publications as Edward Hitchcock's 1840 *Elementary Geology*, popular a decade before his *Religion of Geology* came out, further highlights how Dickinson links religious and scientific paradigms (even as she is mainly interested in deducing a law of human love from them), while also pushing beyond natural theology. Instead of an overarching interest in proving God's grace, her poem, no matter how facetiously, combines notions of spiritual (or transcendental) wholes with a more empirical holism, and her inclusion of humans in nature's processes minimizes "man's" superiority and difference. And while the poem is certainly interested in drawing moral principles from a perfect universe, its "ethical sententiousness" (Pollack, "Emily Dickinson's Valentines" 72) implicitly also deems the earth's manifold phenomena and the globe itself worthy of ethical attention, while the overall flippancy prevents the speaker from taking herself too seriously.

Dickinson's second valentine, "Sic transit gloria mundi" (Fr2), turns the other way and comments ironically on the presumptuousness of totalizing notions of "climb[ing] the 'Hill of Science'" to "'view the landscape o'er.'" Most of its references to schoolbooks and other sources of knowledge allude to instances of global geographical exploration: the speaker pays mock tribute to Peter Parley and Daniel Boone, ridicules views of the stars as a domestic family and of humans regulating the firmaments, and mentions theories of gravitation, the earth's rotation, and Columbus's voyages in ways that draw attention to the mix of human naïveté and overconfidence that have led to various misunderstandings. The humor of these lines derives largely from their shrill tone and apparent arbitrariness.[1]

It is interesting to compare this poem's position to the ways in which nineteenth-century geographers and astronomers, in the midst of their global aspirations, occasionally admitted to the limited reach of their theories. Laura Walls points out that Humboldt, for example, did "not believe that man can ever, 'by the operation of thought [. . .] hope to reduce the immense diversity of phenomena comprised by the Cosmos to the unity of a principle' (I:73)" (*Seeing New Worlds* 87). In a way, Dickinson's poem, which shares the time's fascination with grasping the earth even as it displays people's ultimate inadequacy for the task, deals with a similar tension. For all its excessive punning and overall hyperbole, it does suggest a perplexing mix of scientific curiosity, ironic distance, and, especially, the recognition of human failure in the face of the earth's magnitude.

In a much more mature piece, Dickinson fleshes out the experientially based yet radically imaginary quality of her global poetics. "The Sun went down – no Man looked on – " (Fr1109) casts the earth as local place and global phenomenon, sees humans as outside of yet embedded in nature, and imagines a beautifully suggestive personal relationship between speaker and earth:

The Sun went down – no Man looked on –
The Earth and I, alone,
Were present at the Majesty –
He triumphed, and went on –

The Sun went up – no Man looked on –
The Earth and I and One
A nameless Bird – a Stranger
Were Witness for the Crown –

The curious notion of the earth watching the sun, joined by the speaker in an atmosphere of otherwise complete loneliness, casts the earth as a cosmic entity slowly moving through space. But the idea of the sun going *down* also creates a local situation, since seeing the sun disappear below the horizon depends on a position somewhere on the earth, rather than with it in space. The presence of a bird strengthens this view of the earth as a locale without giving up its cosmic dimension because the bird, although its realm is the air, grounds the speaker's global experience in nearby nature without limiting its scope. By way of a leap of the imagination that intersects a symbolic perspective (the sunset as a religious spectacle) with a metonymic connection (between a local earthly place and the earth as globe), Dickinson makes the earth graspable both as an immediate living ground and as a planet.

Moreover, the personification of the earth as companion ("The Earth and I, alone"), which suggests some degree of equality, evokes a speaker of rather cosmic proportions. Yet the personification of a bird as third partner in this scene ("The Earth and I and One") immediately diminishes the speaker's relative size and significance. In her friendly relations with earth and bird, the speaker is akin to both, a mutuality in which the three recognize each other as common cosmic inhabitants and, paradoxically, common earthly beings. And yet, as both an observer of a cosmic spectacle and embedded in a local scene, the speaker does not herself become nature; instead of imaginatively dissolving the difference, she remains distinct from earth and bird, which grants nature its otherness even at this moment of universal communion turned human-nature partnership. The ethical implications go beyond the ways in which such earth consciousness highlights an otherwise universal human (and specifically male) oblivion, emphasized through the repeated "no Man looked on." Dickinson offers no less than a model of global human-nature interaction as a companionship that implies a certain mutuality, and equality in difference—and that, for all its groundedness in place, remains dependent on the imagination in ways that reinvest religious revelation with eco-ethical meaning.

Wendy Martin has argued that this poem refers to a religious conversion and de-emphasizes God's omnipresence while emphasizing nature's glory (*An American Triptych* 124). I would add that it also slides from a religious toward a more empirically interested vision, and in doing so again talks back to contemporaries like Hitchcock. As a last representative of natural theology, as well as the first who turned geology into a serious science (see Dean 644), his attempts to reconcile divine providence with empirical studies read as follows:

> Is not the God of revelation the God of nature also? and must not his varied works tend to sustain and elucidate, instead of weakening and darkening, one another? Has Christianity suffered because the Copernican system of astronomy has proved true, or because chemistry has demonstrated that the earth is already for the most part oxidized, and therefore cannot literally be burned hereafter? (*Religion of Geology* 28–29)

Dickinson's poem links such perspectives without circling back to God's supreme power. It suggests a personal, almost intimate relationship between speaker and earth that combines yet also transcends local, global, and cosmic scales in ways that ground such a vision in place without delimiting it. The vast earth, and a personal, friendly relationship with it, become thus equally fathomable—while the poem's potentially self-aggrandizing implications are undercut by the fact that the scene's "triumph" belongs to the sun, so that the speaker's religiously inspired sensibility is recharged as environmental humility.

Two other, more skeptical global poems are similarly based on religious and scientific epistemologies, and on an empirical understanding of smaller scales. In "Perhaps I asked too large – " (Fr358), Dickinson imagines cosmic constellations by referring to a local landscape without collapsing their difference, while expressing an abiding doubt that a global vision is attainable:

> Perhaps I asked too large –
> I take – no less than skies –
> For Earths, grow thick as
> Berries, in my native Town –
>
> My Basket holds – just – Firmaments –
> Those – dangle easy – on my arm,
> But smaller bundles – Cram.

It seems as if the metonymic reference to berries as local "Earths," which borders on conceit, and the opposition between small "Earths" and vast "skies" primarily suggest that the speaker is less intrigued by local vistas than by the "Firmaments." Indeed, most critics emphasize how much the confident poet here seems to pull away from the "small" landscape of her "native Town," interested in nothing but "skies." According to Wendy Barker, "smaller" issues constitute a heavy, perhaps oppressive weight for her, whereas the "Firmaments," or "fine philosophy and poetry," are a light burden (65); and ecofeminist Rachel Stein, who discusses the poem's "berries" and "skies" on a more than symbolic level, argues that the titanic speaker is liberated as she "gathers immensities of nature—'Earths,' 'skies,' 'Firmaments'—and refuses the 'smaller bundles' that would, ironically, 'Cram' her within the constricted scope of feminine norms" (42). I suggest here that the speaker seems less interested in replacing local with global perspectives than in their ambivalent relationship, taking the "earth's" two-sided resonance as a starting point. As the mid-nineteenth-century *Webster's* explains: "1. *Earth*, in *its primary sense*, signifies the particles which compose the mass of the globe, but *more particularly*, the particles which form the fine mold on the surface of the globe; or it denotes any indefinite mass or portion of that matter," while also referring to "[t]he terraqueous globe which we inhabit."[2] Part of the effect of this poem's way of combining references to the particles at our feet and their planetary totality is an empirically informed vision of the earth as a whole, which was as difficult to attain in the nineteenth century as it is now and has interesting environmental subtexts.

When the speaker claims that she takes "no less than skies" because "Earths, grow thick as / Berries, in [her] native town – ," she also uses her familiarity with local perspectives as a stepping stone for evoking the entire earth as habitat. For instance, the "thick" "Earths" in which her imagination is grounded even as she pulls away from them refer to "Berries" not only ironically but also as phenomena that can be hugely significant. Similarly, the perplexing statement that "smaller bundles – Cram" may not simply suggest that smaller natural phenomena are oppressive, but also that their meanings point beyond local frameworks, overfilling "baskets." The image of a woman who roams forests thinking about "Firmaments" further connects local to cosmic ventures. In other words, the speaker's outbound yearnings are informed by and refer back to an interest in smaller local natural contexts.

Turning to a passage from Humboldt's *Cosmos* highlights how much such imaginative local-global crossovers were part of geographical discussions about the earth as an interconnected cosmic body:

> If for a moment we could yield to the power of fancy, and imagine the acuteness of our visual organs to be made equal with the extremest bounds of telescopic vision, and bring together that which is now divided by long periods of time, the apparent rest that reigns in space would suddenly disappear. We should see the countless host of fixed stars moving in thronged groups in different directions; nebulae wandering through space, and becoming condensed and dissolved like cosmical clouds; the vail [*sic*] of the Milky Way separated and broken up in many parts, and "motion" ruling supreme in every portion of the vault of heaven, even as on the Earth's surface, where we see it unfolded in the germ, the leaf, and the blossom, the organisms of the vegetable world. (149)

Humboldt's text is still infused with notions of Enlightenment holism, even as it points toward a globally oriented modern ecology. What interests me here is that he not only compares but actually links the dynamics of germs, leaves, and blossoms to the movements of stars, highlighting how Dickinson's image of local "Earths" also makes cosmic realms graspable by way of associations to small nature that are metaphorical as well as metonymic. Moreover, Humboldt's way of basing his argument on "the power of fancy" calls attention not only to the fact that Dickinson's confident speaker also embraces the power of imagination but to her somewhat more pronounced doubts regarding her cosmic reach: the "Perhaps" looms large at the poem's beginning, and the nagging question whether she attempted something "too large" is never resolved. Regardless whether the "skies" she was after or the native "Berries" were "too large," this speaker, with echoes from religious and traditional female humility, balances her proud, cosmic desire with a scientific and ultimately poetic humility, doubting her capability not only to decipher but also to envision the natural world in its small and large manifestations.

A later poem on the relationship between earth and heaven addresses the possibilities and limitations of a global imagination in ways that involve basic premises of human life on earth. Like the inverted wordplays on life and death Dickinson occasionally used in her letters—she wrote to Charles H. Clark in 1883, "I felt it almost a bliss of sorrow that the name so long in Heaven on earth, should be on earth in Heaven" (L827)—it envisions the earth as a heavenly dwelling place:

> The Fact that Earth is Heaven –
> Whether Heaven is Heaven or not
> If not an Affidavit
> Of that specific Spot
> Not only must confirm us
> That it is not for us
> But that it would affront us
> To dwell in such a place – (Fr1435)

At first, this speaker seems to remind readers that earth's "heavenly" qualities do not suffice as evidence for the existence of what lies beyond, but the phrase "that specific Spot" is ambiguous enough to refer to the earth as much as to a hereafter. Collapsing the difference between an imagined heavenly and an earthly place, the poem suggests that we know as little about the one as about the other. That the speaker links religious concerns to questions of the earth's materiality makes this poem resonate in terms not just of a spiritual dilemma but also of her time's religiously informed scientific approaches to the nonhuman world.

For all its abstraction, this poem, too, manages to evoke the earth as a living place—paradoxically, by inverting the conventional religious idea of heaven as a place that she explored in earlier poems. Poem Fr476, for example, in which the speaker asks, "Is Heaven a Place – a Sky – a Tree?," rejects the signifying power of "Location's narrow way," yet relies on geographical paradigms to bring the otherworldly close to home; and poem

Fr241, which begins, "What is – 'Paradise' – / Who live there – / Are they 'Farmers' – / Do they 'hoe' – ," is as much about rural New England as about "the sky." "The Fact that Earth is Heaven – " is less about heaven's earthliness than earth's heavenliness, which contributes to the globe's lyrical presence as place. This only works because the speaker embraces rational (in a language of "Fact" and "Affidavit," specificity and confirmation) and local perspectives (referring to the earth as "specific Spot," and the notion of "dwelling"). Maintaining a connection to nature on the global scale becomes feasible here through the combination of religious and empirical, global and local, views.

In regard to the poem's green implications, I would stress that its numerous negative constructions do not so much blur the clarity of the first line, as Albert J. Gelpi has suggested (*Emily Dickinson: The Mind of the Poet* 81), as they are part of the central idea that we cannot know the earth any more than heaven. In the second part, Dickinson takes this reluctance to claim conceptual control further, toward the cautionary remark that "The Fact that Earth is Heaven" must mean that "it is not for us"—or, as she put it in another poem, that we are but "A Guest in this stupendous place" (Fr572). The poem culminates in what sounds like an admonition, "that it would affront us / To dwell in such a place – ," offering the perplexing conclusion that it would already offend our modesty to assume the familiarity of simply living on this earth as our home—let alone assume scientific or imaginative control. Where James R. Guthrie argues that those who grasp that "Earth is Heaven" "effectively 'own' a chunk of paradise" (83), I would go the other way, stressing that in this poem, knowledge of the earth, or any right to live on it, is not to be had. Considering the rise of scientific studies that promised to take humans to the verge of understanding the earth and the universe, Dickinson's thoughts on life and death also work as a response to these developments. Here is another passage from the first volume of *Cosmos*:

> If we take up the physical description of the universe from the remotest nebulae, we may be inclined to compare it with the mythical portions of history. The one begins in the obscurity of antiquity, the other in that of inaccessible space; and at the point where reality seems to flee before us, imagination becomes doubly incited to draw from its own fullness, and give definite outline and permanence to the changing forms of objects. (88)

Humboldt assumed that a description of the universe would ultimately be impossible because such realms are forever empirically inaccessible. Yet while his notion that in attempting such a project one must therefore rely on the imagination can be taken as an expression of scientific humility, it still leaves the basic ideal of grasping the universe unchallenged. Dickinson's poem, by comparison, declares that even our imagination may fail us. By suggesting that the heavenliness of earth confirms that this earth "is not for us," she links a religiously motivated humility to a more profound reluctance to assume control over the earth, both in epistemological terms and as a local-global "dwelling" place. Whether the primary "place" of this poem is heaven or earth, it advocates a position with respect to both that precludes the common presumption that we are able to grasp our environment, or even fully dwell in it.

In a small but significant group of earth poems, then, Dickinson envisions the earth as an interconnected living place and an autonomous planet, the sum total of our physical environment moving through space, in ways that engage in an indirect dialogue with certain proto-ecological ideas of her time. She does so in part by combining religious views of the earth and heaven as entirely different realms with a more empirically oriented attention to nature and human-nature dynamics in smaller frameworks, without collapsing the difference between religious and scientific epistemologies or local and global scales. Yet her poems also link an unorthodox passion for the earth as heaven's counterpart to daring visions of a quasi-interpersonal relationship with the globe, casting the earth as a local-global companion with whom an egalitarian, ethical relationship might be feasible. At the same time, her poetic forays into an earth epistemology also revisit the ethical question of how humans relate to nature in terms of the realization that the idea of grasping the earth is inseparable from the urge to control it. As such, her meditations on the limits of the imagination are tantamount to realizing the limits of poetic language. Overall, both her attempts to envision the globe as a material presence and the tension between hubris and humility that pervades these poems intersect as well with Whitman's approach to this "vast rondure swimming in space," bringing a new dimension to the comparison between the two poets, which the last chapter of this book will explore.

8

"What is this earth to our affections?"

Whitman's Vision of Cosmic Companionship

Leaves of Grass has been global in scope and aspiration from the first edition, in ways that not only situate America and its poetry in transnational and international contexts but also refer to the whole earth as a natural phenomenon. In his 1855 preface, Whitman talks about the vital relationships he envisioned between America, the poet, and the earth: he not only claims that "[t]he Americans of all nations at any time upon the earth have probably the fullest poetical nature" (*LG* 1855, 616), but also writes that "[t]he land and sea, the animals fishes and birds, the sky of heaven and the orbs, the forests mountains and rivers, are not small themes" (621); that all poets should "[l]ove the earth and sun and the animals"; and that "[t]he known universe has one complete lover and that is the greatest poet" (622). Although such notions are held together by the poet's ability to "see" what is impossible to experience, the earth takes shape here as a physical basis for diverse natural phenomena, human-nature interactions, and democratic relationships; as an autonomous cosmic body; and as an object of the poet's affection—at a time when geographers and other earth scientists were faced with the double challenge of grasping the globe empirically and formulating what would now be called a global environmental ethics.

Still, Whitman's global imagination appears to be as elusive and ambivalent a candidate for an environmental reappraisal of his poetry as Dickinson's is for hers, mainly because it is more directly linked to colonizing perspectives that view the earth's material riches from the perspective of an emerging industrial capitalism. In such a reading of Whitman, the earth becomes a passive stage for a manifest destiny that does not stop at California's shores; in "Passage to India," for example, the speaker imaginatively merges with colonial explorers and becomes "the true son of God" who "shall indeed pass the straits and conquer the mountains" (*LG* 349). Critics have therefore expressed reservations about Whitman's global poetry. Cecelia Tichi, for instance, stresses that Whitman "understood and believed in—and risked the creation of—a world autonomous in language alone" (224) and echoed an anthropocentric reform ideal that aspired to the global management and control of nature. Bruce Piasecki also insists that Whitman advocated "the utter domestication and utilization of the globe," "a complete humanization of nature" ("Conquest of the Globe" 43–44), adding that his idea of an immensely fecund earth (31) "considers the entire globe uniformly receptive to the comprehension and material transformations of humankind" (36). And M. Jimmie Killingsworth finds that Whitman's poetry often "suffers from overextension": "when he tries to expand to global proportions, or even when he strives for continental and national coverage, his rhetoric appears falsely inflated," treating "nature as an abstraction" and embracing technological progress and the dynamics of a global imperialism (*Whitman and the Earth* 74–75).

Yet the paradoxical ways in which Whitman's often grand, controlling, colonizing views intersect with strands of the environmental debates of his time also invite different readings without being apologetic. In particular, the green implications of his global poems have more to do with the Humboldtian worldview than has previously been acknowledged. While it is well known that Whitman was so fascinated with reading Humboldt's *Cosmos* that he included the word in one of the most famous sections of "Song of Myself," copied passages from *Cosmos* to his *Notebooks*, and read *The Letters of Humboldt* with appreciation (Piasecki, "American Literary Environmentalism before Darwin" 13), Humboldt's role as the most important ecological thinker before Darwin has not been discussed by Whitman's critics.[1] In particular, a closer look at Humboldtian holism offers a new angle on the colonizing dynamic that makes some of Whitman's poems so disturbing. While Mary Louise Pratt has stressed that Humboldt's travels to South America were framed by Spanish colonial interests (116), the links between Humboldt's scientific ambitions and colonial structures have been reinterpreted. Laura Walls, for instance, differentiates between Humboldt's own interests as the founder of a holistic ecology and those of nineteenth-century American expansionists who claimed that his theories proved "that empire was America's Manifest Destiny" (*Seeing New Worlds* 105). Aaron Sachs stresses that Humboldt relentlessly criticized colonial oppression and slavery, although his new ecological paradigm could not avoid being entangled in colonial projects (124–28), and that he moved toward "a socially conscious ecology, a positive vision of humanity in nature" on a global scale (118), even as his vision was abused to control the natural and cultural phenomena of distant colonies (119). And Richard H. Grove's *Green Imperialism: Colonial Expansion, Tropical Island Edens and the Origins of Environmentalism, 1600–1860* (1995) shows that for centuries, such links between environmentalism and colonialism were less the exception than the norm, since colonialism both generated ecologically devastating conditions and "helped to create a context that was conducive to rigorous analytical thinking about the actual processes of ecological change as well as thinking about the potential for new forms of land control" (6–7). While such arguments do not suggest that colonialism was a green endeavor, they make the ideologically difficult move of acknowledging that the emergence of a global environmental awareness was in part propelled by the dynamics of early capitalist global expansion. In terms of reading Whitman, they imply that his grand global visions, even as they echo perspectives of a colonizing culture and economy, are not automatically ecologically despicable.

The juxtaposition with Dickinson reveals a number of unexpected affinities between the two, while drawing further attention to the specific ambivalences of Whitman's poetry. The previous chapter has shown that Dickinson's poetry about earth and heaven participated in a shift from natural theology and its scientifically informed holism toward a more empirically based recognition of natural phenomena in their global interconnectedness. I have also argued that Dickinson envisioned experiential, potentially ethical relationships with the earth, while at the same time expressing a lingering sense of doubt. A comparison shows that in similar ways, Whitman's global poetry was inspired by transcendental perspectives and embraced the empiricism that informed the new. Moreover, Whitman too made global nature and humankind's involvement with it fathomable by imagining personal relationships with the earth, while pointing to the limits of such a vision, especially when it can never fully step outside of an imperial, colonial, and, in his case, not only anthropocentric but also androcentric framework. As such, Whitman's embrace of the material earth also includes potentially chauvinistic, oppressive relationships, which highlights a suggestive elision in Dickinson's work. The New England poet, who only reluctantly turned toward economic issues in her regional poetry, completely refrains from utilitarian perspectives on a global scale. And yet both poets reflect upon the sense of vision it takes to imagine a global nature and living planet, including the realization that such a grandiose enterprise cannot but falter, no matter how boldly, or humbly, one enters into it.

Whitman's most passionate lines about the globe can be found in the luscious night scene in section 21 of "Song of Myself," in which the speaker is both walking the earth and encountering it as his stunningly beautiful female lover:

> I am he that walks with the tender and growing night,
> I call to the earth and sea half-held by the night.
>
> Press close bare-bosom'd night – press close magnetic nourishing night!
> Night of south winds – night of the large few stars!
> Still nodding night – mad naked summer night.
>
> Smile O voluptuous cool-breath'd earth!
> Earth of the slumbering and liquid trees!
> Earth of departed sunset – earth of the mountains misty-topt!
> Earth of the vitreous pour of the full moon just tinged with blue!
> Earth of shine and dark mottling the tide of the river!
> Earth of the limpid gray of clouds brighter and clearer for my sake!
> Far-swooping elbow'd earth – rich apple-blossom'd earth!
> Smile, for your lover comes.
>
> Prodigal, you have given me love – therefore I to you give love!
> O unspeakable passionate love. (*LG* 43)

This passage recalls the baffling simultaneity of local and global nature in Dickinson's "The Sun went down – no Man looked on – " (Fr1109). Here the notion of walking and calling out to "the earth and sea" while evoking the sensuous presence of trees, mountains, and rivers creates a local situation, perhaps a seashore at dusk, with "the earth" resonating as ground or soil. Yet this earth is equally vivid in its presence as celestial body, an interconnected natural entity characterized by such interlinking local-global phenomena as rivers, winds, and tides. Also as in Dickinson's poem, a personal relationship contributes to the earth's poetic presence; this time, the experience of a man who is so overcome with love for all creation that he extends his embrace of a specific place to the entire planet increases this global there-ness.

The ethical implications of such a move are interesting as well. Recalling Dickinson's poem, whose speaker enjoys a moment of intimate companionship with the earth, the embrace of the earth as lover seems to inflate the speaker to cosmic proportions. In Whitman's case this dynamic is particularly prominent because it is in tune with the proud gestures of the previous section of "Song of Myself," where the speaker seeks to emancipate himself and his readers from subservient positions by picturing himself as the center of the universe. Yet Whitman, too, counteracts this dynamic. Where in Dickinson's poem the speaker's parallel companionship with a bird relativizes the self-aggrandizing aspect of her cosmic vision, Whitman's speaker remains an attentive local walker, which counterbalances his self-assertiveness to a certain degree. Finally, both poems evoke autonomous earths that will not be contained or controlled, yet in Whitman's case, the earth lover's sexualized desire complicates the constellation. As Killingsworth puts it in his fine reading of this passage from the 1855 edition, the "winkingly self-ironic hyperbole may mask sinister implications," including notions of the earth as an abundant female body to be used (*Whitman and the Earth* 50, 51).

It is interesting to note how expressions of love for the earth also played a part in some of the proto-ecological discourses of the day, albeit in more subtle ways. Alexander von Humboldt, for instance, who emphasized how crucial it was to study relationships in nature, also and especially on a global scale, and from whom Whitman borrowed the idea of *Cosmos* in the first place, expressed a tender affection for nature that, as Ottmar Ette explains, was dialectically related to his lifelong love for his male companions:

> It may not have been pure chance that made him write, in the same letter, the formula he always dedicated to his best and intimate friends, reminding them of the "happiest hours" spent together, adapting it now to another object the lonely "Weltbürger" never stopped loving: "Das Studium der Natur füllt meine ganze Muße aus, es gewährt ein so reines Vergnügen, dem ich kein anderes gleichzuschäzen weis, an das sich jedes moralische Gefühl ankettet und das mir die glücklichsten Stunden meines Lebens geschenkt hat." (182)[2]

It may not have been "pure chance" either that Whitman's "Song of Myself" echoes sentiments Humboldt expressed in his letters—that the "happiest hours" he spent loving his intimate friends and loving nature were of a similar, unmatched quality. By fusing an interest in the earth with expressions of passionate intimacy in his poetry, he too sees global nature as more than a grand object of study that yields scientific truths and moral, social, and political lessons. In his daring personification, the earth becomes a seductive and loving partner in a potentially reciprocal relationship. Yet that these lines remain so full of yearning, that the speaker keeps calling and urging the earth as if in doubt, also expresses a subliminal awareness of the impossible tensions between mutuality and mastery that come with his global embrace.

In his 1856 poem "Salut au Monde," Whitman imagines the earth and people's interactions with global nature in a much more public and political framework. The poem has been both praised for its cosmopolitanism and criticized for its imperial gestures; what interests me here is how Whitman intertwines his struggle with America's global double role as democracy and imperial power, on the one hand, and views of the earth as planetary body, on the other. As Harry Warfel stressed in an early essay, the poem's guiding vision of a democratic internationalism is based on nature's cosmic interconnectedness: "[t]he logical method is that of demonstrating that what is true of the whole of nature is true of every individual, since each person is a micro-cosmic part of nature" (154). My point here is that as such, the poem's earth is not just the proof of a metaphysical principle, as Warfel says, but also matters as an interconnected, living entity in its own right, and that Whitman employs the ideal of universal brotherhood in ways that to some extent counter manifest destiny's imperial gestures toward the earth.

At first, the poem seems to offer little in terms of engaging the actual natural world. In answer to the question "What widens within you Walt Whitman?" it unfolds like a transcendentalist's credo, with latitudes, longitudes, and continents appearing as mere spectacles of the poet's mind (*LG* 117), and with dozens of lines that begin with "I hear" and "I see," so that this "I" seems to be the poem's true spine. Yet its central image of a "great round wonder rolling through space" (*LG* 118) is environmentally quite compelling. The planet is strikingly vital ("'Banding the bulge of the earth winds the hot equator, / Curiously north and south turn the axis-ends"; *LG* 117); it consists of mountains, rivers, oceans, and diverse "regions of snow and ice," of "the fig-tree, tamarind, date," and is populated by various peoples whose stories, religions, and occupations are often defined by their relationships to the land. As such, a differentiated web of natural and cultural communities gives the earth a global material presence as planet and place. In a way, people's culturally specific connections to the earth, intertwined with and sometimes indistinguishable from the web of natural phenomena, emerge as one of this poem's themes, which intersects with nineteenth-century geography's interest in links between the earth's biophysical features and cultural patterns.

Again, Whitman also talks about human-nature relations in ethically suggestive ways. When the speaker celebrates "Such join'd unended links, each hook'd to the next, / Each answering all, each sharing the earth with all" (*LG* 117), this implies that humans potentially "share" the earth with each other and with nonhuman creatures and are eternally interlinked. The ideal of international brotherhood that the poem is so invested in as a democratic principle further accentuates its view of the earth. The poem's two gestures—of saluting and of taking someone's hand—which the eager speaker uses metonymically for the earth's diverse peoples, are also gestures with which he relates to the actual globe. The salutation of the title "Salut Au Monde" alone implies this earth-orientedness. This exchange of a respectful greeting that implicitly includes the earth itself comes up again in section 4, where the speaker asks himself (or is asked by his soul) "Who are they you salute, and that one after another salute you?" and begins his answer with the line "I see a great round wonder rolling through space" (118). The poem's second gesture of political brotherhood—enacted here in taking someone's hand—is referred to in the first line, "O take my hand Walt Whitman!," where the preceding title and the next image of "Such gliding wonders! such sights and sounds!" make it possible to see Whitman taking the planet's hand, as if including it in the new bond of equality and solidarity.

That the poem's concluding section shifts from gestures of brotherhood toward those of a more passionate love, however, again changes its global green subtext:

> My spirit has pass'd in compassion and determination around the whole
>   earth,
> I have look'd for equals and lovers and found them ready for me in all lands,
> I think some divine rapport has equalized me with them.
> You vapors, I think I have risen with you, moved away to distant continents,
>   and fallen down there, for reasons,
> I think I have blown with you you winds;
> You waters I have finger'd every shore with you,
> I have run through what any river or strait of the globe has run through,
> I have taken my stand on the bases of peninsulas and on the high embedded
>   rocks, to cry thence:
>
> *Salut au monde!* (*LG* 125–26)

The eco-ethical subtexts of this political love are less vexed than those of the heterosexual encounter between speaker and earth in "Song of Myself," yet its egalitarian implications are still relativized by how the titanic speaker stresses his role as a "determined" unifying agent. Throughout the poem, the vision of democratic internationalism, which subtly resounds as brotherly nature-culture interaction, is further compromised by echoes of imperialist utilitarianism and homocentrism. Walter Grünzweig has shown how the poem's Americanizing rhetoric "implies a Western bias in favor of expansion, economic exploitation, and technology" ("Walt Whitman as an International(ist) Poet" 247); I would add that the rhetoric of "each of us with his or her right upon the earth, / Each of us allow'd the eternal purports of the earth" (*LG* 125) betrays how much Whitman's noteworthy combination of the ideal of global human rights with views of the earth as a living body still privileges humans as those who not only have rights *on* the earth but *to* this earth, including the right to a full grasp of the earth's "eternal purports."

At this point it is again helpful to consider nineteenth-century discussions, especially the ways in which Humboldt tried to link his environmental and political ideas. Humboldt's holistic view of the earth included the connections among all kinds of natural phenomena, as well as interactions between humans and natural, built, and social-cultural environments, stretching from the most immediate to the global level. At the same time, he was passionate about the ideals of political equality, and especially "since the French Revolution," as Walls stresses, he "dreamed of a future in which republicanism would sweep the globe and bring liberty and equality to all its peoples" (*Passage to Cosmos* 147). Here is how Walls summarizes the Humboldtian worldview:

> [T]hat a harmony might emerge from the free interaction of democratic peoples; that in appropriating nature for our own ends, humanity will lead not to destruction but to a new and higher creative union; that the mind is not separate from nature, exerting control over it, but emerges from contact with nature in a social ecology by which each is constantly composing and recomposing the other. ("'Hero of Knowledge, Be Our Tribute Thine'" 133)

This implies that Humboldt at times sought to reconcile his appreciation for nature with what seems like humanity's necessary appropriation of the world by de-emphasizing the human ability to exert full control. In this light, Whitman's "Salut Au Monde" expresses a similar vision of a wonderfully ordered natural whole in which humankind is fully embedded, even though the poem is centrally concerned with people's political equality.

Yet while it is true that, as David Reynolds remarks, "for Whitman as for Humboldt, 'cosmos' signified both the order of nature and the centrality of human beings" (*Walt Whitman's America* 244–45), Whitman's way of including relationships not only among the world's peoples but also between them and the earth in his ideal of global brotherhood imagines the earth as an equal partner, without negating the limitations of such a utopia. If "Salut Au Monde" expresses a vision of internationalism and solidarity that is in line with the political implications of the French title (see Erkkila, "The Politics of Language" 29), it also suggests an ecological vision of a global natural-cultural system in which no one wholly dominates the other, as was put forward by Humboldt's *Cosmos*, originally titled *Physique du monde*.

Whitman's much later "Passage to India" (1871) poses perhaps the greatest challenge for a green reappraisal of his global poetry, because its focus on a transcendental journey and excitement over technological achievements as a basis for a new spiritual unity (see Mason 507) de-emphasize the earth's natural geography and its own vital interrelatedness. Betsy Erkkila, who has read the poem's push beyond the physical as a critique of the time's crude materialism, but also as a push away from democracy, explains that Whitman here becomes Emerson's "Poet" who has "lost touch with the stubborn particularity of the physical world" (*Political Poet* 273). In his ecocritical reading, M. Jimmie Killingsworth argues that although "Passage to India" is in part "a web-making poem," it "opens the door to the kind of thinking all too easily enrolled in the service of political imperialism"; he also explains how the poet tries to resolve the conflict between his "propagandistic commitment to the full sweep of manifest destiny" and his doubts by further aggrandizing his own role (*Whitman and the Earth* 77–78), reducing natural particulars to "mere objects without value, used and discarded resources" (81). Walter Grünzweig, however, argues that "Passage to India" also empowers imperial subjects by imagining them as actively growing together, performing a "divinely ordained movement towards an integrated, universalized world" ("Imperialism" 160–61). Following these investigations I want to emphasize how, if only to a degree, "Passage to India" also gives space to earthly interconnections that precede and outlast those forged by industrial contrivances, and how the allusion to an unreciprocated love relationship with the earth, while it may not fully undercut the speaker's prominent rhetoric of mastery, acknowledges certain tensions between America's colonizing practices and more reciprocal notions of dealing with the nonhuman world.

On one level, this poem's "One World" is certainly achieved by way of modern technologies, "the strong light works of engineers" for which nature figures as a passive stage and object ("[t]he seas inlaid with eloquent gentle wires"; "[t]he oceans to be cross'd, the distant brought near, / The lands to be welded together"; *LG* 346). And yet, as the speaker celebrates this newly linked world, these technological accomplishments also increase his awareness of the ways in which it has been interconnected all along:

> In one again, different, (yet thine, all thine, O soul, the same,)
> I see over my own continent the Pacific railroad surmounting every barrier,
> I see continual trains of cars winding along the Platte carrying freight and
> passengers,
> I hear the locomotives rushing and roaring, and the shrill steam-whistle,
> I hear the echoes reverberate through the grandest scenery in the world,
> I cross the Laramie plains, I note the rocks in grotesque shapes, the buttes,
> I see the plentiful larkspur and wild onions, the barren, colorless,
> sage-deserts,
> I see in glimpses afar or towering immediately above me the great mountains,
> I see the Wind river and the Wahsatch mountains,
> I see the Monument mountain and the Eagle's Nest, I pass the Promontory,
> I ascend the Nevadas,
> I scan the noble Elk mountain and wind around its base,
> I see the Humboldt range, I thread the valley and cross the river,
> I see the clear waters of lake Tahoe, I see forests of majestic pines,
> Or crossing the great desert, the alkaline plains, I behold enchanting mirages
> of waters and meadows,
> Marking through these and after all, in duplicate slender lines,
> Bridging the three or four thousand miles of land travel,
> Tying the Eastern to the Western sea,
> The road between Europe and Asia. (*LG* 347)

Although the speaker perceives all kinds of natural phenomena as being united by the railroad here, the alliterative force of his lines also casts these geographical particulars as an already interconnected entity, a preexisting, analogous transcontinental network. Similarly, when he reviews the accomplishments of explorers such as Columbus and Vasco da Gama, celebrating "Thou rondure of the world at last accomplish'd," the idea that these connections are solely human-made is belied by the way in which this "vast Rondure" is "swimming in space / Cover'd all over with visible power and beauty," surrounded by "sun and moon and countless stars above" (*LG* 348). Although this poem is greatly invested in celebrating human achievements in terms of creating a new global reality, it gives space to the globe as a natural entity and cosmic body. Similarly, the speaker's desire to leave all materiality behind and unite with the soul, to move "to primal thought / Not lands and seas alone," makes his imaginary "circumnavigation of the world" appear to be uninterested in earthly geographies. Yet in his search for the earth's ultimate "secret" he remains bound back to, and subtextually recognizes, the physical connectedness of the waters of the sea, creeks and rivers, woods and fields, mountains, prairies, rocks, clouds, rain and snow, sun, moon, and stars (*LG* 353).

In terms of imagining an interaction with the world as a personal relationship, I am less interested here in the speaker's notion of uniting "continents, climates and oceans" "As brides and bridegrooms hand in hand" (*LG* 349), or with his intense connection to the soul, "yield[ing]" and "melt[ing]" in the arms of God in a mix of friendship, love, and brotherhood. What I want to draw attention to is the idea of people's "restless explorations" as a yearning for the earth's love and affection:

> Ah who shall soothe these feverish children?
> Who justify these restless explorations?
> Who speak the secret of impassive earth?
> Who bind it to us? what is this separate Nature so unnatural?
> What is this earth to our affections? (unloving earth, without a throb to
> answer ours,
> Cold earth, the place of graves.) (*LG* 348–49)

The speaker's compassion for generations of "feverish children," in their desperate desire to gain the earth's love and especially in their doubts, merges with his own sense that the earth might not respond to such advances. Killingsworth's detailed interpretation of the poem has shown how Whitman's doubts "virtually shout at the reader here" and how "[t]he earth itself seems to resist the poet's sweeping claims" (*Whitman and the Earth* 78). I fully concur with this assessment, but where Killingsworth reads the passage mainly as part of Whitman's shift away from the environmental sensibilities expressed in the first editions of *Leaves of Grass* toward the more abstract, distanced, globalizing poems of his later years, I want to suggest that this passage is also meaningful in the context of how nineteenth-century scientists tried to negotiate their environmental sensibilities with the colonial dynamics on which their global explorations were necessarily based. Humboldt's *Cosmos*, for instance, includes passages in which he almost excuses himself for devising "an extended and perhaps too boldly imagined [. . .] plan" of a global geography, based on what he sees as the unparalleled privilege of exploring "the interior" of "vast continents" (8). In other passages, he describes feelings of "sadness" and "unsatisfied longing" that affect his attempts "perfectly to represent" all of this earth:

> A considerable portion of the qualitative properties of matter [. . .] is doubtlessly still unknown to us, and the attempt perfectly to represent unity in diversity must therefore necessarily prove unsuccessful. Thus, besides the pleasure derived and tinged with a *shade of sadness, an unsatisfied longing* for something beyond the present—a striving toward regions yet unknown and unopened. Such a sense of longing binds still faster the links which, in accordance with the supreme laws of our being, connect the material with the ideal world, and animates the mysterious relation existing between that which the mind receives from without, and that which it reflects from its own depths to the external world. *If, then, nature (understanding by the term all natural objects and phenomena) be illimitable in extent and contents, it likewise presents itself to the human intellect as a problem which can not be grasped, and whose solution is impossible,* since it requires a knowledge of the combined action of all natural forces. [. . .] But, although the incessant effort to embrace nature in its universality may remain unsatisfied, the history of the contemplation of the universe (which will be considered in another part of this work) will teach us how, in the course of ages, mankind has gradually attained to a partial insight into the relative dependence of phenomena. (*Cosmos* 1:80–81; emphasis added)

It is interesting to note that Humboldt, as he expresses a deep sense of scientific humility, calmly binds even his doubts back into the grand cosmic scheme he is interested in, and how he admits to the impossibility of grasping nature while still celebrating humankind's gradual progress. Whitman's speaker, by way of personalizing this conflict as a vexed love affair, can give himself over more fully to expressing a "feverish," perhaps almost insane desire to "speak the secret" of the earth, while also voicing a more shattering sense of inadequacy that is on the verge of turning into anger, deriding the earth as "impassive," "cold," "unloving," and even "unnatural." Humboldt saw his new geography as a major contribution to humankind's comprehension of nature, and yet he tried not to subject the earth to systems of total epistemological control and spoke out against colonial practices. In "Passage to India," Whitman's sense that global imperial expansionism promises a new cosmic consciousness is linked to a similar dilemma; as he celebrates his era's ideal of completely embracing the earth materially and imaginatively, he seems, at times, almost overcome by the political and ethical conundrum posed by such an agenda.

Whitman's global poetry, then, is not antithetical to environmental sensibilities. Such a perspective emerges from a contextual reading that explores Whitman's echoes of the time's national and international forays into a globally oriented ecology, an approach that also brings his poetry, which has long been noted for its prophetic reach, into the imaginative vicinity of Dickinson's interest in "this earth." On this largest geographical scale, where the imagination seems limited to abstractions, Whitman joins Dickinson in making the earth and human interactions with it fathomable by metonymically linking the nearby and familiar to global, even cosmic, phenomena, as well as by envisioning the earth as a partner, be it a companion, sibling, or lover. Furthermore, where Dickinson's global poems resonate as meditations on the interrelations between earth and heaven, and Whitman's earth-spanning visions express transcendentalist and more specific political ideals, they too matter as empirically based epiphanies of a global ecology that includes and enfolds humankind. Unlike Dickinson, however, who remains comparatively silent on the intersections between trying to understand global nature and its colonial subjugation, Whitman's poetry shows the entanglements of the globalizing American poet in such structures of domination, expressing a longing for human-natural interactions that are not primarily exploitative. On all these levels, the global emerges as these two poets' most visionary scale. For Dickinson and Whitman, as for such nineteenth-century naturalists and scientists as Edward Hitchcock, George Perkins Marsh, and Alexander von Humboldt, the desire not only to grasp nature and to maintain a connection to it on a global level, but also to achieve a boundless cosmic mutuality and human-natural fusion, ultimately remains just beyond the reach even of the imagination. Despite the unattainability of such mutuality, Dickinson and Whitman are moving toward a nature-centered global vision that does not subject the earth to human schemes, a vision that must remain unstable and ineffable, forever a project for the future.

Conclusion

The main point of the readings I have offered here is that Dickinson's and Whitman's widely divergent bodies of poetry share a fundamental interest in imagining more equitable relationships with the natural world, an interest that specifically responds to a number of nineteenth-century environmental discourses. In many ways their related poetic projects are so deeply resonant with the development of a modern environmental consciousness that they mark a foundational moment in the history of American environmental literature. Together, Dickinson and Whitman have contributed to the creation of a lyrical idiom that brings nature as autonomous subject matter, a nature-oriented aesthetic, and ethics into a dynamic interrelationship that propels the poetic speaker toward rethinking our conflicted ways of being in the world. As the previous chapters have demonstrated, reading them against their culture's upsurge of proto-ecological sciences, natural history prose, and popular environmental concern reveals with particular saliency how their poems absorb and also revise the shifting environmental perspectives of their time. This is true even though, or precisely because, they do so in works whose significance reaches far beyond their eco-ethical implications.

"'Nature' is what we see – / The Hill – the Afternoon – / Squirrel – Eclipse – the Bumble bee – " (Fr721), Dickinson wrote, letting her lyrical definition of nature start out from the tension between the mind's creative faculties and its embrace of the world's physical diversity. The preceding chapters have shown that the green resonances of Dickinson's and Whitman's poetry often begin with such a move of making room for sincere attentiveness to natural phenomena, in conjunction with their overarching concerns with perception, language, and the self. Both poets seek to talk about nature and human-nonhuman relationships as they are specific to particular natural and cultural contexts in a language "proportionate to Nature," developing a differentiated poetics of place that is responsive to the environmental debates of their historical moment while reaching far beyond them.

For example, on the microscale, Dickinson's snapshots of seemingly "needless" creatures bring the language and perspectives of the emerging proto-ecological sciences together with sentimental discourses, forging an idiosyncratic poetic language that not only amplifies certain concerns of taxonomy, botany, and ornithology but also revises the limiting identification of women with (small) nature through an aesthetic that empowers the natural environment. Whitman's poetry, too, echoes the time's scientifically informed attention to previously overlooked life-forms, in numerous lines on weeds and insects that often serve as remedial gestures and link the speaker's transcendental urge to a subtle critique of ecological myopia. At the same time, their quick gestures of noticing selected small phenomena also respond to the scientific challenge of dealing with a wealth of physiological detail by means of nuanced lyrical modes of their own. Similarly, on the local scale, their poems engage the descriptive mode of environmentally oriented nature essayists, in particular, and devise different yet related poetic descriptions of familiar naturescapes that relatively de-center the human observer. On the regional scale, they access their culture's conflicting narratives about how to relate to nature as resource or value and thus indirectly talk back to emerging conservationist debates. And on the global scale, they envision the earth in ways that face the challenge of making an unfathomably vast entity graspable by grounding their work in a more empirical understanding of nature's smaller realms, as well as by imagining personal relationships with the earth, taking up perspectives of the time's globally oriented scientists and conservationists. Across all scales, Dickinson and Whitman develop poetic strategies that connect the transcendent and metaphysical with the concrete, corporeal encounter between self and nature as it is specific to particular geographies, yielding a differentiated and environmentally resonant poetics of place that is an integral part of their overall aesthetic achievement.

Throughout the previous chapters I have also argued that apart from their shared investment in turning toward specific natural phenomena and human-nature relations, the environmental resonance of Dickinson's and Whitman's poetry is vitally linked to how they face the ineffability of the nonhuman world. As Dickinson writes in the final stanza of her "definition" of nature:

Nature is what we know –
Yet have no art to say –

So impotent Our Wisdom is
To her Simplicity.

In Dickinson's and Whitman's poetry, the insight into nature's alterity goes beyond the acceptance of philosophical skepticism. It also goes beyond confronting the limited ability of language, even lyrical language, to grasp or embody the phenomenal world. Dickinson and Whitman frequently express a sense of humans as being always outside of and apart from nature and thus not only essentially incapable of knowing nature but also potentially disruptive and appropriative. Yet both of them keep attempting the impossible: to carve out a language that allows their speakers to relate to nature in nondominating ways. In this they again echo perspectives, or rather a profound dilemma, that permeated the environmental discussions around them, while their finely modulated lyrical language moves beyond the edge of what most natural scientists, activists, and essayists would be interested in or could afford to explore.

On the microlevel, this becomes manifest in their speakers' attempts to move close to and identify with specific natural phenomena and become like them to the point that human subjectivity is allowed to dissolve. Yet such dissolution into nature comes with the realization that even at the point of death, language can never bridge the gap, never overcome nature's alterity or undo the mechanisms of control inherent in the act of speaking. On the local level, Dickinson and Whitman similarly try to familiarize nature, often through ecologically resonant household metaphors or notions of organicism, while also granting the land a dynamic presence that ultimately unsettles such attempts. At the same time, the two poets' revisions of popular forms of nature description, to the point of writing the speaker's linguistic agency almost completely out of the scene, cannot keep them from asserting symbolic power over the object of description. On all geographic scales, their poems push toward an idiom that attempts to speak about nature or let nature speak itself by minimizing linguistic mastery, while communicating the dilemma that even in the most radical linguistic self-effacement, elimination of all human control is impossible.

The term I have found most appropriate in talking about the epistemological and ethical import of Dickinson's and Whitman's nature-oriented poetry is humility. While the concept may seem to be fraught with outdated notions of human conduct, its groundedness in the nineteenth century also serves as a conceptual bridge between the ethical assumptions that guided environmentally oriented debates of Dickinson's and Whitman's time and their equivalents today. It has been my argument throughout that humility as it figures in Dickinson's and Whitman's nature-related poetry reconfigures traditional virtues as eco-ethical positions in ways that enter into a conversation with the environmental debates of their time while also pointing forward to twentieth- and twenty-first-century green discourses, especially debates around eco- and anthropocentrism.

Dickinson and Whitman enter this conversation from different positions. To Dickinson's female speakers, gestures of nature-centeredness are more readily available than for her male contemporaries, by way of the gendered notion of modesty that was so central to standard concepts of nineteenth-century womanhood. However, this nexus between environmental humility and conventional feminine modesty renders Dickinson's "bashful" regard for nature also more at risk of collapsing back into conventional female domesticity and self-effacement, quite remote from any sense of self-sustained individuality, which is a necessary condition for an ethical stance. Yet a number of her environmentally sensitive poems push such modesty toward an eco-ethical speaking position by sounding out the dialectical relationship between humility and hubris. Her assertiveness and pride in particularly compelling poetic renditions of nature (as in "Blazing in Gold and quenching in Purple") tend to include a subtextual recognition of nature's vulnerability and ultimate inaccessibility. Conversely, the conspicuously unassuming pose she sometimes assumes toward natural phenomena is not the disingenuous modesty for which it tends to be taken but stakes out the claims of a female speaker as subject, either through the paradoxical notion of achieved humility or by letting the self re-emerge on the other side of its apparent self-effacement, "with modesties enlarged" (as in "Our little Kinsmen – after Rain," "The Sun went down – no Man looked on – ," and "Sweet Mountains – Ye tell Me no lie – ").

For Whitman, the problem is the reverse, since his poetry is informed by ideas of masculine independence, arrogance, and pride as grounding for humanity and citizenship. Humility, toward nature as well, indirectly threatens to submit the male speaker to conventional religiosity and even emasculation. And yet Whitman admits humility into perspectives largely guided by pride, from the 1855 preface to *Leaves of Grass*, in which he claims that great poetry emerges from a soul that "has sympathy as measureless as its pride and the one balances the other," to his late "Backward

Glance O'er Travel'd Roads": "Defiant of ostensible literary and other conventions, I avowedly chant 'the great pride of man in himself,' and permit it to be more or less a *motif* of nearly all my verse. I think this pride Indispensable to an American. I think it not inconsistent with obedience, humility, deference, and self-questioning" (*CPCP* 667–68). Like Dickinson, he probes the poetic potential of the tension between hubris and humility in many of his nature-related poems. And even though he speaks from a perspective that can never fully step outside of an androcentric, imperial, even colonial framework, he likewise moves to the verge of dissolving the human subject vis-à-vis nature (most hauntingly in "As I Ebb'd"). Moving through such dissolution, his speaker ultimately emerges with a reconstituted subjecthood, assertive of his human capacity to speak, yet with his poetic pride forever changed by such profoundly humbling encounters.

It has also turned out that, although Dickinson expresses ecosensitive perspectives that are particularly available to those who occupy positions defined by social subjugation, while Whitman more often critically reflects human actions against the natural world that imperil its continued existence, both poets challenge conceptual constraints of nineteenth-century morality and gender roles. They turn a prescribed female submissiveness and a culturally condoned male destructiveness into new forms of humility that resonate as an environmentally oriented speaking position. It is a humble, and humbling, position that moves toward a complex ethical understanding of the interconnectedness of human and nonhuman life. In the nineteenth century, "humility" referred not simply to "freedom from pride or arrogance" (Webster, *Dictionary* [1847]), but was increasingly understood as a position that "consists in rating our claims low, in being *willing to waive our rights*, and take a lower place than might be our due" yet that "does *not require of us to underrate ourselves*" (Webster, *Dictionary* [1859]; emphasis added). Whitman and Dickinson transform this remedial, relative, and relational mode of provisionally yielding control into a way of responding poetically to the natural environment, making it the foundation for an environmentally sensitive epistemology.

Considering the resonance of such humility in terms of twenty-first-century environmental discourses, I have argued that one of its strengths is that it runs counter to the opposition between ecocentrism and anthropocentrism still common in ecocritical and other discussions. The humility that is so vital to Dickinson's and Whitman's poetry acknowledges human failure, including the poetic limitations of the speaking subject, also and especially in recognition of the agency of the nonhuman other, even if this agency is not expressed in language. In contrast to Whitman's term "sympathy," such humility does not expect a response in kind; it establishes a relationship that is not based on exchange or dialogue but on a sense of common createdness, or being in the world. At the same time, complete self-effacement is not a position from which one can be humble. The notion of humility as it emerges from these poems is quite distinct from the ideal of complete human relinquishment, in that it courageously takes on the human need to subsist on nature while also emphasizing the significance of the poetic imagination to the ecological project. Indeed, such relinquishment, even if it strives for an ecocentric position, actually presupposes a monodirectional economy that must by definition be human-centered.

By contrast, the environmental humility of Whitman's and Dickinson's poetry makes the self accountable for its own actions, and in this sense it is always provisionally human-centered. Such a poetic humility concedes a human-centeredness that inevitably attends the act of speaking, yet it is a human-centeredness that is grounded in doubt. As such, it is not only skeptical about the human ability to achieve a balance between the interests of the self and those of the natural environment, but also passionate about the responsibility of the self to keep striving for such a balance. This is ultimately the most radical implication of the environmental humility that is such a central feature of their art. Their poetic projects, in dialogue with their time and each other, create an ethical stance that accomplishes a vision of the impossible without settling for a safe position on some middle ground. Even at the beginning of the twenty-first century, their poetry may be seen to keep moving toward the verge of the unspeakable.

Notes

Introduction

1. For a succinct discussion of this new, "postmodern" ecology, see also Garrard 56–58.
2. Ecocritical survey studies on American environmental poetry include John Elder's *Imagining the Earth: Poetry and the Vision of Nature* (1985), Leonard M. Scigaj's *Sustainable Poetry: Four American Ecopoets* (1999), Bernard W. Quetchenbach's *Back from the Far Field: American Nature Poetry in the Late 20th Century* (2000), David Gilcrest's *Greening the Lyre: Environmental Poetics and Ethics* (2002), J. Scott Bryson's *Ecopoetry: A Critical Introduction* (2002), Jed Rasula's *This Compost: Ecological Imperatives in American Poetry* (2002), Angus Fletcher's *New Theory for American Poetry: Democracy, the Environment, and the Future of Imagination* (2004), and Scott Knickerbocker's *Ecopoetics: The Language of Nature, the Nature of Language* (2012).
3. Even though the two are sometimes used synonymously, "place," not "space," has been the key category for analyses of nature in literature. Lawrence Buell discusses this juncture in "Space, Place, and Imagination from Local to Global" (*The Future of Environmental Criticism*, esp. 63–65). Concise geographical discussions of the place-space conjunction can be found in David Harvey, "From Space to Place and Back Again: Reflections on the Condition of Postmodernity" (1993), Edward S. Casey, "How to Get from Space to Place in a Fairly Short Stretch of Time" (1996), and Yi-Fu Tuan, "Space and Place: Humanistic Perspective" (1996). Among the classic monographs on space and place are Tuan's *Space and Place: The Perspective of Experience* (1977), David Harvey's *The Condition of Postmodernity: An Enquiry into the Origins of Cultural Change* (1989), and *Space and Place: of Identity and Location*, edited by Erica Carter, James Donald, and Judith Squires (1993).
4. In terms of her regionalism, studies range from Anne-Marie Brumm's "The Poetry of Regionalism: Feminine Voices of the Nineteenth-Century, Emily Dickinson and Annette Von Droste-Huelshoff" (1985) to the Dickinson chapter in Christopher Benfey's *American Audacity: Literary Essays North and South* (2008). For studies on how the scientific discourses of the time have informed Dickinson's work, including her conceptions of place, see, for instance, James Guthrie, who in *Emily Dickinson's Vision: Illness and Identity in Her Poetry* (1998) reads

Dickinson's spatial tropes as attempts to redefine locality as a new kind of locus within her poetry (6); Robin Peel, *Emily Dickinson and the Hill of Science* (2010), especially the chapters on geography and Darwin; and Paul Giles, who claims that the conceptual range of her work negotiates theological and scientific notions of time and place, and that her local and especially her global imagination are informed by transhistorical and geophysical perspectives ("'The Earth Reversed Her Hemispheres': Dickinson's Global Antipodality," 2011).

5. Concentric circles themselves are becoming, as J. A. Wiens puts it, "a new ecological buzzword" (385), used to measure natural phenomena on different scales. In environmental ethics, Peter Wenz has developed a concentric circles theory of moral responsibility in order to negotiate human responsibilities toward people and other elements of the environment, such as animals and the soil, in terms of relative closeness to the center (316–17).

6. Dickinson used an 1844 printing of the 1841 edition of Noah Webster's *American Dictionary of the English Language* (Cristanne Miller, *Emily Dickinson: A Poet's Grammar*, 189n3), while Whitman used the 1846 edition "religiously" (Folsom, "Prairie Paradise" 49). For the entries I am using in this study, I quote mainly from the 1847 edition; the differences between these editions are minimal.

7. For a detailed discussion of Tupper's probable influence on Whitman, see Matt Cohen, "Martin Tupper, Walt Whitman, and the Early Reviews of *Leaves of Grass*."

8. In Dickinson criticism, humility is occasionally mentioned, but usually in passing, and mostly with regard to the role of women and religious positions. Particularly noteworthy here is Charles Anderson's comment regarding Dickinson's "coy" poems on nature having an "inner secret," in which she seems to prefer ignorance over scientific or theological dogma (84)—a move he links to religious humility: "Her religious training taught humble resignation since all would be made clear in heaven, but the ambiguity of the grave's meaning to her set up an ironic discontent with mortal limitations," especially the limitations of human knowledge (85). A related discussion is offered by Brantley's *Experience and Faith*, which includes a brief section on "Unassuming Knowledge" that talks about Dickinson's "modest claim to knowledge" (75) in terms of a scientifically informed, empirically grounded outlook that reaches back to religious epistemologies. In Whitman criticism, the concept is hardly mentioned. David S. Reynolds links Whitman's life and work to Benjamin Franklin's famous thirteen virtues, including "Humility," and argues that Whitman's humility, always in combination with arrogance, finds an expression in his identification with the "divine average" and the "commonest and cheapest," as well as in his decision to keep his name off most editions of *Leaves of Grass* ("Benjamin Franklin's Representative Man" 38).

9. Apart from Weinstein's thesis, and two of his essays on Marianne Moore (2010) and Susan Cooper (2012), the concept of humility also plays a critical role in Bonnie Costello's chapter on Marianne Moore in her *Shifting Ground: Reinventing Landscape in Modern American Poetry* (2003).
10. Leopold's argument is often taken as an expression of ecocentrism, since it involves changing the role of humans from conqueror to mere member of the biotic community (Leopold 204). This does not mean, however, that Leopold's notion of humility is in itself ecocentric; after all, it is also a distinct quality that sets humans apart in their specific responsibility.
11. There are also a number of analyses on *Specimen Days* (1882) that explore Whitman's approach to the natural world. Betsy Erkkila's *Whitman the Political Poet* (1989) includes a discussion of how Whitman "depicts again and again the presence of self in nature, nature in self," in both descriptive and interactive terms (296–97); Daniel J. Philippon's "'I Only Seek to Put You in Rapport': Message and Method in Walt Whitman's *Specimen Days*" (1998) argues that Whitman does not represent nature as an inanimate entity for aesthetic consumption but re-presents it for readers to have a "healthful" rapport with it.
12. See my own "Managing the Wilderness: Walt Whitman's Southern Landscapes" (2004) and "'Syllabled to Us for Names': Native American Echoes in Walt Whitman's Green Poetics" (2006), Paul Outka's "(De)Composing Whitman" (2005), Maria Farland's "Decomposing City: Walt Whitman's New York and the Science of Life and Death" (2007), and Steve Mentz's "After Sustainability" (2012).
13. See Midori Asahina's "'Fascination Is Absolute of Clime': Reading Dickinson's Correspondence with Higginson as Naturalist" (2005), my own "'Often Seen – but Seldom Felt': Emily Dickinson's Reluctant Ecology of Place" (2006), Hubert Zapf's "Literary Ecology and the Ethics of Texts" (2008), Scott Knickerbocker's "Emily Dickinson's Ethical Artifice" (2008), Robert Kern's "Birds of a Feather: Emily Dickinson, Alberto Manguel, and the Nature Poet's Dilemma" (2009), and Cecily Parks's "The Swamps of Emily Dickinson" (2013). And while not explicitly ecocritical in outlook, Colleen Boggs's "Emily Dickinson's Animal Pedagogies" (2009) and Aaron Shackelford's "Dickinson's Animals and Anthropomorphism" (2010) are also noteworthy here, for their discussion of the ethical and epistemological implications of Dickinson's animal poems.

Part I

1. The most recent discussion of the resemblance between Parton's *Fern Leaves* and Whitman's 1855 *Leaves of Grass* can be found in Ed Folsom's *Whitman Making Books, Books Making Whitman* (14).

Chapter 1

1. Judith Farr argues that Dickinson shares a "respect for definition and detail" with Ruskin's Pre-Raphaelites" and that she "achieves visual representation of [Ruskinian] downright fact" ("Dickinson and the Visual Arts" 72). Paula Bennett writes that "the care and feeding of flowers were themselves [. . .] supremely important" for Dickinson, emphasizing that in her art, flowers serve as references to "poetry and the poetic process, to individuals and to generic human beings, to Jesus and the soul, to Eden and bliss, and, perhaps most important, to women and the female genitalia" ("Flowers" 116).
2. For a discussion of the related concept of anthropomorphism, both in the mid-nineteenth-century sciences and in Dickinson's animal poetry, see Aaron Shackelford's "Dickinson's Animals and Anthropomorphism."
3. Hubert Zapf offers a detailed and insightful reading of the poem as an ecological text, emphasizing its referential qualities and, especially, its "semantic indeterminacy and [. . .] metaphoric, narrative, and aesthetic dimensions"; fascinatingly, Zapf reads the poem as a key example of literature's ethical function, namely, "a self-reflexive form of knowledge staging complex life processes at the boundary line of the culture-nature interaction" (858, 860).
4. Charles Anderson's interpretation of a shorter version of the poem (consisting of the second and third stanzas) comes to a very different conclusion than I do here. To him, the poem suggests that even a child never gets "admission," since all one sees at a circus is a mere spectacle, and that "man must remain forever a child incapable of growing up to true knowledge" (84).
5. I am grateful to Ed Folsom for an extended conversation about this poem in 2006, which helped me to articulate this interpretation.

Chapter 2

1. It is, for example, central to Val Plumwood's work, who defines it as a noninstrumental way of relating to the other (*Feminism and the Mastery of Nature*, esp. 154, 188).
2. See, for instance, Beaver; Reynolds, *Whitman's America*; and Matteson.
3. I thank Ed Folsom for his generosity in discussing this crucial connection with me.
4. John Burroughs had already marveled that "[b]efore Darwin or Spencer [Whitman] proclaimed the doctrine of evolution" (*Birds and Poets* 138); and Joseph Beaver's detailed chapter on evolution stresses that this passage is "specific and orderly," a progression from minerals, via plant and animal life, including "occasional 'throwbacks' or regression" in the evolutionary process (111–12).

Chapter 3

1. Angus Fletcher's revaluation of poetic description also takes a very brief look at Dickinson. He posits "From Cocoon forth a Butterfly" (Fr610) as a model for "the most intensely deep descriptive poetic form, the *chorographic* poem" (117), and argues that the poem emphasizes "space rather than place," while its objects matter mainly because they surround the observer (118).
2. How much landscape painting was part of nineteenth-century environmental discourses is underscored by the fact that Alexander von Humboldt dedicated a long section of his *Cosmos* to it because it ideally fused the two key principles of his science, accurate measurement and visual representation (cf. Walls, *Seeing New Worlds* 101).
3. Other environmental revaluations of Ruskin include Brian J. Day's "The Moral Intuition of Ruskin's 'Storm-Cloud' " (2005) and Donald Winch's "Thinking Green, Nineteenth-Century Style: John Stuart Mill and John Ruskin" (2004). While the green undertones of Ruskin's work certainly do not compensate for his "romantic neofeudalism," as Jonathan Bate has called it (268), they nevertheless invite us to reconsider the upper-class perspectives that often fed into landscape painting as complex responses to an emerging sense of environmental crisis.
4. In her ecofeminist discussion of swamps in Dickinson's work, Cecily Parks links the fourth stanza to Dickinson's tendency "to pair feminized flowers with the ambiguous bog" (20).
5. For instance, Joanne Feit Diehl has linked the poem's "absence of assured meaning either in the trees' relation to other natural facts or to an ordering principle" to Dickinson's own "sense of dislocation" ("Ransom in a Voice" 164–65); E. Miller Budick has argued that the poem's "confusion and fragmentation" have less to do with "external nature" than with surpassing disunities of "the human thought process" (16–17); and Cynthia Griffin Wolff has read the poem as an example of Dickinson's view of a "demythologized world" that is "emancipated from the tyranny of God's rule," a universe that "has been evacuated of meaning and intrinsic relationships" (459). Turning to the poem's "external nature," Shira Wolosky still stresses that it confronts a "world of radical disorder," "of discrete details without interconnection," through a syntax that is "as discontinuous as the scene it presents" ("A Syntax of Contention" 163); and Susan Howe writes that this poem is "viewing Emptiness without design or plan, neighborless in winter blank, or blaze of summer. This is waste wilderness" (21).

Chapter 4

1. As early as 1887, Walter Lewin compared Whitman's nature notes to Thoreau's prose, claiming that the latter "was a disinterested student of nature, whereas

Whitman is always more or less concerned with the relation of nature to himself. [. . .] There is, however, no lack of sympathetic understanding in his intercourse with nature. He seems to include the very plants, and animals, and sea, and sky in his 'comradeship'" (390–91). In 1933, Sculley Bradley stressed that Whitman's notes "compare favorably with the writings of the poet's great friend, John Burroughs, who admired them so much" (235). Both mention the role of description in Whitman's nature notes in passing—Lewin finds that "[s]ome of his descriptions of natural scenery are exceedingly fine" (390), and Bradley stresses their fidelity and groundedness in sincere experience. Recently, Daniel J. Philippon has argued that Whitman tried to "re-present" an indescribable nature by a rhetoric of spontaneity, artlessness, and intimacy, as well as by a structure of loosely connected fragments, yet without discussing the role of description in this text.

2. In an earlier version of this argument I have compared "As I Ebb'd" to Dickinson's "I started Early – Took my Dog – " (Fr656) in terms of their interest in the tensions between recognizing the sea as a dynamic place and force and the ensuing crisis of the speaker's stable sense of self ("Sounding Together: Walt Whitman, Emily Dickinson and the Ocean of Organic Life").
3. That the *Atlantic* would also print excerpts from Louis Agassiz's "Methods of Study in Natural History" (1862), which combined rich accounts of the seas—especially "the slow growth of coral reefs, those wonderful sea-walls raised by the little ocean-architects whose own bodies furnish both the building-stones and the cement that binds them together" (571)—with blatantly racist arguments against Darwin's views of evolution, shows to what extent novel ideas about the natural environment were part of controversial social and political discussions.
4. This personification has been interpreted in terms of heterosexual fulfillment, homoerotic passion, and a vision of a renewed bond with Whitman's father (cf. Gutman 32–33). Revisiting this juncture from a green perspective, Killingsworth finds that the "identity with the island-father seems to give the poet the strength to face again the ocean's ebb-tide dirge," and suggests that the father figure serves Whitman as a symbolic means for expressing the human insignificance for which his own father was an actual example (*Whitman and the Earth* 126–27). I would claim that while the island-father indeed consists of small sands and drifts, it also figures as a prominent physical entity with which the desperate poet hopes to reconcile as much as with his ocean-mother, and that this double personification of nature as complex parental figures also has environmental implications outside of the biographical paradigm.
5. Regarding the hermit thrush, Lawrence Buell writes that knowledge of the ornithological reasons for Whitman's choice increases the appreciation of the poem in terms of its "outer mimesis" (*The Environmental Imagination* 97).

Earlier, Lutwack found the passages on the thrush ornithologically consistent ("bird and habitat are carefully described in the Lincoln poem"; 69) and speculated that Whitman may have refrained from presenting the thrush as expressing grief in reaction to Burroughs's complaint about interpretations that have no grounding in natural history (70). Berbrich linked the botanically correct references to lilacs to Whitman's biography (171), and Beaver offered a detailed discussion of Whitman's exact references to Venus as the poem's "great star" (31).

6. Killingsworth argues convincingly that "the bird reminds the poet of his faculty of openness" and claims that "in the notion of 'tallying'—[. . .] a pattern of responses repeated in all the seashore and wetland poems—lies perhaps [Whitman's] greatest contribution to ecopoetics, the willingness and capacity of the sensitive person to be transformed in the face of undeniable otherness, both human and natural" (*Whitman and the Earth* 119).

Part III

1. The narrativity of Dickinson's poems is discussed in two essays, Michael Ryan's "Dickinson's Stories" and Elizabeth Willis's "Dickinson's Species of Narrative" (both 2009). Cristanne Miller also stresses that Dickinson's poetry tested the possibilities and limitations of narrative properties, and may well have been influenced by the very popular long narrative poems of the time even if she did not write any herself (*Reading in Time* 23).

Chapter 5

1. Even though this is a letter and not a poem, its double-edged agricultural commentary can also be linked to Betsy Erkkila's important argument that Dickinson's "poetic revolution was grounded in the privilege of her class position [. . .] whose elitist, antidemocratic values were at the very center of her work" ("Dickinson and Class" 23).
2. Of special interest here is William Mulder's "Seeing 'New Englandly': Planes of Perception in Emily Dickinson and Robert Frost," which argues that her New England poetry contains an elementary level of description, which celebrates "the land and life on the land" pictorially; a didactic level of reading nature as a manual for ethical instruction; and a symbolic level that yearns for transcendence (550–51).
3. Dickinson critics, who occasionally mention nostalgia in context-oriented interpretations, have so far not linked it to America's environmentalist debates. In particular, Domhnall Mitchell writes that "[t]he modern machine [in "I like to see it lap the Miles"] is made over into a nostalgic, agrarian vision of highly strung animals and their bemused but tolerant masters" at a time when writers opposed "the urban-industrial transformation of the landscape and its ac-

companying demographic changes with a nostalgic vision of empty fields and grazing cows" (43, 35); Elizabeth Petrino explains that the era's nature writers seldom distinguished between "science observation and nostalgic reverie" (131); and Adam Sweeting has shown Samuel Bowles's texts about Indian summer in the *Springfield Republican* to be both deeply nostalgic and attentive to the season's evocations of death and guilt (143).

4. For a detailed discussion of nineteenth-century ballads in connection with the formal features of Dickinson's poetry, see Cristanne Miller, *Reading in Time* (49–81).

Chapter 6

1. See also early biographical studies such as Joan D. Berbrich's *Three Voices from Paumanok* (1969) and Bertha H. Funnel's *Walt Whitman on Long Island* (1971).
2. For a book-length discussion of industrialization's devastating effects on New England waters, see Theodore Steinberg's *Nature Incorporated: Industrialization and the Waters of New England* (1991).
3. For an interesting historical context for this move, see Selzer 163–64.
4. In a related but different argument, Linda Selzer claims that the workers are the crucial force in the poem, their hard labor serving to increase, paradoxically, the awe for the trees (160–61).
5. An early exception is Deborah Kolb's "Walt Whitman and the South," which argues that "Whitman's fascination with the South grows from a delight in the exotic landscape and manners of New Orleans to a highly complex artistic concern for the unity of the nation and the unity of an individual" (13).
6. Cowdrey explains this situation as follows: "The agricultural fixation of the South, spreading ruin in one place, protected or at any rate ignored other woodlands; distance from rivers, a low population, rugged or nonarable land could still provide adequate protection in a section which still held its frontier character until the Gilded Age. The spirit of the Old South was seemingly quite willing to cut down its forests, almost to the last tree; but performance was incurably weak" (93).
7. For a critical discussion of the initial attempts to maintain an anachronistic façade of wilderness in national parks, and of the century-long clash between proponents of resource management in national parks and those who favored strict protective measures, see Richard West Sellars, *Preserving Nature in the National Parks: A History* (1997). The first American wetlands to be protected were Florida's Everglades (in 1947), after the national park concept had shifted from its initial focus on areas of supreme natural beauty to a "broader desire to protect the biological integrity of water, energy, and land" (Siry 373).

Part IV

1. In particular, Ursula K. Heise's *Sense of Place and Sense of Planet* (2008) analyzes recent "eco-cosmopolitan" narrative texts whose stylistic features enable an imaginative engagement with the entire globe.

Chapter 7

1. Critics have found that Dickinson makes fun of her schooling here (Sewall 350; Peel 61), pays happy homage to it (Eberwein, "Dickinson's Local, Global, and Cosmic Perspectives" 34), or formulates a more serious critique of pedagogical practices (Pollack, "Emily Dickinson's Valentines"; Robson 107). Robin Peel's chapter on geology offers detailed discussions of the scientific subfields and publications that the poem alludes to, especially magazines and educational books under the name Peter Parley (160–61).
2. As I mentioned above, Dickinson used an 1844 printing of the 1841 Webster's *American Dictionary of the English Language* and Whitman an 1846 edition; I am using an 1847 edition here, which is largely identical with the earlier two.

Chapter 8

1. The only exception I am aware of is Bruce Piasecki's essay on teaching environmental literature, "American Literary Environmentalism before Darwin" (1985), which provides an important survey of pre-Darwinian environmental publications and briefly links almost all of them, including Humboldt's *Cosmos*, to Whitman.
2. "Studying nature fills all my leisure; it bestows such a pure pleasure to which I know no other to compare, to which every moral feeling is chained and which has gifted me with the happiest hours of my life" (translation mine).

Bibliography

Agassiz, Louis. "Methods of Study in Natural History." *Atlantic Monthly* 9.55 (May 1862): 570–78.

Allen, Gay Wilson. "How Emerson, Thoreau, and Whitman Viewed the Frontier." *Toward a New American Literary History: Essays in Honor of Arlin Turner.* Eds. Louis J. Budd, Edwin H. Cady, and Carl L. Anderson. Durham, NC: Duke University Press, 1980. 111–28.

———. "The Influence of Space on the American Imagination." *Essays on American Literature in Honor of Jay B. Hubbell.* Ed. Clarence Gohdes. Durham, NC: Duke University Press, 1967. 329–42.

———. *The New Walt Whitman Handbook.* New York: New York University Press, 1986.

———. *The Solitary Singer: A Critical Biography of Walt Whitman.* 1955. New York: New York University Press, 1967.

Allen, T. F. H., and Thomas W. Hoekstra. *Toward a Unified Ecology.* New York: Columbia University Press, 1992.

Anderson, Charles Roberts. *Emily Dickinson's Poetry: Stairway of Surprise.* New York: Holt Rinehart, 1960.

Anderson, Douglas. "Presence and Place in Emily Dickinson's Poetry." *New England Quarterly* 57.2 (1984): 205–24.

Ando, Midori. "Birds." Eberwein, *An Emily Dickinson Encyclopedia* 23–24.

Angelo, Ray. "Catalog of Plant Specimens." *Emily Dickinson's Herbarium: A Facsimile Edition.* By Emily Dickinson. Cambridge, MA: Belknap Press, 2006. 169–92.

Asahina, Midori. "'"Fascination" Is Absolute of Clime': Reading Dickinson's Correspondence with Higginson as Naturalist." *Emily Dickinson Journal* 14.2 (2005): 103–19.

Ashworth, William. *The Encyclopedia of Environmental Studies.* New York: Facts on File Science Library, 1991.

Aspiz, Harold. "Science and Pseudoscience." Kummings, *A Companion to Walt Whitman* 216–32.

———. "'There Was a Child Went Forth' (1855)." LeMaster and Kummings 714–15.

Baker, Dorothy Z. "Domesticity, as Subject." Eberwein, *An Emily Dickinson Encyclopedia* 86–87.

Ball, Ian R. "Nature and Formulation of Biogeographical Hypotheses." *Systematic Zoology* 24.4 (1975): 407–30.

Barker, Wendy. *Lunacy of Light: Emily Dickinson and the Experience of Metaphor.* Carbondale: Southern Illinois University Press, 1987.

Bate, Jonathan. *The Song of the Earth.* Cambridge, MA: Harvard University Press, 2000.

Baym, Nina. *American Women of Letters and the Nineteenth-Century Sciences: Styles of Affiliation.* New Brunswick, NJ: Rutgers University Press, 2002.

———. "Thoreau's View of Science." *Journal of the History of Ideas* 26 (1965): 221–34.

Beaver, Joseph. *Walt Whitman—Poet of Science.* New York: King's Crown, 1951.

Benfey, Christopher. *American Audacity: Literary Essays North and South.* Ann Arbor: University of Michigan Press, 2008.

———. *Dickinson and the Problem of Others.* Amherst: University of Massachusetts Press, 1984.

———. *Emily Dickinson: Lives of a Poet.* New York: George Braziller, 1986.

———. "Emily Dickinson and the American South." *The Cambridge Companion to Emily Dickinson.* Ed. Wendy Martin. Cambridge: Cambridge University Press, 2002. 30–50.

Bennett, Paula. *Emily Dickinson: Woman Poet.* London: Harvester Wheatsheaf, 1990.

———. "Flowers." Eberwein, *An Emily Dickinson Encyclopedia* 115–16.

Berbrich, Joan D. *Three Voices from Paumanok: The Influence of Long Island on James Fenimore Cooper, William Cullen Bryant, and Walt Whitman.* Port Washington, NY: Ira J. Friedman, 1969.

Black, Stephen A. "*Leaves of Grass.*" LeMaster and Kummings 352–54.

Blackhawk, Terry. "'Flowers-Well-If Anybody.'" Eberwein, *An Emily Dickinson Encyclopedia* 116–17.

Blakemore, Steven, and Jon Noble. "Whitman and 'the Indian Problem': The Texts and Contexts of 'Song of the Redwood-Tree.'" *Walt Whitman Quarterly Review* 22.2–3 (Fall 2004): 108–25.

Boggs, Colleen. "Emily Dickinson's Animal Pedagogies." *PMLA* 124.2 (2009): 533–41.

Botkin, Daniel B. *Discordant Harmonies: A New Ecology for the Twenty-First Century.* New York: Oxford University Press, 1992.

Bowler, Peter J. *The Earth Encompassed: A History of the Environmental Sciences.* New York: Norton, 2000.

Bradley, Sculley. "Walt Whitman on Timber Creek." *American Literature* 5.3 (1933): 235–46.

Brantley, Richard E. *Experience and Faith: The Late-Romantic Imagination of Emily Dickinson.* New York: Palgrave Macmillan, 2004.

Brumm, Anne-Marie. "The Poetry of Regionalism: Feminine Voices of the Nineteenth-Century, Emily Dickinson and Annette Von Droste-Huelshoff." *Colby Library Quarterly* 21 (1985): 83–91.

Bryson, J. Scott. *Ecopoetry: A Critical Introduction.* Salt Lake City: University of Utah Press, 2002.

Budick, E. Miller. *Emily Dickinson and the Life of Language: A Study in Symbolic Poetics.* Baton Rouge: Louisiana State University Press, 1985.

Buell, Janet. "'A Slow Solace': Emily Dickinson and Consolation." *The New England Quarterly* 62.3 (1989): 323–45.

Buell, Lawrence. "Ecocriticism: Some Emerging Trends." *Qui Parle: Critical Humanities and Social Sciences* 19.2 (Spring-Summer 2011): 87–115.

———. *The Environmental Imagination: Thoreau, Nature Writing, and the Formation of American Culture.* Cambridge: Harvard University Press, 1995.

———. *The Future of Environmental Criticism: Environmental Crisis and Literary Imagination.* Malden, MA: Blackwell, 2005.

———. "The Timelessness of Place: Response to the Presidential Address." *American Quarterly* 58.1 (2006): 17–22.

———. *Writing for an Endangered World: Literature, Culture, and Environment in the U.S. and Beyond.* Cambridge, MA: Belknap Press, 2001.

Burroughs, John. *Birds and Poets with Other Papers.* 1877. Boston: Houghton Mifflin, 1899.

———. *Notes on Walt Whitman, as Poet and Person.* 2nd ed. New York: J. S. Redfield, 1871.

———. "Real and Sham Natural History." *Atlantic Monthly* 91.545 (March 1903): 298–309.

———. *Wake-Robin.* 1871. Boston: Houghton Mifflin, 1913.

———. *Whitman: A Study.* New York: AMS Press, 1969.

Byers, Thomas B. "Believing Too Much in Words: W. S. Merwin and the Whitman Heritage." *Missouri Review* 3.2 (1980): 75–89.

Cabot, James Elliot. "Our Birds, and Their Ways." *Atlantic Monthly* 1.2 (1857): 209–16.

Carter, Erica, James Donald, and Judith Squires, eds. *Space and Place: Theories of Identity and Location.* London: Lawrence & Wishart, 1993.

Casey, Edward S. "How to Get from Space to Place in a Fairly Short Stretch of Time." *Sense of Place.* Eds. Steven Feld and Keith H. Basso. Santa Fe: School of American Research Press, 1996. 13–52.

Ceniza, Sherry. "Gender." Kummings, *A Companion to Walt Whitman* 180–96.

Cheever, David William. "The Aquarium." *Atlantic Monthly* 8.47 (September 1861): 322–37.

Cobb, Edith. *The Ecology of Imagination in Childhood.* London: Routledge, 1977.

Cohen, Matt. "Martin Tupper, Walt Whitman, and the Early Reviews of Leaves of Grass." *Walt Whitman Quarterly Review* 16 (Summer 1998): 23–31.

Cohen, Michael P. "Blues in the Green: Ecocriticism under Critique." *Environmental History* 9.1 (2004): 9–36.

Constanzo, Angelo. "Organicism." LeMaster and Kummings 490–91.
Cooper, Susan Feminore. *Rural Hours.* 1850. Eds. Rochelle Johnson and Daniel Patterson. Athens: University of Georgia Press, 1998.
Cosgrove, Denis E. "John Ruskin and the Geographical Imagination." *Geographical Review* 69.1 (1979): 43–62.
Costello, Bonnie. *Shifting Ground: Reinventing Landscape in Modern American Poetry.* Cambridge, MA: Harvard University Press, 2003.
Cowdrey, Albert E. *This Land, This South: An Environmental History.* Lexington: University Press of Kentucky, 1983.
Crumbley, Paul. "Child Role." Eberwein, *An Emily Dickinson Encyclopedia* 44.
Dandurand, Karen. "New Dickinson Civil War Publications." *American Literature* 56.1 (1984): 17–27.
Day, Brian J. "The Moral Intuition of Ruskin's 'Storm-Cloud.'" *SEL Studies in English Literature 1500–1900* 45.4 (2005): 917–33.
Dean, Dennis R. "Hitchcock's Dinosaur Tracks." *American Quarterly* 21.3 (1969): 639–44.
Dettelbach, Michael. "Alexander von Humboldt between Enlightenment and Romanticism." *Northeastern Naturalist* 8.1 (2001): 9–20.
Dickinson, Emily. *The Letters of Emily Dickinson.* Eds. Thomas H. Johnson and Theodora Ward. Cambridge, MA: Harvard University Press, 1986 (1958).
——. *The Poems of Emily Dickinson.* Ed. R. W. Franklin. 3 vols. Cambridge, MA: Harvard University Press, 1998.
Diedrich, Deborah. "'Song of Joys' (1860)." LeMaster and Kummings 653–54.
Diehl, Joanne Feit. *Dickinson and the Romantic Imagination.* Princeton, NJ: Princeton University Press, 1981.
——. "Ransom in a Voice: Language as Defense in Dickinson's Poetry." *Feminist Critics Read Emily Dickinson.* Ed. Suzanne Juhasz. Bloomington: Indiana University Press, 1983. 156–75.
——. *Women Poets and the American Sublime.* Bloomington: Indiana University Press, 1990.
Dorman, Robert L. *A Word for Nature: Four Pioneering Environmental Advocates, 1845–1913.* Chapel Hill: University of North Carolina Press, 1998.
Doudna, Martin K. "Nature." LeMaster and Kummings 451–54.
Doughty, Robin W. "Land Use." *Encyclopedia of Southern Culture.* Eds. Charles Reagan Wilson and William R. Ferris. Chapel Hill: University of North Carolina Press, 1989. 343–44.
Eberwein, Jane Donahue. *Dickinson: Strategies of Limitation.* Amherst: University of Massachusetts Press, 1985.
——. "Dickinson's Local, Global, and Cosmic Perspectives." *The Emily Dickinson Handbook.* Eds. Cristanne Miller, Roland Hagenbüchle, and Gudrun Grabher. Amherst: University of Massachusetts Press, 1998. 27–45.
——, ed. *An Emily Dickinson Encyclopedia.* Westport, CT: Greenwood, 1998.

——. "Nature." Eberwein, *An Emily Dickinson Encyclopedia* 205–6.

Eitner, Walter H. "Emily Dickinson's Awareness of Whitman: A Reappraisal." *Walt Whitman Review* 22 (1976): 111–15.

Elder, John. *Imagining the Earth: Poetry and the Vision of Nature*. Urbana: University of Illinois Press, 1985.

Erkkila, Betsy. "Emily Dickinson and Class." *American Literary History* 4.1 (1992): 1–27.

——. "Walt Whitman: The Politics of Language." *American Studies* 24.2 (Fall 1983): 21–34.

——. *Whitman the Political Poet*. New York: Oxford University Press, 1989.

Ette, Ottmar. "The Scientist as *Weltbürger*: Alexander von Humboldt and the Beginning of Cosmopolitics." *Northeastern Naturalist* 8.1 (2001): 157–82.

Farland, Maria Magdalena. "Decomposing City: Walt Whitman's New York and the Science of Life and Death." *ELH* 74.4 (Winter 2007): 799–827.

——. "'That Tritest/Brightest Truth': Emily Dickinson's Anti-Sentimentality." *Nineteenth-Century Literature* 53.3 (1998): 364–89.

Farr, Judith. "Dickinson and the Visual Arts." *The Emily Dickinson Handbook*. Eds. Gudrun Grabher, Roland Hagenbüchle, and Cristanne Miller. Amherst: University of Massachusetts Press, 1998. 61–92.

——. *The Gardens of Emily Dickinson*. With Louise Carter. Cambridge, MA: Harvard University Press, 2004.

Flagg, Wilson. "Among the Trees." *Atlantic Monthly* 6.35 (1860): 257–71.

——. "Trees in Assemblages." *Atlantic Monthly* 8.46 (August 1861): 129–41.

——. "The Winter-Birds." *Atlantic Monthly* 3.17 (1859): 319–30.

Fletcher, Angus. *A New Theory for American Poetry: Democracy, the Environment, and the Future of Imagination*. Cambridge, MA: Harvard University Press, 2004.

Foerster, Norman. *Nature in American Literature: Studies in the Modern View of Nature*. 1923. New York: Russell, 1950.

Folsom, Ed. *Walt Whitman's Native Representations*. Cambridge: Cambridge University Press, 1994.

——. "Walt Whitman's Prairie Paradise." *Recovering the Prairie*. Ed. Robert F. Sayre. Madison: University of Wisconsin Press, 1999. 47–60.

——. *Whitman Making Books, Books Making Whitman: A Catalogue and Commentary*. Iowa City: Obermann Center for Advanced Studies, 2005.

Folsom, Ed, and Kenneth M. Price. *Re-Scripting Walt Whitman: An Introduction to His Life and Work*. Malden, MA: Blackwell, 2005.

Friztell, Peter A. *Nature Writing and America: Essays upon a Cultural Type*. Ames: Iowa State University Press, 1990.

Funnel, Bertha H. *Walt Whitman on Long Island*. Port Washington, NY: Ira J. Friedman, 1971.

Fuss, Diana. "Corpse Poem." *Critical Inquiry* 30 (2003): 1–30.

Garrard, Greg. *Ecocriticism*. The New Critical Idiom. New York: Routledge, 2004.

Gelpi, Albert. *Emily Dickinson: The Mind of the Poet*. Cambridge, MA: Harvard University Press, 1965.

———. *The Tenth Muse: The Psyche of the American Poet*. Cambridge, MA: Harvard University Press, 1975.

Genoways, Ted. "An Unknown Daguerreotype." *Virginia Quarterly Review* 81.2 (Spring 2005): 11.

Gerhardt, Christine. "'Earth Adhering to Their Roots': Dickinson, Whitman, and the Ecology of Bookmaking." *American Studies as Media Studies*. Eds. Frank Kelleter and Daniel Stein. Heidelberg: Winter, 2008. 37–46.

———. "Managing the Wilderness: Walt Whitman's Southern Landscapes." *Forum for Modern Language Studies* 40.2 (Spring 2004): 225–35.

———. "'Often Seen – but Seldom Felt': Emily Dickinson's Reluctant Ecology of Place." *Emily Dickinson Journal* 15.1 (2006): 56–78.

———. "Sounding Together: Walt Whitman, Emily Dickinson and the Ocean of Organic Life." *Words on Water: Literary and Cultural Representations*. Eds. Maureen Devine and Christa Grewe-Volpp. Trier: WVT, 2008. 131–46.

———. "'Syllabled to Us for Names': Native American Echoes in Walt Whitman's Green Poetics." *Nature in Literary and Cultural Studies: Transatlantic Conversations on Ecocriticism*. Eds. Catrin Gersdorf and Sylvia Mayer. Amsterdam: Rodopi, 2006. 209–28.

Gibson, Robert B. "Respecting Ignorance and Uncertainty." *Achieving Environmental Goals: The Concept and "Often Seen – but Seldom Felt" Practice of Environmental Performance Review*. Ed. Erik Lykke. London: Belhaven, 1992. 158–78.

Gilcrest, David W. *Greening the Lyre: Environmental Poetics and Ethics*. Reno: University of Nevada Press, 2002.

Giles, Paul. "'The Earth Reversed Her Hemispheres': Dickinson's Global Antipodality." *Emily Dickinson Journal* 20.1 (2011): 1–21.

Glotfelty, Cheryll. "Introduction: Literary Studies in an Age of Environmental Crisis." *The Ecocriticism Reader: Landmarks in Literary Ecology*. Eds. Cheryll Glotfelty and Harold Fromm. Athens: University of Georgia Press, 1996. xv–xxxvii.

Godlewska, Anne Marie Claire. "Humboldt's Visual Thinking: From Enlightenment Vision to Modern Science." *Geography and Enlightenment*. Eds. David N. Livingstone and Charles W. J. Withers. Chicago: University of Chicago Press, 1999. 236–79.

Gonnaud, Maurice. "Nature, Apocalypse or Experiment: Emerson's Double Lineage in American Poetry." *Vistas of a Continent: Concepts of Nature in America*. Ed. Teut Andreas Riese. Heidelberg: Winter, 1979. 123–42.

Gottlieb, Robert. *Forcing the Spring: The Transformation of the American Environmental Movement*. 1993. Washington, DC: Island Press, 2005.

Goudie, Andrea. "Another Path to Reality: Emily Dickinson's Birds." *Concerning Poetry* 7 (Spring 1974): 31–38.

Gould, Stephen Jay. *Wonderful Life: The Burgess Shale and the Nature of History.* New York: Norton, 1989.

Greenberg, Robert M. *Splintered Worlds: Fragmentation and the Ideal of Diversity in the Work of Emerson, Melville, Whitman, and Dickinson.* Boston: Northeastern University Press, 1993.

Grove, Richard H. *Green Imperialism: Colonial Expansion, Tropical Island Edens and the Origins of Environmentalism, 1600–1860.* Cambridge: Cambridge University Press, 1995.

Grünzweig, Walter. "'For America – for All the Earth': Walt Whitman as an International(ist) Poet." *Breaking Bounds: Whitman and Amerian Cultural Studies.* Eds. Betsy Erkkila and Jay Grossman. New York: Oxford University Press, 1996. 238–50.

———. "Imperialism." Kummings, *A Companion to Walt Whitman* 151–63.

Guthrie, James R. *Emily Dickinson's Vision: Illness and Identity in Her Poetry.* Gainesville: University Press of Florida, 1998.

Gutman, Huck. "'As I Ebb'd with the Ocean of Life' (1860)." LeMaster and Kummings 31–33.

Habegger, Alfred. *My Wars Are Laid Away in Books: The Life of Emily Dickinson.* New York: Random House, 2001.

Handley, George. *New World Poetics: Nature and the Adamic Imagination of Whitman, Neruda, and Walcott.* Athens: University of Georgia Press, 2007.

Hart, George "Postmodernist Nature/Poetry: The Example of Larry Eigner." *Reading under the Sign of Nature: New Essays in Ecocriticism.* Eds. John Tallmadge and Henry Harrington. Salt Lake City: University of Utah Press, 2000. 315–32.

Harvey, David. *The Condition of Postmodernity: An Enquiry into the Origins of Cultural Change.* Oxford: Blackwell, 1989.

———. "From Space to Place and Back Again: Reflections on the Condition of Postmodernity." *Mapping the Future: Local Cultures, Global Change.* Ed. Jon Bird et al. London: Routledge, 1993. 3–29.

Heise, Ursula K. *Sense of Place and Sense of Planet: The Environmental Imagination of the Global.* New York: Oxford University Press, 2008.

Herod, Andrew. "Scale: The Local and the Global." *Key Concepts in Geography.* Eds. S. P. Rice, S. L. Holloway, and G. Valentine. London: Sage, 2003. 229–47.

Higginson, Thomas Wentworth. "The Life of Birds." *Atlantic Monthly* 10.59 (September 1862): 368–76.

———. *Out-Door Papers.* 1863. Michigan Reprint Series. Ann Arbor: Scholarly Publishing, University of Michigan University Library, 2006.

———. "Water-Lilies." *Atlantic Monthly* 22.11 (September 1858): 465–74.

Hitchcock, Edward. *Religion of Geology and Its Connected Sciences.* Boston: Phillips, Sampson, 1857.

Hitchcock, Edward, and Charles Henry Hitchcock. *Elementary Geology.* 1849. New York: Ivison, Phinney, 1862.

Hochman, Jhan. "Green Cultural Studies." *The Green Studies Reader: From Romanticism to Ecocriticism*. Ed. Laurence Coupe. London: Routledge, 2000. 187–92.

Holland, Josiah Gilbert. "Farming Life in New England." *Atlantic Monthly* 2.10 (1858): 334–41.

Howe, Susan. *My Emily Dickinson*. Berkeley, CA: North Atlantic Books, 1985.

Hubert, Denise Dawn. "Where's Walt? Situating the Poet-Speaker in His Nation." *Mickle Street Review* 17–18 (2005): http://micklestreet.rutgers.edu/archives/Issue%201718/index.html.

Hudgins, Andrew. "Walt Whitman and the South." *Southern Literary Journal* 15 (1982): 91–100.

Huffstetler, Edward W. "The American South." LeMaster and Kummings 671–72.

———. "'O Magnet-South' (1860)." LeMaster and Kummings 475.

Humboldt, Alexander von. *Cosmos: A Sketch of a Physical Description of the Universe*. 1845. Ed. Nicolaas A. Rupke. Vol. 1. Baltimore: Johns Hopkins University Press, 1997.

Hutchinson, Coleman. "'Eastern Exiles': Dickinson, Whiggery, and War." *Emily Dickinson Journal* 13.2 (2004): 1–26.

Hutchinson, George. *The Ecstatic Whitman: Literary Shamanism and the Crisis of the Union*. Columbus: Ohio State University Press, 1986.

Judd, Richard W. *Common Lands, Common People: The Origins of Conservation in Northern New England*. Cambridge, MA: Harvard University Press, 1997.

———. "A 'Wonderfull Order and Ballance': Natural History and the Beginning of Forest Conservation in America, 1730–1830." *Environmental History* 11.1 (2006): 8–36.

Keller, Karl. *The Only Kangaroo among the Beauty: Emily Dickinson and America*. Baltimore: Johns Hopkins University Press, 1979.

Kern, Robert. "Birds of a Feather: Emily Dickinson, Alberto Manguel, and the Nature Poet's Dilemma." *Isle: Interdisciplinary Studies in Literature and Environment* 16.2 (2009): 327–42.

Kher, Inder Nath. *The Landscape of Absence: Emily Dickinson's Poetry*. New Haven, CT: Yale University Press, 1974.

Killingsworth, M. Jimmie. "Nature." Kummings, *A Companion to Walt Whitman* 311–24.

———. "The Voluptuous Earth and the Fall of the Redwood Tree: Whitman's Personifications of Nature." *Whitman East and West*. Ed. Ed Folsom. Iowa City: University of Iowa Press, 2002. 14–25.

———. *Walt Whitman and the Earth: A Study in Ecopoetics*. Iowa City: University of Iowa Press, 2004.

Kirk, Diane Moore. "Landscapes of Old Age in Walt Whitman's Later Poetry." Ph.D. dissertation. Texas A&M University, 1994.

Knickerbocker, Scott. *Ecopoetics: The Language of Nature, the Nature of Language*. Amherst: University of Massachusetts Press, 2012.

———. "Emily Dickinson's Ethical Artifice." *Isle: Interdisciplinary Studies in Literature and Environment* 15.2 (2008): 185–97.

Kohn, David, et al. "What Henslow Taught Darwin: How a Herbarium Helped to Lay the Foundations of Evolutionary Thinking." *Nature* 436.4 (2005): 643–45.

Kolb, Deborah S. "Walt Whitman and the South." *Walt Whitman Review* 22 (1976): 3–14.

Kolodny, Annette. *The Lay of the Land: Metaphor as Experience and History in American Life and Letters.* Chapel Hill: University of North Carolina Press, 1975.

Krieg, Joann P. "Literary Contemporaries." Kummings, *A Companion to Walt Whitman* 392–408.

Kroeber, Karl. *Ecological Literary Criticism: Romantic Imagining and the Biology of Mind.* New York: Columbia University Press, 1994.

Kummings, Donald D., ed. *A Companion to Walt Whitman.* Malden, MA: Blackwell, 2006.

Lakoff, George, and Mark Turner. *More than Cool Reason: A Field Guide to Poetic Metaphor.* Chicago: University of Chicago Press, 1989.

Larson, Kerry C. "Song of Myself." Kummings, *A Companion to Walt Whitman* 471–83.

Lawson, Andrew. *Walt Whitman and the Class Struggle.* Iowa City: University of Iowa Press, 2006.

LeMaster, J. R., and Donald D. Kummings, eds. *Walt Whitman: An Encyclopedia.* Garland Reference Library of the Humanities. New York: Garland, 1998.

Leopold, Aldo. *A Sand County Almanac and Sketches Here and There.* New York: Oxford University Press, 1949.

Levin, Simon A. "The Problem of Pattern and Scale in Ecology: The Robert H. MacArthur Award Lecture." *Ecology* 73.6 (1992): 1943–67.

Lewin, Walter. "Walt Whitman's Specimen Days and Collect." *Academy* (4 June 1887): 390–91.

Lincoln, Almira H. *Familiar Lectures on Botany.* Hartford, CT: H. & F. J. Huntington, 1829.

Lloyd, David. "The Adult Voice in Dickinson's Child Poems." *Dickinson Studies* 49 (June 1984): 22–31.

Loeffelholz, Mary. *Dickinson and the Boundaries of Feminist Theory.* Urbana: University of Illinois Press, 1991.

Loving, Jerome. *Emerson, Whitman, and the American Muse.* Chapel Hill: University of North Carolina Press, 1982.

———. *Walt Whitman: The Song of Himself.* Berkeley: University of California Press, 1999.

Lowell, James Russell. "Humanity to Trees." *Crayon* 55 (October 1857): 96.

Lowenthal, David. *George Perkins Marsh: Prophet of Conservation.* Seattle: University of Washington Press, 2000.

———. "Introduction." *Man and Nature; or, Physical Geography as Modified by Human*

Action. 1864. By George Perkins Marsh. Cambridge, MA: Belknap Press, 1965. ix–xxix.

Lucas, Dolores D. *Emily Dickinson and Riddle*. DeKalb: Northern Illinois University Press, 1969.

Lutwack, Leonard. *Birds in Literature*. Gainesville: University Press of Florida, 1994.

Lyon, Thomas J., ed. *This Incomperable Lande: A Book of American Nature Writing*. New York: Penguin, 1991.

Madigan, Francis V., Jr. "Mermaids in the Basement: Emily Dickinson's Sea Imagery." *Greyfriar: Siena Studies in Literature* 23 (1982): 39–56.

Mancuso, Luke. *The Strange Sad War Revolving: Walt Whitman, Reconstruction, and the Emergence of Black Citizenship, 1865–1876*. Columbia, SC: Camden House, 1997.

Marsh, George Perkins. *Man and Nature; or, Physical Geography as Modified by Human Action*. 1864. Ed. David Lowenthal. Cambridge, MA: Belknap Press, 1965.

———. *So Great a Vision: The Conservationist Writings of George Perkins Marsh*. Ed. Stephen C. Trombulak. Hanover, NH: University Press of New England, 2001.

Martin, Wendy. *An American Triptych: Anne Bradstreet, Emily Dickinson, Adrienne Rich*. Chapel Hill: University of North Carolina Press, 1984.

Martz, Louis L. *The Poem of the Mind: Essays on Poetry, English and American*. New York: Oxford University Press, 1966.

Mason, John B. "'Passage to India' (1871)." LeMaster and Kummings 507–9.

Matteson, John T. "Justus Liebig." LeMaster and Kummings 392.

Mazel, David. *American Literary Environmentalism*. Athens: University of Georgia Press, 2000.

McKibben, Bill. "The Call of the Not So Wild." *Sharp Eyes: John Burroughs and American Nature Writing*. Ed. Charlotte Zoe Walker. Syracuse, NY: Syracuse University Press, 2000. 12–18.

McTier, Rosemary Scanlon. *"An Insect View of Its Plain": Insects, Nature and God in Thoreau, Dickinson and Muir*. Jefferson, NC: McFarland, 2013.

Melosi, Martin V. "Environment." *Encyclopedia of Southern Culture*. Eds. Charles Reagan Wilson and William R. Ferris. Chapel Hill: University of North Carolina Press, 1989. 315–21.

Mentz, Steve. "After Sustainability." *PMLA* 127.3 (May 2012): 586–92.

Merchant, Carolyn. *The Columbia Guide to American Environmental History*. New York: Columbia University Press, 2002.

———. *Ecological Revolutions: Nature, Gender, and Science in New England*. Chapel Hill: University of North Carolina Press, 1989.

Miller, Cristanne. *Emily Dickinson: A Poet's Grammar*. Cambridge, MA: Harvard University Press, 1987.

———. *Reading in Time: Emily Dickinson in the Nineteenth Century*. Amherst: University of Massachusetts Press, 2012.

Miller, James E., Jr. "'Song of Myself' (1855)." LeMaster and Kummings 654–57.

Mitchell, Domhnall. *Emily Dickinson: Monarch of Perception*. Amherst: University of Massachusetts Press, 2000.

Mitchell, W. J. T., ed. *Landscape and Power*. Chicago: University of Chicago Press, 2002.

Muir, John. *Nature Writings: The Story of My Boyhood and Youth; My First Summer in the Sierra; The Mountains of California; Stickeen; Selected Essays*. Ed. William Cronon. Washington, DC: Library of America, 1997.

Mulder, William. "Seeing 'New Englandly': Planes of Perception in Emily Dickinson and Robert Frost." *New England Quarterly* 52.4 (1979): 550–59.

Murray, Aife. *Maid as Muse: How Servants Changed Emily Dickinson's Life and Language*. Durham: University of New Hampshire Press, 2010.

Murray, Martin G. "Specimen Days." *A Companion to Walt Whitman*. Ed. Donald D. Kummings. Malden, MA: Blackwell, 2006. 553–65.

Naess, Arne. "Identification as Source of Deep Ecological Attitudes." *Deep Ecology*. Ed. Michael Tobias. San Diego: Avant Books, 1985. 256–70.

Nash, Roderick Frazier. *The Rights of Nature: A History of Environmental Ethics*. Madison: University of Wisconsin Press, 1989.

———. *Wilderness and the American Mind*. 1967. New Haven, CT: Yale University Press, 1982.

Nassauer, Joan Iverson. "Cultural Sustainability: Aligning Aesthetics and Ecology." *Placing Nature: Culture and Landscape Ecology*. Ed. Nassauer. Washington, DC: Island Press, 1997. 65–84.

Nelson, Howard. "'Crossing Brooklyn Ferry' (1860)." LeMaster and Kummings 156–58.

Newman, Lance. *Our Common Dwelling: Henry Thoreau, Transcendentalism, and the Class Politics of Nature*. New York: Palgrave Macmillan, 2005.

Nissenbaum, Stephen. "New England as Region and Nation." *All over the Map: Rethinking American Regions*. Eds. Edward L. Ayers et al. Baltimore: Johns Hopkins University Press, 1996. 38–61.

Norwood, Vera. "Women's Roles in Nature Study and Environmental Protection." *OAH Magazine of History* 10.3 (Spring 1996): 12–17.

Oelschlaeger, Max. *The Idea of Wilderness: From Prehistory to the Age of Ecology*. New Haven, CT: Yale University Press, 1991.

O'Gorman, Francis. "Ruskin's Memorial Landscapes." *Worldviews: Environment, Culture, Religion* 5.1 (March 2001): 20–34.

Oliver, Virginia H. *Apocalypse of Green: A Study of Emily Dickinson's Eschatology*. New York: Lang, 1989.

Olson, Steven. *The Prairie in Nineteenth-Century American Poetry*. Norman: University of Oklahoma Press, 1994.

Outka, Paul. "(De)Composing Whitman." *Isle: Interdisciplinary Studies in Literature and Environment* 12.1 (2005): 41–60.

Palmer, Douglas. "John Ruskin (1819–1900), Man of Art and Science." *Nature* 403 (24 February 2000): 830.

Parks, Cecily. "The Swamps of Emily Dickinson." *Emily Dickinson Journal* 22.1 (2013): 1–29.

Patterson, Rebecca. *Emily Dickinson's Imagery*. Amherst: University of Massachusetts Press, 1979.

Payne, Daniel G. *Voices in the Wilderness: American Nature Writing and Environmental Reform*. Hanover, NH: University Press of New England, 1996.

Peel, Robin. *Emily Dickinson and the Hill of Science*. Madison, NJ: Fairleigh Dickinson University Press, 2010.

Petrino, Elizabeth A. *Emily Dickinson and Her Contemporaries: Women's Verse in America, 1820–1885*. Hanover, NH: University Press of New England, 1998.

Philippon, Daniel J. "'I Only Seek to Put You in Rapport': Message and Method in Walt Whitman's Specimen Days." *Reading the Earth: New Directions in the Study of Literature and Environment*. Eds. Michael P. Branch et al. Moscow: University of Idaho Press, 1998. 179–93.

Phillips, Elizabeth. *Emily Dickinson: Personae and Performance*. University Park: Pennsylvania State University Press, 2004 (1988).

Piasecki, Bruce. "American Literary Environmentalism before Darwin." *Teaching Environmental Literature: Materials, Methods, Resources*. Ed. Frederick O. Waage. New York: MLA, 1985. 9–18.

———. "Conquest of the Globe: Walt Whitman's Concept of Nature." *Calamus* 23 (June 1983): 29–44.

Plumwood, Val. *Feminism and the Mastery of Nature*. London: Routledge, 1993.

Pollack, Vivian. *Dickinson: The Anxiety of Gender*. Ithaca, NY: Cornell University Press, 1984.

———. "Emily Dickinson (1830–1886)." LeMaster and Kummings 182–83.

———. "Emily Dickinson's Valentines." *American Quarterly* 26.1 (March 1974): 60–78.

Pratt, Mary Louise. *Imperial Eyes: Travel Writing and Transculturation*. London: Routledge, 1992.

Quetchenbach, Bernard W. *Back from the Far Field: American Nature Poetry in the Late 20th Century*. Charlottesville: University Press of Virginia, 2000.

Rasula, Jed. *This Compost: Ecological Imperatives in American Poetry*. Athens: University of Georgia Press, 2002.

Relph, Edward. *Place and Placelessness*. London: Academic Press, 1976.

Reveal, James L., and James S. Pringle. "Taxonomic Botany and Floristics." *Flora of North America North of Mexico*. Ed. Flora of North America Editorial Committee. Vol. 1. New York: Oxford University Press, 1993. 157–92.

Reynolds, David S. "Walt Whitman: Benjamin Franklin's Representative Man." *Modern Language Studies* 28 (Spring 1998): 29–39.

———. *Walt Whitman's America: A Cultural Biography*. New York: Knopf, 1995.

Richards, Eliza, ed. *Emily Dickinson in Context*. Cambridge: Cambridge University Press, 2013.

Richards, Robert J. *The Romantic Conception of Life: Science and Philosophy in the Age of Goethe*. Chicago: University of Chicago Press, 2002.

Robson, Catherine. "Reciting Alice: What Is the Use of a Book without Poems?" *The Feeling of Reading: Affective Experience and Victorian Literature*. Ed. Rachel Ablow. Ann Arbor: University of Michigan Press, 2010. 93–112.

Roche, John. "Democratic Space: The Ecstatic Geography of Walt Whitman and Frank Lloyd Wright." *Walt Whitman Quarterly Review* 6 (1988): 16–32.

Rotella, Guy. *Reading and Writing Nature: The Poetry of Robert Frost, Wallace Stevens, Marianne Moore, and Elizabeth Bishop*. Boston: Northeastern University Press, 1991.

Rupke, Nicolaas A. "Introduction to the 1997 Edition." *Cosmos: A Sketch of a Physical Description of the Universe*. 1845. By Alexander von Humboldt. Baltimore: Johns Hopkins University Press, 1997. vii–xlii.

Ruskin, John. *Modern Painters: Volume 1. Of General Principles, and of Truth*. N.p.: Elibron Classics, 2005.

Ryan, Michael. "Dickinson's Stories." *American Poetry Review* 38.2 (March–April 2009): 5–6.

Sachs, Aaron. "The Ultimate 'Other': Post-Colonialism and Alexander von Humboldt's Ecological Relationship with Nature." *History and Theory* 42.4 (December 2003): 111–35.

Salska, Agnieszka. *Walt Whitman and Emily Dickinson: Poetry of the Central Consciousness*. Philadelphia: University of Pennsylvania Press, 1985.

Sánchez-Eppler, Karen. *Touching Liberty: Abolition, Feminism, and the Politics of the Body*. Berkeley: University of California Press, 1993.

Sattelmeyer, Robert. "Introduction." *Henry David Thoreau: The Natural History Essays*. Ed. Sattelmeyer. Salt Lake City: Peregrine Smith Books, 1989. vii–xxxiv.

Scanlan, Sean. "Introduction: Nostalgia." *Iowa Journal of Cultural Studies* 5.1 (2005): 3–9.

Scigaj, Leonard M. *Sustainable Poetry: Four American Ecopoets*. Lexington: University Press of Kentucky, 1999.

Sellars, Richard West. *Preserving Nature in the National Parks: A History*. New Haven, CT: Yale University Press, 1997.

Selzer, Linda Furgerson. "Walt Whitman, Clarence Major, and Changing Thresholds of American Wonder." *Walt Whitman Quarterly Review* 29 (2012): 159–70.

Sewall, Richard. *The Life of Emily Dickinson*. New York: Farrar, Straus & Giroux, 1974.

Shackelford, Aaron. "Dickinson's Animals and Anthropomorphism." *Emily Dickinson Journal* 19.2 (2010): 47–66.

Sielke, Sabine. "Natural Sciences." *Emily Dickinson in Context*. Ed. Eliza Richards. Cambridge: Cambridge University Press, 2013.

Siry, Joseph V. "Wetlands." *Encyclopedia of Southern Culture.* Eds. Charles Reagan Wilson and William R. Ferris. Chapel Hill: University of North Carolina Press, 1989. 371–73.

Slicer, Deborah. "Toward an Ecofeminist Standpoint Theory: Bodies as Grounds." *Ecofeminism: Women, Animals, Nature.* Ed. Greta Gaard. Philadelphia: Temple University Press, 1993. 49–73.

Slovic, Scott. *Seeking Awareness in American Nature Writing: Henry David Thoreau, Annie Dillard, Edward Abbey, Wendell Berry, and Barry Lopez.* Salt Lake City: University of Utah Press, 1992.

———. "The Third Wave of Ecocriticism: North American Reflections on the Current Phase of the Discipline." *Ecozon@* 1.1 (2010): 4–10.

Smallwood, J. B. "Environmental Movements." *Encyclopedia of Southern Culture.* Eds. Charles Reagan Wilson and William R. Ferris. Chapel Hill: University of North Carolina Press, 1989. 332–35.

Smith, Neil. "Homeless/Global: Scaling Places." *Mapping the Futures: Local Cultures, Global Change.* Eds. Jon Bird et al. London: Routledge, 1993. 87–119.

St. Armand, Barton Levi. *Emily Dickinson and Her Culture: The Soul's Society.* Cambridge: Cambridge University Press, 1984.

Stein, Rachel. *Shifting the Ground: American Women Writers' Revision of Nature, Gender, and Race.* Charlottesville: University Press of Virginia, 1997.

Steinberg, Ted [Theodore]. *Down to Earth: Nature's Role in American History.* New York: Oxford University Press, 2002.

———. *Nature Incorporated: Industrialization and the Waters of New England.* Cambridge: Cambridge University Press, 2003.

Steiner, Dieter, and Markus Nauser. "General Introduction." *Human Ecology: Fragments of Anti-Fragmentary Views of the World.* Eds. Steiner and Nauser. London: Routledge, 1993. 1–12.

Stewart, Frank. *A Natural History of Nature Writing.* Washington, DC: Island Press, 1995.

Stonum, Gary Lee. *The Dickinson Sublime.* Madison: University of Wisconsin Press, 1990.

Strysick, Michael. "Cultural Studies, as an Approach." Eberwein, *An Emily Dickinson Encyclopedia* 58–59.

Sweeting, Adam. *Beneath the Second Sun: A Cultural History of Indian Summer.* Hanover: University of New Hampshire Press, 2003.

Temin, Peter. "The Industrialization of New England, 1830–1880." *Engines of Enterprise: An Economic History of New England.* Ed. Temin. Cambridge, MA: Harvard University Press, 2000. 109–52.

Thaxter, Celia. "Among the Isles of Shoals I." *Atlantic Monthly* 24.142 (1869): 177–87.

———. "Among the Isles of Shoals VI." *Atlantic Monthly* 25.151 (1870): 579–89.

Thomas, M. Wynn. *The Lunar Light of Whitman's Poetry.* Cambridge, MA: Harvard University Press, 1987.

Thoreau, Henry David. "Autumnal Tints." *The Essays of Henry D. Thoreau*. Ed. Lewis Hyde. New York: North Point, 2002. 215–42.

———. *Cape Cod*. 1865. Ed. Joseph M. Moldenhauer. Princeton, NJ: Princeton Paperback, 1993.

———. "Chesuncock." *Atlantic Monthly* 2.10 (1858): 305–17.

———. "Huckleberries." *Henry David Thoreau: Collected Essays and Poems*. Ed. Elizabeth Hall Witherell. New York: Library of America, 2001. 468–501.

———. *Walden and Resistance to Civil Government*. Ed. William Rossi. New York: Norton, 1992.

———. "Walking." *Atlantic Monthly* 9.56 (1862): 657–74.

———. "Wild Apples." *Henry David Thoreau: Collected Essays and Poems*. Ed. Elizabeth Hall Witherell. New York: Library of America, 2001. 444–67.

———. "A Winter Walk." *The Essays of Henry D. Thoreau*. Ed. Lewis Hyde. New York: North Point, 2002. 27–41.

Tichi, Cecelia. *New World, New Earth: Environmental Reform in American Literature from the Puritans through Whitman*. New Haven, CT: Yale University Press, 1979.

Trachtenberg, Alan. "Whitman's Lesson of the City." *Breaking Bounds: Whitman and American Cultural Studies*. Eds. Betsy Erkkila and Jay Grossman. New York: Oxford University Press, 1996. 163–73.

Tuan, Yi-Fu. "Humanistic Geography." *Annals of the Association of American Geographers* 66.2 (June 1976): 266–76.

———. "Language and the Making of Place: A Narrative-Descriptive Approach." *Annals of the Association of American Geographers* 81.4 (1991): 684–96.

———. "Space and Place: Humanistic Perspective." *Human Geography: An Essential Anthology*. Eds. John Agnew, David N. Livingstone, and Alisdair Rogers. Oxford: Blackwell, 1996. 444–57.

———. *Space and Place: The Perspective of Experience*. 1977. Minneapolis: University of Minnesota Press, 1995.

———. *Topophilia: A Study of Environmental Perception, Attitudes, and Values*. Englewood Cliffs, NJ: Prentice-Hall, 1974.

Tyrrell, Ian R. *True Gardens of the Gods: Californian-Australian Environmental Reform, 1860–1930*. Berkeley: University of California Press, 1999.

Waldman, John R. *Heartbeats in the Muck: The History, Sea Life and Environment of New York Harbor*. New York: Lyons Press, 1999.

Walls, Laura Dassow. *Emerson's Life in Science: The Culture of Truth*. Ithaca, NY: Cornell University Press, 2003.

———. "'Hero of Knowledge, Be Our Tribute Thine': Alexander von Humboldt in Victorian America." *Northeastern Naturalist* 8.1 (2001): 121–34.

———. *The Passage to Cosmos: Alexander von Humboldt and the Shaping of America*. Chicago: University of Chicago Press, 2009.

———. "Science and the Shaping of Nineteenth-Century American Nature Literature." *Literature of Nature: An International Sourcebook*. Eds. Patrick Dickinson Murphy, Terry Gifford, and Katsunori Yamazato. Chicago: Fitzroy Dearborn, 1998. 18–25.

———. *Seeing New Worlds: Henry David Thoreau and Nineteenth-Century Natural Science*. Madison: University of Wisconsin Press, 1995.

Wardrop, Daneen. *Word, Birth, and Culture: The Poetry of Poe, Whitman, and Dickinson*. Westport, CT: Greenwood, 2002.

Warfel, Harry R. "Whitman's *Salut au Monde*: The Ideal of Human Brotherhood." *Phylon Quarterly* 19.2 (1958): 154–56.

Warren, James Perrin. "Contexts for Reading 'Song of the Redwood-Tree.'" *Reading under the Sign of Nature: New Essays in Ecocriticism*. Eds. John Tallmadge and Henry Harrington. Salt Lake City: University of Utah Press, 2000. 165–78.

———. *John Burroughs and the Place of Nature*. Athens: University of Georgia Press, 2006.

Webster, Noah. *An American Dictionary of the English Language*. Springfield, MA: Merriam, 1847.

———. *An American Dictionary of the English Language*. Revised and enlarged by Chauncey A. Goodrich. Springfield, MA: Merriam, 1856.

———. *An American Dictionary of the English Language*. Springfield, MA: Merriam, 1859.

Weiner, Jacob. "On Self-Criticism in Ecology." *Oikos* 85.2 (1999): 373–74.

Weinstein, Josh Aaron. "Humility and the Face of Nature: Towards an Ecological Ethics of Humility in the Works of Henry Thoreau, Susan Cooper, Walt Whitman, and Marianne Moore." Ph.D. dissertation, State University of New York at Buffalo, 2007.

———. "Marianne Moore's Ecopoetic Architectonics." *Isle: Interdisciplinary Studies in Literature and Environment* 17.2 (2010): 373–88.

———. "Susan Cooper's Humble Ecology: Humility and Christian Stewardship in Rural Hours." *Journal of American Culture* 35.1 (March 2012): 65–77.

Weisbuch, Robert. *Emily Dickinson's Poetry*. Chicago: University of Chicago Press, 1975.

Wenz, Peter S. *Environmental Justice*. Albany: State University of New York Press, 1988.

Whitman, Walt. *An American Primer by Walt Whitman*. Ed. Horace Traubel. 1904. Stevens Point, WI: Holy Cow!, 1987.

———. *Complete Poetry and Collected Prose*. Ed. Justin Kaplan. Washington, DC: Library of America, 1982.

———. *The Complete Writings of Walt Whitman*. 10 vols. Eds. Richard M. Bucke, Thomas B. Harned, and Horace L. Traubel. New York: Putnam, 1902.

———. *I Sit and Look Out: Editorials from the Brooklyn Daily Times*. Eds. Emory Holloway and Vernolian Schwarz. New York: Columbia University Press, 1932.

———. *Leaves of Grass, and Other Writings*. Ed. Michael Moon. New York: Norton, 2002.

Wiens, J. A. "Spatial Scaling in Ecology." *Functional Ecology* 3.4 (1989): 385–97.

Willis, Elizabeth. "Dickinson's Species of Narrative." *Emily Dickinson Journal* 18.1 (2009): 22–31.

Wilson, Anthony. *Shadow and Shelter: The Swamp in Southern Culture*. Jackson: University Press of Mississippi, 2006.

Wilson, Edward O. *The Future of Life*. New York: Vintage, 2003.

Wilson, Eric. *Romantic Turbulence: Chaos, Ecology, and American Space*. New York: St. Martin's Press, 2000.

Winch, Donald. "Thinking Green, Nineteenth-Century Style: John Stuart Mill and John Ruskin." *Markets in Historical Contexts: Ideas and Politics in the Modern World*. Eds. Mark Bevir and Frank Trentmann. Cambridge: Cambridge University Press, 2004. 105–28.

Wolff, Cynthia Griffin. *Emily Dickinson*. New York: Knopf, 1987.

Wolosky, Shira. "Dickinson's Emerson: A Critique of American Identity." *Emily Dickinson Journal* 9.2 (Fall 2000): 134–41.

———. *Emily Dickinson: A Voice of War*. New Haven, CT: Yale University Press, 1984.

———. "Poetry and Public Discourse, 1820–1910." *The Cambridge History of American Literature*. Ed. Sacvan Bercovitch. Vol. 4: Nineteenth-Century Poetry. New York: Chelsea House, 2004. 145–480.

———. "A Syntax of Contention." *Emily Dickinson*. Ed. Harold Bloom. Bloom's Major Poets. New York: Chelsea House, 1999. 161–85.

Worster, Donald. *Nature's Economy: A History of Ecological Ideas*. Cambridge: Cambridge University Press, 1994.

———. "New West, True West: Interpreting the Region's History." *Western Historical Quarterly* 18.2 (1987): 141–56.

———. *Rivers of Empire: Water, Aridity and the Growth of the American West*. Oxford: Oxford University Press, 1985.

———. *The Wealth of Nature: Environmental History and the Ecological Imagination*. New York: Oxford University Press, 1993.

Zapf, Hubert. "Literary Ecology and the Ethics of Texts." *New Literary History* 39.4 (Autumn 2008): 847–68.

Zimmerer, Karl S. "Human Geography and the 'New Ecology': The Prospect and Promise of Integration." *Annals of the Association of American Geographers* 84.1 (1994): 108–25.

Index

Following standard practice in Dickinson scholarship, Dickinson's poems are alphabetized strictly by the first word of the first line of each poem, even if that word is "The," "An," or "A," and each title is followed by the number of the poem in R. W. Franklin's *The Poems of Emily Dickinson* (Harvard University Press, 1998). All other titles, including those of Whitman's poems, are alphabetized under the first word immediately following the articles. A list of Dickinson's and Whitman's works can also be found at the conclusion of their respective entries.

THE IOWA WHITMAN SERIES

Conserving Walt Whitman's Fame: Selections from Horace Traubel's "Conservator," 1890–1919, edited by Gary Schmidgall

Democratic Vistas: The Original Edition in Facsimile, by Walt Whitman, edited by Ed Folsom

Intimate with Walt: Selections from Whitman's Conversations with Horace Traubel, 1888–1892, edited by Gary Schmidgall

Leaves of Grass, 1860: The 150th Anniversary Edition, by Walt Whitman, edited by Jason Stacy

A Place for Humility: Whitman, Dickinson, and the Natural World, by Christine Gerhardt

The Pragmatic Whitman: Reimagining American Democracy, by Stephen John Mack

Supplement to "Walt Whitman: A Descriptive Bibliography," by Joel Myerson

Transatlantic Connections: Whitman U.S., Whitman U.K., by M. Wynn Thomas

Visiting Walt: Poems Inspired by the Life and Work of Walt Whitman, edited by Sheila Coghill and Thom Tammaro

Walt Whitman: The Correspondence, Volume VII, edited by Ted Genoways

Walt Whitman and the Class Struggle, by Andrew Lawson

Walt Whitman and the Earth: A Study in Ecopoetics, by M. Jimmie Killingsworth

Walt Whitman, Where the Future Becomes Present, edited by David Haven Blake and Michael Robertson

Walt Whitman's Reconstruction: Poetry and Publishing between Memory and History, by Martin T. Buinicki

Walt Whitman's Songs of Male Intimacy and Love: "Live Oak, with Moss" and "Calamus," edited by Betsy Erkkila

Whitman among the Bohemians, edited by Joanna Levin and Edward Whitley

Whitman East and West: New Contexts for Reading Walt Whitman, edited by Ed Folsom

Whitman Noir: Black America and the Good Gray Poet, edited by Ivy G. Wilson